A One-Man Manifesto

Herbert Read (1893-1968) *photo by V. Richards 1946*

HERBERT READ

A One-Man Manifesto
and other writings for Freedom Press

Edited with an Introductory Essay

by

David Goodway

Freedom Press
London
1994

First Published
by
FREEDOM PRESS
84b Whitechapel High Street
London E1 7QX
in
1994

ISBN 0 900384 72 7

PRINTED in GREAT BRITAIN
by ALDGATE PRESS
LONDON E1 7RQ

Contents

Introduction by David Goodway   **1**

1. 'The Prerequisite of Peace', *Spain and the World*, Supplement, May 1938 (extracted from *Poetry and Anarchism* (1938))   **27**
2. 'Berneri's Creed' (translation), *Spain and the World*, 20 May 1938 (printed in full in *The Knapsack* (1939))   **30**
3. 'The Method of Revolution', *Spain and the World*, 16 September 1938   **31**
4. 'The Method of Revolution: An Answer', *Spain and the World*, 12 November 1938   **37**
5. 'The Open Fields System', *Spain and the World*, Supplement, December 1938   **40**
6. 'Lament for Spain', *Spain and the World*, 23 December 1938   **44**
7. 'Nearer to Reality', *Revolt!*, 11 February 1939   **46**
8. 'Democratic Hospitality', *Revolt!*, 1 May 1939   **48**
9. 'The Russian Terror', *War Commentary*, September 1940   **50**
10. 'Use of Land', *War Commentary*, November 1940   **53**
11. 'Eric Gill: Anarchist', *War Commentary*, February 1941   **57**
12. 'Bedlam Politics', address to the inaugural meeting of the Friends of Freedom Press, 28 September 1941 (printed in *War Commentary*, November 1941)   **61**
13. *The Education of Free Men* (Freedom Press, 1944) (reprinted in *Education for Peace* (1950) and *The Redemption of the Robot* (1966))   **65**
14. Speech before the trial of the editors of *War Commentary*, (printed in *War Commentary*, 21 April 1945, and *Freedom: Is It a Crime?* (Freedom Press Defence Committee, 1945))   **96**
15. Speech after the trial (from *Freedom: Is It a Crime?*)   **99**

16. 'Amnesty Campaign', *Freedom*, 25 August 1945 — **104**
17. 'The Centenary of *The Ego and His Own*', *Freedom*,
    27 July 1946 (reprinted in *The Tenth Muse* (1957)) — **106**
18. 'Neither Communism nor Liberalism', BBC talk
    (printed in *Freedom*, 4 January 1947) — **112**
19. 'Anarchism: Past and Future', lecture to the London
    Anarchists (printed in *Freedom*, 17 May 1947) — **117**
20. 'The Problem of War and Peace', BBC talk
    (printed in *Freedom*, 20 September 1947) — **126**
21. 'The End of an Age', *Freedom*, 13 November 1948 — **131**
22. 'Jankel Adler: The Artist', *Freedom*, 28 May 1949 — **134**
23. 'Culture and Religion', BBC talk
    (printed in *Freedom*, 23 July, 6 August 1949) — **137**
24. 'Americanism', *Freedom*, 1 April 1950 — **144**
25. 'Marie Louise Berneri', *Freedom*, 15 April 1950 — **148**
26. 'The Utopian Mentality', *Freedom*, 23 December 1950 — **150**
27. 'A One-Man Manifesto', *Freedom*, 3 March 1951 — **153**
28. 'The Death of Kropotkin', *Freedom*, 31 March 1951
    (reprinted in *Moon's Farm* (1955) and *Collected Poems*)) — **157**
29. *Art and the Evolution of Man* (Freedom Press, 1951)
    (Conway Memorial Lecture, 10 April 1951) — **159**
30. 'Kicks and Ha'pence', *Freedom*, 2 June 1951 — **179**
31. 'Kicks and Ha'pence: Machinism', *Freedom*, 7 July 1951 — **181**
32. 'Kicks and Ha'pence', *Freedom*, 18 August 1951 — **184**
33. 'The Problem of Survival', BBC talk
    (printed in *Freedom*, 29 September 1951) — **187**
34. 'Postscript to Posterity', *Freedom*, 1 March 1952 — **190**
35. 'Ancient War and Modern Peace', *Freedom*, 15 March 1952 — **194**
36. 'The Ape of Hitler', *Freedom*, 29 March 1952 — **196**
37. 'We Protest against This Spanish Tyranny...', speech at
    London protest meeting (printed in *Freedom*, 5 April 1952) — **199**
38. 'Beyond Nihilism', *Freedom*, 30 August 1952
    (reprinted as Foreword to the English translation
    of Albert Camus, *The Rebel* (1953)) — **201**
39. 'A Statement', *Freedom*, 17 January 1953 — **204**

1
Introduction

Herbert Read was born on 4 December 1893 at Muscoates Grange, a farm near Kirkbymoorside in North Yorkshire. When his father died in 1903, the family, being tenants, had to leave the farm – and the arcadian life that Read was to describe in *The Innocent Eye* – and he was sent in an orphanage in a very different part of Yorkshire: Crossley's School, Halifax. He left school in 1908, aged fifteen, went to Leeds and worked at the Leeds, Skyrac and Morley Savings Bank. In 1912, having borrowed some money from an uncle, he enrolled at Leeds University, where he studied a diversity of subjects although economics was possibly the only one, he later recalled, in which he ever received 'what pedagogues would call a "thorough grounding"'[1].

He left university before finishing his degree to join the army (he was an eager volunteer) and in 1915 was commissioned as a Second Lieutenant in the Green Howards. The same year saw the publication of his first book, *Songs of Chaos*, a volume of poetry. Read had a good war – he was awarded the MC for conducting a raid and capturing an enemy officer and the DSO for leading a retreat during the Germans' Spring Offensive of 1918 – and he seriously considered pursuing a military career.

In the event he went to work at the new Ministry of Labour and then the Treasury in 1919 and was able in 1922 to transfer, within the Civil Service, to the Department of Ceramics at the Victoria and Albert Museum. This provided the springboard for his highly influential involvement for the rest of his life with the visual arts. Books soon appeared on *English Pottery* (1924), *English Stained Glass* (1926) and *Staffordshire Pottery Figures* (1929). A long and prolific association began in 1929 with Read contributing art criticism to the *Listener*; and his widely-read *The Meaning of Art* (1931), one of the very few of his books to have remained in print, was adapted from some of these articles.

He left the V&A in 1931 to become Watson Gordon Professor of Fine

Art at Edinburgh University, but was obliged to resign the following year on account of personal scandal. Already married, he had met Margaret Ludwig ('Ludo'), a Lecturer in Music, who was to become his second wife. Back in London he earned a living partly by becoming editor of the art-historical (and establishment) *Burlington Magazine* from 1933 until 1939.

Read was by now the foremost propagandist in Britain for modern art. He was the author of *Art Now* (1933), of the first book on his close friend Henry Moore (1934) and of a seminal work on industrial design, *Art and Industry* (1934). His avant-gardism led to a close association with the International Surrealist Exhibition of 1936; but his fundamental, persistent advocacy was for abstraction. *Art and Society* (1937), originally delivered as the Sydney Jones Lectures at Liverpool University, was a pioneering contribution to the sociology of art.

Parallel to these important activities in the world of art was an equally distinguished and productive literary output. Read became a regular contributor from its first issue in 1923 to the *Criterion*, the periodical edited by his lifelong intimate, T.S. Eliot. He wrote also for the *Times Literary Supplement* (from 1925) and the *Nation and Athenaeum* (from 1927). Collections of his literary essays were published as *Reason and Romanticism* (1926), *The Sense of Glory* (1929), *In Defence of Shelley* (1936) and a large *Collected Essays in Literary Criticism* (1938).

A first volume of *Collected Poems* appeared as early as 1926; and the greatly admired *English Prose Style* in 1928. There were also *Phases of English Poetry* (1928) and *Form in Modern Poetry* (1932). In 1929 he delivered the Clark Lectures at Trinity College, Cambridge, and these were published as *Wordsworth* (1930); and his deep engagement with the Romantic poets continued with *In Defence of Shelley* and later writings. *The Innocent Eye*, his first autobiographical volume and a small masterpiece, came out in 1932 and *The Green Child*, a mysterious utopian work and his only novel, in 1934. In total, when Herbert Read announced in 1937 that he was an anarchist he was already a figure of considerable cultural authority, at the height of a dual career in literature and writing about the visual arts.[2]

It was the impact of the Spanish Revolution of 1936 and the ensuing Civil War that caused Read in 1937 to declare for anarchism – in the *Left Review* survey, *Authors Take Sides on the Spanish War*, and in 'The Necessity of Anarchism', a three-part article in the *Adelphi*. This latter was included the following year in a substantial manifesto, *Poetry and Anarchism*:

'To declare for a doctrine so remote as anarchism at this stage of history will be regarded by some critics as a sign of intellectual bankruptcy; by others as a sort of treason, a desertion of the democratic front at the most acute moment of its crisis; by still others as merely poetic nonsense. For myself it is not only a return to Proudhon, Tolstoy, and Kropotkin, who were the predilections of my youth, but a mature realisation of their essential rightness, and a realisation, moreover, of the necessity, or the probity, of an intellectual confining himself to essentials.

'I am thus open to a charge of having wavered in my allegiance to the truth. In extenuation I can only plead that if from time to time I have temporised with other measures of political action – and I have never been an active politician, merely a sympathising intellectual – it is because I have believed that such measures were part way to the final goal, and the only immediately practical measures. From 1917 onwards and for as long as I could preserve the illusion, communism as established in Russia seemed to promise the social liberty of my ideals. So long as Lenin and Stalin promised a definitive "withering away of the State" I was prepared to stifle my doubts and prolong my faith. But when five, ten, fifteen, and then twenty years passed, with the liberty of the individual receding at every stage, a break became inevitable. It was only delayed so long because no other country in the world offered a fairer prospect of social justice. It comes now because it is possible to transfer our hopes to Spain, where anarchism, so long oppressed and obscured, has at last emerged as a predominant force in constructive socialism'.

'The will to power', he continued,

'which has for so long warped the social structure of Europe, and which has even possessed the minds of socialists, is renounced by a party that can claim to represent the vital forces of a nation. For that reason I do not see why intellectuals like myself, who are not politicians pledged to an immediate policy, should not openly declare ourselves for the only political doctrine which is consistent with our love of justice and our need for freedom'.[3]

Who and what, more exactly, were the 'predilections' of Read's youth? In later writings he was very precise about these. In 'My Anarchism', a review article of 1968, the year of his death, he said

'my own anarchist convictions...have now lasted for more than fifty years – I date my conversion to the reading of a pamphlet by Edward Carpenter with the title *Non-Governmental Society*, which took place in 1911 or

1912, and immediately opened up to me a whole new range of thought –
not only the works of professed anarchists such as Kropotkin, Bakunin
and Proudhon, but also those of Nietzsche, Ibsen, and Tolstoy which
directly or indirectly supported the anarchist philosophy, and those of
Marx and Shaw which directly attacked it'.[4]

In *Annals of Innocence and Experience* (1940) he had also named Marx
and Bakunin, and went on: '...I was much influenced by Kropotkin's
Fields, Factories and Workshops, and by his pamphlets on *Anarchist Morality* and *Anarchist Communism* (published by the Freedom Press in 1912
and 1913). A pamphlet by Edward Carpenter on *Non-Governmental Society* (1911) was even more decisive ...'[5] To these writers must be added
also Max Stirner and Georges Sorel.

Another question that demands an answer is why Read's political
convictions of the pre-1914 years, formed around the time when he
was a student at Leeds University, were not manifested until a quarter
of a century later. He accounts for this partly in the passage already
quoted from *Poetry and Anarchism* (by confessing to the hold over him
of the Bolshevik Revolution); makes clear his support of Guild Socialism during World War One and his occasional advocacy of it in the
New Age and the *Guildsman*; and also says:

> '...when, after the war, I entered the Civil Service, I found myself under a
> much stricter censorship, and though I never "dropped" politics, I ceased
> to write about them. When in 1931 I left the Civil Service and was once
> more at liberty to take part in the public discussion of political issues,
> some people assumed that I had "just discovered Marx", that the turn of
> political events had forced me from the seclusion of an ivory tower, that
> I had adopted anarchism as a logical counterpoint to my views on art.
> Actually there was an unfailing continuity in my political interests and
> political opinions. I would not like to claim that they show an unfailing
> consistency, but the general principles which I found congenial thirty
> years ago are still the basic principles of such political philosophy as I
> now accept'.[6]

(What is missing here is any mention – by Read himself or by his
biographers – of his adherence to Social Credit. This was a common
enthusiasm in the 1920s and 1930s amongst members of Read's milieu.
It was his mentor, A.R. Orage, who in the *New Age* had 'discovered'
and edited Major C. H. Douglas and led a section of Guild Socialism in
support of Social Credit. Other followers, temporary or for life, of Douglas included Ezra Pound, Edwin Muir and Hugh MacDiarmid. The

scale of Read's involvement remains to be documented; but it is readily apparent that *Essential Communism*, a pamphlet of 1935, a 'drastic revision' of which was incorporated in *Poetry and Anarchism*, was a Douglasite tract – and it was indeed reprinted in *The Social Credit Pamphleteer* (1935).)[7]

Read continues, in *Annals of Innocence and Experience:*

> 'In calling these principles Anarchism I have forfeited any claim to be taken seriously as a politician, and have cut myself off from the main current of socialist activity in England. But I have often found sympathy and agreement in unexpected places, and there are many intellectuals who are fundamentally anarchist in their political outlook, but who do not dare to invite ridicule by confessing it.'[8]

There is considerable irony in the ultra-modern trend-setter in the visual arts electing for so permanently unfashionable a political creed as anarchism. Read has been accused, especially by bitter figurative painters, whose work he caused to be shunned, of jumping ceaselessly on to the bandwagon of the latest artistic novelty, of imposing upon practising artists a procrustean schema of aesthetic evolution culminating in the abstract. As his thoroughgoing enemy, Wyndham Lewis, put it in 1939:

> 'Mr Herbert Read has an unenviable knack of providing, at a week's notice, almost any movement, or sub-movement, in the visual arts, with a neatly-cut party-suit – with which it can appear, appropriately caparisoned, at the cocktail-party thrown by the capitalist who has made its birth possible, in celebration of the happy event'.[9]

In *The Demon of Progress in the Arts*, his extended assault of 1954, Lewis attacked Read

> 'for having been for years ready to plug to the hilt, to trumpet, to expound, any movement in painting or sculpture – sometimes of the most contradictory kind – which was obviously hurrying along a path as opposite as possible from what had appealed to civilised man through the ages.'[10]

In politics, however, for half a century, Read went resolutely (and, with exception of his knighthood, consistently) against the tide by professing his anarchist convictions.

Emma Goldman spent the years of the Spanish Revolution and Civil War largely in London, acting as representative for the CNT-FAI and running a propaganda office for them. So after Read had announced his anarchism in 1937 he was contacted by Goldman and recruited as a sponsor for the English Section of the SIA (Solidaridad Internacional Antifascista).[11] For several months they worked together fairly closely. Goldman later told Read that he and the novelist Ethel Mannin were the only 'two real comrades and friends' she had made during her entire three-year stay in London.[12] Read donated small sums of money; reviewed anarchist books for the *Criterion*; acted on behalf of anarchist authors with the two publishers, Heinemann and Routledge, for which he worked; spoke on anarchist platforms; and published articles and poetry in *Spain and the World* (the paper launched in 1936 by the twenty-year-old Vernon Richards).

This set the pattern for the fifteen years of Read's association with the Freedom Press Group. *Spain and the World* became *Revolt!*, which was revived as *War Commentary*, which in turn became, in 1945, a resurrected *Freedom*. Read published in these titles the articles collected in this volume. In addition he wrote or edited for Freedom Press (which also reprinted *Poetry and Anarchism*) six books and pamphlets: *The Philosophy of Anarchism* (1940), *Kropotkin: Selections from His Writings* (1942), *The Education of Free Men* (1944), *Freedom: Is It a Crime?* (Freedom Press Defence Committee,1945), *Existentialism, Marxism and Anarchism* (1949) and *Art and the Evolution of Man* (1951).

Anarchists have always revered the written word but, traditionally, they have esteemed public speaking almost as much; and so Read was pressed to participate in this area also. But, as Vernon Richards remembered in his affectionate obituary of Read,

> 'he not only reluctantly agreed to speak at meetings but... having agreed to he wrote out his speech and delivered it with all the revolutionary fervour he could summon up for the occasion. Which meant that more often than not some of the public were so disappointed by his delivery that they failed to take into account the important things he had to say!'[13]

All this came to a dramatic end with Read's acceptance of a knighthood in the New Year's Honours for 1953. It is significant for two reasons that this was awarded 'for services to literature', not to art. The State was unable to stomach his promotion of contemporary art; and Read, who always thought of himself as primarily a poet and that his literary achievement had been unfairly overshadowed by his other activities, felt it was at last properly recognised. Anarchists, not unnaturally, found his conduct insupportable – in any case they found themselves the laughing-stock of their revolutionary rivals on the left for what was perceived as the opportunism or, at best, ingenuousness of their most prominent advocate – and he was ostracised by *Freedom*.

Yet as far as Read himself was concerned he remained an anarchist, even if an anarchist knight. His gravestone at St Gregory's Minster, Kirkdale, bears the now scarcely legible inscription: 'KNIGHT, POET, ANARCHIST' – wording which George Woodcock, his first biographer, suspects was chosen by Lady Read.[14] Benedict, Read's youngest son, commented In 1974: 'Read attempted to justify his decision to accept, but it is clear that there was more behind it than he cared to state publicly; perhaps the heart had its reasons. In any case it did not in any way lessen the strength of his [political] views.'[15]

Read's new biographer, James King, has now disclosed how eager Ludo Read was to become Lady Read: 'Ludo had no doubt that Herbert had to accept the Palace's invitation.' T.S. Eliot had in 1948 been appointed to the Order of Merit, but Ludo asked 'what's the use of being Mrs OM?'. The couple were partially estranged because of a passionate friendship which Read had formed with Ruth Francken, a woman painter thirty years his junior, in Venice earlier in 1952. The relationship was platonic, but he had wanted it otherwise and been so foolhardy as to tell Ludo so. Thus King concludes: 'Finally, Read succumbed to Ludo's considerable powers of persuasion.'[16]

All the same, I still find it very relevant that Read was a countryman, coming from a Conservative farming family – his first politics (from the age of fifteen) was a romantic, Disraelian Toryism.[17] In 1949 he had returned to Yorkshire: to live in Stonegrave, only two or three miles from his birthplace and childhood home at Muscoates. He had explained in *Poetry and Anarchism:*

> 'In spite of my intellectual pretensions, I am by birth and tradition a peasant. I remain essentially a peasant. I despise the whole industrial epoch – not only the plutocracy which it has raised to power, but also the industrial proletariat which it has drained from the land and proliferated in hovels of indifferent brick. The only class in the community for which I feel any real sympathy is the agricultural class, including the genuine remnants of a landed aristocracy. This perhaps explains my early attraction to Bakunin, Kropotkin, and Tolstoy, who were also of the land, aristocrats and peasants. A man cultivating the earth – that is the elementary economic fact; and as a poet I am only concerned with elementary facts.'[18]

Read's anarchist political theory was unremarkable. He was an anarcho-syndicalist – at the outset at least – with respect to means. 'The ethical anarchism of Bakunin has been completed by the economic syndicalism of Sorel'; and '...wherever anarchism is a considerable political force, as in Spain, it is combined with syndicalism. Anarcho-syndicalism is a clumsy mouthful, but it describes the present-day type of anarchist doctrine.'[19] In terms of ends, Read seems always to have been an anarchist communist. Kropotkin is the anarchist theorist most frequently (and approvingly) mentioned by him.

In 1942 Read concluded:

> '...all the practical aspect of Kropotkin's work is astonishingly apt for the present day. Though written more than fifty years ago, a work like *Fields, Factories and Workshops* only needs to have its statistics brought up-to-date; its deductions and proposals remain as valid as on the day when they were written.'[20]

Colin Ward has, of course, now done just this for Kropotkin in his edition of *Fields, Factories and Workshops Tomorrow* (1974; 2nd edn., 1985). On a visit to China in 1959 Read wrote:

> 'All these communes are virtually self-supporting – the only things they need to get from outside are heavy machinery like tractors & perhaps coal & minerals like cobalt. It is the complete decentralisation of industry advocated by Kropotkin in *Fields, Factories and Workshops...*'[21]

George Woodcock recalls how

> 'On his return from his first visit to the United States after World War II ...he came to see me and talked mostly about supermarkets, which he had seen for the first time, and which interested him because people took what they wanted from the shelves; it seemed to him that, if only the cash desks at the entrances could be removed, the supermarket would be the perfect model for free anarchist communist distribution as envisaged by Kropotkin in *The Conquest of Bread.*'[22]

These three comments demonstrate one of Read's most attractive qualities: keeping abreast of modern developments and assessing the continuing relevance of anarchist analysis – and, if necessary, pointing out how it needed to be updated. From the mid-1940s he often anticipates the 'new anarchism' of Alex Comfort and Paul Goodman, Colin Ward and Murray Bookchin – an anarchism informed by such disciplines as psychology, sociology, biology and ecology. His impressive lecture of 1947 to the London Anarchists, 'Anarchism: Past and Future', reprinted for the first time here, is particularly noteworthy in this respect.

It remains the case, though, that the broad outlines of Read's anarchism are unexceptional:

> 'I have said little about the actual organisation of an anarchist community, partly because I have nothing to add to what has been said by Kropotkin and by contemporary syndicalists like Dubreuil;[23] partly because it is always a mistake to build *a priori* constitutions. The main thing is to establish your principles – the principles of equity, of individual freedom, of workers' control. The community then aims at the establishment of these principles from the starting-point of local needs and local conditions. That they must be established by revolutionary methods is perhaps inevitable....An insurrection is directed against the State as such, and this aim will determine our tactics. It would obviously be a mistake to create the kind of machinery which, at the successful end of a revolution, would merely be taken over by the leaders of the revolution, who then assume the functions of a government. That is out of the frying-pan into the fire....
>
> 'The natural weapon of the working classes is the strike, and if I am told that the strike has been tried and has failed, I must reply that the strike as a strategic force is in its infancy. This supreme power which is in the hands of the working classes has never yet been used with intelligence and with courage.... The real protagonists in this struggle are the community and the State – the community as an organic and inclusive body and the State as the representative of a tyrannical minority....The General Strike of the future must be organised as a strike of the community against the State....
>
> 'An insurrection is necessary for the simple reason that when it comes to the point, even your man of good will, if he exercises power, will not sacrifice his personal advantages to the general good.... For the last fifty years it has been obvious to anyone with an inquiring mind that the capitalist system has reached a stage in its development at which it can only continue under cover of imperial aggression – at which it can only extend its markets behind a barrage of high explosives.... Nowhere – not even in Russia – have they abandoned the economic values upon which every society since the Middle Ages has vainly tried to base itself.... Half-measures have failed and now the inevitable catastrophe has overwhelmed us.... Faith in the fundamental goodness of man; humility in the presence of natural law; reason and mutual aid – these are the qualities that can save us. But they must be unified and vitalised by an insurrectionary passion, a flame in which all virtues are tempered and clarified, and brought to their most effective strength.'[24]

Theoretically, this is unexceptional. Yet since Read is a professional writer and a poet, what he says is frequently extremely well-expressed – and lucidly inspiring – as in the two concluding sentences of the preceding long extract from *The Philosophy of Anarchism*, a pamphlet of 1940. On the other hand, Murray Bookchin, the most innovative anarchist theorist since Kropotkin, has revealed that

> Kropotkin had no influence on my turn from Marxism to anarchism –nor, for that matter, did Bakunin or Proudhon. It was Herbert Read's *The Philosophy of Anarchism* that I found most useful for rooting the views I slowly developed over the fifties and well into the sixties in a libertarian pedigree...[25]

During the twentieth century one of the most damning criticisms of anarchism has been as to how an anti-statist and anti-bureaucratic ideology can be regarded as relevant to the needs of contemporary societies and economies. Read replies:

> 'Actually, of course, in a society of rich and poor nothing is more necessary [than a State]. If it is necessary to protect an unfair distribution of property, a system of taxation and speculation, a monopolist money system; if you have to prevent other nations from claiming your ill-gotten territorial gains, your closed markets, your trade routes; if as a consequence of these economic inequalities you are going to do any or all these things you will need a bureaucracy.'

As he was formerly a civil servant, Read's further comments are of particular interest:

> 'Every country has the bureaucracy it deserves. Ours, trained in public school and university, is efficient, unimaginative, unfeeling, dull, and honest. In other countries the bureaucracy has no such gentlemanly traditions; it is lazy, lousy, and corrupt. In any case, lazy or efficent, honest or corrupt, a bureaucracy has nothing in common with the people; it is a parasitic body, and has to be maintained by taxation and extortion. Once established (as it has been established for a century in England and as it is newly established in Russia) it will do everything possible to consolidate its position and maintain its power. Even if you abolish all other classes and distinctions and retain a bureaucracy you are still far from the classless society, for the bureaucracy is itself the nucleus of a class whose interests are totally opposed to the people it supposedly serves.'[26]

Read's libertarian alternative is, save for a slight Social Credit twist, traditionally anarchist but bearing the stamp of the experience of the Spanish Revolution:

> 'The syndicalist – the anarchist in his practical rather than his theoretical activity – proposes to liquidate the bureaucracy first by federal devolution. Thereby he destroys the idealistic concept of the State – that nationalistic and aggressive entity which has nearly ruined Western civilisation. He next destroys the money monopoly and the superstitious structure of the gold standard, and substitutes a medium of exchange based on the productive capacity of the country – so many units of exchange for so many units of production. He then hands over to the syndicates all other administrative functions – fixing of prices, transport, and distribution, health, and education. In this manner the State begins to wither away! It is true that there will remain local questions affecting the immediate interests of individuals – questions of sanitation, for example; and the syndicates will elect a local council to deal with such questions – a council of workers. And on a higher plane there will be questions of co-operation and exchange between the various productive and distributive syndicates, which will have to be dealt with by a central council of delegates – but again the delegates will be workers. Until anarchism is complete there will be questions of foreign policy and defence, which again will be dealt with by delegated workers. But no whole-time officials, no bureaucrats, no politicians, no dictators. Everywhere there will be cells of workers, working according to their abilities and receiving according to their needs.'

As Read himself observes:

> 'I realise that there is nothing original in this outline of an anarchist community: it has all the elements of essential communism as imagined by Marx and Engels; it has much in common with Guild Socialism and Christian Socialism. It does not matter very much what we call our ultimate ideal. I call it anarchism because that word emphasises, as no other, the central doctrine – the abolition of the State and the creation of a co-operative commonwealth.'[27]

Read breaks with the classic anarchist political thinkers in just one way, but it is of decisive importance. This is his rejection of force. 'Anarchism', he says, 'naturally implies pacifism'.[28] Writing in 1938, he explained:

> 'There is no problem to which, during the last twenty years, I have given more thought than this problem of war and peace; it has been an

obsession with my generation. There is no problem which leads so inevitably to anarchism. Peace is anarchy. Government is force; force is repression, and repression leads to reaction, or to a psychosis of power which in its turn involves the individual in destruction and the nations in war. War will exist as long as the State exists. Only a non-governmental society can offer those economic, ethical and psychological conditions under which the emergence of a peaceful mentality is possible.'[29]

He explicates further, in 1953:

'Revolt, it will be said, implies violence; but this is an outmoded, an incompetent conception of revolt. The most effective form of revolt in this violent world we live in is non-violence. Gandhi temporarily inspired his followers to practise such a form of revolt, but we are still far from a full awareness of its potentialities.'[30]

Read became a member, one of the 'names', of the Committee of 100, the most important anarchist – or near-anarchist – political organisation of modern Britain; but he resigned, after only a year, in 1961 in protest against the mass action at the Wethersfield air-base, regarding the intention as aggressive:

'Such a policy is not passive. It is an organised threat to authority that provokes the threat of counter-forces to preserve public order or protect public property. In their immediate effect such demonstrations are directed against the police and military forces and not against the real enemy, which is the people in their massive ignorance and stupidity'.[31]

Read's anarchism was not peripheral to his other, varied activities. Rather it was – knighthood and all – at the core of how he viewed the world in general. He remarked of William Morris: 'It is customary to consider Morris in his threefold aspect as poet, craftsman, and socialist. In this way we break down the fundamental unity of the man'.[32] The same applies to Read himself. To understand any one of his activities that activity needs to be considered in the context of the totality; to assess the stature of the man each of his individual achievements has to added together (and the total is greater than the sum of the parts); and his anarchist politics has to be regarded as central in all of this. When he came to collect the essays he had written 'specifically on the subject of Anarchism' he very rightly insisted:

'There is no categorical separation ... between what I have written on this subject and what I have written on social problems generally (*The*

Politics of the Unpolitical) or on the social aspects of art (*Art and Society* and *The Grass Roots of Art*) or on the social aspects of education (*Education through Art* and *Education for Peace*). The same philosophy reappears in my literary criticism and in my poetry'.[33]

In his aesthetics Read attempted to assimilate classicism and romanticism. As he explained in 1937: 'From 1918 I have been a close friend of T.S. Eliot, and to some extent his influence is responsible for my early attempt to reconcile reason and romanticism – not entirely, because the contradiction exists in my own personality'. Other major influences on Read in this respect were Orage and T.E. Hulme, whose *Speculations* he edited for posthumous publication.[34]

'Wisdom, as I have insisted ever since I became intellectually conscious, is the needle which comes to rest between reason and romanticism (a word which comprises instinct, intuition, imagination, and fantasy).'[35]

So it is when Read deliberately situates his politics within his overall philosophy that what he has to say is at its most unusual and, I think, impressive. Let me, in Read's own style, quote two more lengthy extracts in illustration:

'When we follow reason...in the medieval sense, we listen to the voice of God; we discover God's order, which is the Kingdom of Heaven. Otherwise there are only the subjective prejudices of individuals, and these prejudices inflated to the dimensions of nationalism, mysticism, megalomania, and fascism. A realistic rationalism rises above all these diseases of the spirit and establishes a universal order of thought, which is a necessary order of thought because it is the order of the real world; and because it is necessary and real, it is not man-imposed, but natural; and each man finding this order finds his freedom.

'Modern anarchism is a reaffirmation of this natural freedom, of this direct communion with universal truth. Anarchism rejects the man-made systems of government, which are instruments of individual and class tyranny; it seeks to recover the system of nature, of man living in accordance with the universal truth of reality. It denies the rule of kings and castes, of churches and parliaments, to affirm the rule of reason, which is the rule of God.

'The rule of reason – to live according to natural laws – this is also the release of the imagination. We have two possibilities: to discover truth, and to create beauty. We make a profound mistake if we confuse these two activities, attempting to discover beauty and to create truth. If we attempt to create truth, we can only do so by imposing on our fellow-men an arbitrary and idealistic system which has no relation to reality; and if we attempt to discover beauty we look for it where it cannot be found – in reason, in logic, in experience. Truth is in reality, in the visible and tangible world of sensation; but beauty is in unreality, in the subtle and unconscious world of the imagination... We must surrender our minds to universal truth, but our imagination is free to dream; is as free as the dream; is the dream.

'I balance anarchism with surrealism, reason with romanticism, the understanding with the imagination, function with freedom'.[36]

'This Heraclitean principle of flux, of chance, of fortuity issues out of the tragedy of war, and is basic to my anarchism and romanticism... That I can combine anarchism with order, a philosophy of strife with pacifism, an orderly life with romanticism and revolt in art and literature – all this is inevitably scandalous to the conventional philosopher. This principle of flux, the Keatsian notion of "negative capability", justifies everything I have done (or not done) in my life, everything I have written, every attack and defence. I hate all monolithic systems, all logical categories, all pretences to truth and inevitability. The sun is new every day.

'A fatalistic philosophy should imply more resignation than I have shown. But fatalism does not imply inactivity; on the contrary, since we are counters in a child's game, we are condemned to action. It is in changing, as Heraclitus said, that things find repose. I have called my politics 'the politics of the unpolitical', but I have striven for change, even for revolution. My understanding of the history of culture has convinced me that the ideal society is a point on a receding horizon. We move steadily towards it but can never reach it. Nevertheless we must engage with passion in the immediate strife – such is the nature of things and if defeat is inevitable (as it is) we are not excused. The only excusable indifference is that of Zeus, the divine indifference'.[37]

As this second passage in particular suggests, Read was, as Henry Moore considered, 'fundamentally...a romantic'.[38] So Read could write:

'It is true that we come into the world trailing clouds of glory; a Heaven which is universal and impersonal lies about us in our infancy, and though the shades of the social prison-house begin to close on the growing boy, he is still, in Wordsworth's exact phrase, "Nature's Priest"'.[39]

At root Read adhered to the values of romanticism: sincerity, simplicity, organicism, spontaneity, emotion, individualism. (I would contend that the politics of romanticism is most naturally and properly anarchism.) And it is when he is writing as a Yorkshire romantic (even if balancing this with classicism) rather than as an internationalist revolutionary that his political voice is most distinctive.

The point at which Read's anarchist thought is most grievously lacking is in his failure to extend his professional concern with the visual arts into a generalised theory of human emancipation. George Orwell, reviewing a collection of his essays, astutely chose 'to concentrate mainly on one point – the clash between Read's political beliefs and his aesthetic theory.'[40] In the title essay of *The Politics of the Unpolitical* Read names the six modern 'philosophers and prophets... whose message is still insistent, and directly applicable to our present condition – Ruskin and Kropotkin, Morris and Tolstoy, Gandhi and Eric Gill.'[41] Although Read is sincere in his admiration of Morris as a 'great artist and great socialist', he is withering in his dismissal of Morris's rejection of the machine:

> 'I am no yearning medievalist, and have always denounced the sentimental reaction of Morris and his disciples. I have embraced industrialism, tried to give it its true aesthetic principles, all because I want to be through with it, want to get to the other side of it, into a world of electric power and mechanical plenty when man can once more return to the land, not as a peasant but as a lord.'[42]

Read is, of course, fully aware of the way in which the names and ideas of Ruskin, Morris and Gill are interlinked,[43] but neither Ruskin nor Gill receive the stick which he gives in his writings to Morris. Ruskin he reveres as as a great and visionary writer and as a master of English prose. His high opinion of Gill, a personal friend, is indicated by his surprising inclusion among 'the Six' and influenced by Gill's having come to terms with mechanisation and mass production (as actually Read considered Morris would also have done).[44]

Read's predominant concern is with the role of the designer in modern industry rather than, as Morris was, with the liberation of the worker. But in one important and provocative lecture, 'The Future of Art in an Industrial Civilisation' (later retitled 'Towards a Duplex Civilisation'), he speculates on the future not only of industrial design and the industrial designer but also of 'industrial man in general'.[45] He envisages a future in which the

> 'defects in the existing economic system have been removed, and...there are no further obstacles to the full and free application of design to the

products of the industrial system. Production is for use rather than profit, everything is made fit for the purpose it is to serve, and everyone has the necessary means to acquire the essentials of a decent life at the highest level of prevailing taste... virtually the industrial designer's paradise will have come into being, and we shall have not only a machine age but also, what we have so far lacked, a machine art.'

The standards for machine art are 'economy, precision, fitness for purpose – all qualities of classical beauty.' 'It is', says Read, 'a very possible, and even a very probable utopia.'

What problems could afflict such a utopia?

'We shall have factories full of clean automatic machines moulding and stamping, punching and polishing innumerable objects which are compact in form, harmonious in shape, delectable in colour. Gone are the jointed and fragile objects which today we ingeniously construct from wood and metal; almost everything will be made from one basic plastic material, and beds and bath-tubs, plates and dishes, radio cabinets and motor-cars, will spill out of the factories in an unending stream of glossy jujubes. I am perhaps exaggerating: if we get tired of glossiness, we can have our surfaces matt. Nothing will be impossible. The technologist and the designer between them will be able satisfy every whim and fancy. From a technical point of view, it will all be fearfully easy, and we may well ask ourselves: where is the restraint to come from? What is to prevent this search for quality and variety degenerating into an avalanche of vulgarity?'[46]

Technological advances will have largely eliminated the human element from production and so, in addition to the problem of leisure, there will be the problem of 'the atrophy of sensation': so few people will be required 'to use their hands in creative contact with a material' that they will be 'quite unable to check a general atrophy of sensibility...'

Read's solution to these interrelated problems, 'if we are to go forward to the logical conclusion of the machine age,' is to 'create a movement in a parallel direction, and not in opposition.' It will be necessary to establish a 'double-decker' or 'duplex civilisation', in which there will be a division between a public machine art, abstract and geometrical, and a private naturalistic or humanistic art.[47] He gives the example of ancient Egypt, where a religious art, mainly of public buildings and sculptured monuments, and which was geometric, rational, objective, abstract, co-existed for centuries with a domestic art, largely of paintings, small carvings and various kinds of decorated vessels, and which was naturalistic, lyrical, even sentimental. Obviously contemporary society already exemplifies to a significant extent a double-decker civilization. What, in addition Read prescribes is to

> 'let every individual serve an apprenticeship in handicrafts...creative arts of every kind should be made the basis of our educational system. If, between the ages of five and fifteen, we could give all our children a training of the senses through the constructive shaping of materials... then we need not fear the fate of those children in a wholly-mechanised world. They would carry within their minds, within their bodies, the natural antidote to objective rationality, a spontaneous overflow of creative energies into their hours of leisure.
>
> 'The result would be a private art standing over against the public art of the factories. But that – in our painting and sculpture, our poetry and dancing, our artist-potters and artist-weavers – we already have. That is to say, we have a tiny minority of people calling themselves artists. I am recommending that everyone should be an artist.'[48]

Here, belatedly, in a lecture given in 1943 and first published in 1947, we have Read standing more-or-less foursquare alongside his great predecessors – Ruskin, Morris, Gill – and stressing the fundamental, liberatory importance of the arts and crafts in any free society. It must be noted, though, that the argument is not unproblematical for, as the reviewer of *The Grass Roots of Art* in *Freedom* observed, it is

> 'not one that would be acceptable to anarchists; indeed, the argument as it stands seems to be in sharp contradiction to the general thesis of the book... the anarchist would argue that the syndicate and the commune, operating a decentralised industry, would exert a direct influence upon design as well as distribution and exemplify the kind of communal creativity Read has in mind. This particular essay in speculation is a brilliant one, but the steps by which Read mounts to its launching would seem to the anarchist reader to be conspicuously shaky'.[49]

Read's views continued to develop to such an extent that by 1961, as the designer Misha Black, who as a young man had been fired by *Art and Industry*, recalled, 'he had completely changed his attitude' and believed that 'one must accept that most things which are made by industry have no real aesthetic value at all and one must look for aesthetic satisfaction in other things....and he was getting very close in fact to...a kind of William Morris attitude'.[50]

Read's undeniably original contribution to anarchism was as an educational theorist. When the British Council was established in 1940, it was decided to 'project' British art overseas during wartime not by sending valuable works by professional artists but to substitute collections of drawings by British children. Read was given the task of selecting the works and visited schools throughout the country. In the year before his death he was to recall it as 'an experience that may be said to have redirected the course of my life'.[51] He was appointed to a Leon Fellowship at London University for the two years, 1940-42, and the result was the magisterial *Education through Art*, published in 1943.

As Read was to stress:

'It is not often realised how deeply anarchist in its orientation... *Education through Art* is and was intended to be. It is of course humiliating to have to confess that its success (and it is by far the most influential book I have written) has been in spite of this fact. I must conclude that I did not make my intention clear enough...'[52]

He himself admitted: 'It is a general complaint that my book, *Education through Art*, is a difficult one – too difficult for the people it might most benefit'.[53] Freedom Press brought out *The Education of Free Men* in 1944, the year of the Butler Act, as 'a shorter statement of the theory of education' put forward in *Education through Art*, announcing:

'We are glad to publish this pamphlet by Herbert Read because, even though it does not pretend to deal with the whole problem of education (it purposely omits the history of and discussion on the different aspects of education, and the organisation of teachers in the new society) it covers new ground by relating the problem of education to that of liberty. This is particularly important at a time when many people think that the question of education can be solved by State legislation'.

The Education of Free Men was reprinted in Read's other important educational volume, *Education for Peace* (1950), later reissued in a new edition with, in typically confusing manner, a different title, *The Redemption of the Robot: My Encounter with Education through Art* (New York, 1966; London, 1970). (To what extent were such changes of title governed by the need to produce a new book and a part of the 'hack work' necessitated by the financial desperation of his final years?).[54]

Back in 1940 what had so moved Read was the gestural and emotional content of the children's art. In particular, it was a working-class girl of five from a Cambridgeshire village who gave him 'something in the nature of an apocalyptic experience' with the drawing she described as 'a snake going round the world and a boat'. Not only had the child drawn a mandala, 'a magic circle divided into segments', 'one of the oldest symbols in the world', but she had found a verbal equivalent, for 'the snake surrounding the world is one of the most ancient of primordial images'. Read was a convinced Freudian and had been one of the first in Britain to apply psychoanalytical concepts to literary and art criticism. What he had previously known largely from reading Jung and regarded as merely an interesting hypothesis 'suddenly became an observed phenomenon, a proof', as he recognised the girl's drawing as 'a symbol that was archetypal and universal'. (He now transferred his allegiance to Jung and was to become both publisher and editor-in-chief of the collected works of Jung in English.) In total Read recognised in the children's drawings a range of imagery that suggested that young children were naturally in harmony with deeply-embedded cultural and social experiences. As he put it:

'The more I considered my material the more convinced I became of the basic significance of the child's creative activities for the development of consciousness and for the necessary fusion of sensibility and intellect'.[55]

What are the implications for anarchism of all this? Read begins *Education through Art* by stating:

'The purpose of education can... only be to develop, at the same time as the uniqueness, the social consciousness or reciprocity of the individual. As a result of the infinite permutations of heredity, the individual will inevitably be unique, and this uniqueness, because it is something not possessed by anyone else, will be of value to the community... But uniqueness has no practical value in isolation. One of the most certain lessons of modern psychology and of recent historical experiences, is that education must be a process, not only of individuation, but also of *integration*, which is the reconciliation of individual uniqueness with social unity... the individual will be "good" in the degree that his individuality is realized within the organic wholeness of the community'.

Here we have the egoism of Max Stirner assimilated in the anarchist communism of Kropotkin. (Read mentions Stirner in *The Education of Free Men*; writes approvingly of him elsewhere, recounting how he bought his copy of the first British edition of Stirner's great book, *The Ego and His Own*, in 1915; and goes so far as to conclude that 'Jung sometimes seems to echo Stirner's very words'.)[56]

As we have already seen, in Read's discussion of a duplex civilisation, Read advocates that 'creative arts of every kind should be made the basis of our educational system'. On the one hand, 'a child's drawings, produced as a result of spontaneous activity, are direct evidence of the child's physiological and psychological disposition' and 'once the psychological tendency or trend of a child is known, its own individuality can be developed by the discipline of art, till it has its own form and beauty...'; on the other hand: 'We know that a child absorbed in drawing or any other creative activity is a happy child. We know just as a matter of everyday experience that self-expression is self-improvement'. As a result: 'We do not claim an hour or a day of the child's time: we claim the whole child'.[57]

For Read the choice between authoritarianism and a free, libertarian society therefore lies in the schoolroom:

> 'The first charge on the educator...is to bring the uniqueness of the individual into focus, to the end that a more vital interplay of forces takes place within each organic grouping of individuals within the family, within the school, within society itself. The possibilities are at first evenly weighed between *hatred*, leading to crime, unhappiness and social antagonism, and *love*, which ensures mutual aid, individual happiness and social peace.'[58]

Only a few years later Alex Comfort was to conclude that the task of modern revolutionaries is to abandon political intrigue and insurrectionary fantasy and instead become practitioners – or at least propagandists – of 'child psychiatry, social psychology and political psychology.'[59] Similarly, and rather more practically, Read is in effect calling on anarchists to bring about the social revolution by becoming schoolteachers, trained in the pedagogy of his freedom in education:

> '...a choice must be made which inevitably dictates the form which our society will take. In one direction we can institute objective codes of conduct and morality to which our children are introduced before the age of understanding and to which they are compelled to conform by a system of rewards and punishments. That way conducts us to an authoritarian society, governed by laws and sanctioned by military power. It is the kind of society in which most of the world now lives, ridden by neuroses, full of envy and avarice, ravaged by war and disease.
>
> 'In the other direction we can avoid all coercive codes of morality, all formal conceptions of "right" and "wrong". For a morality of obedience we can substitute a morality of attachment or reciprocity... Believing that

the spontaneous life developed by children among themselves gives rise to a discipline infinitely nearer to that inner accord or harmony which is the mark of the virtuous man, we can aim at making our teachers the friends rather than the masters of their pupils; as teachers they will not lay down ready-made rules, but will encourage their children to carry out their own co-operative activities, and thus spontaneously to elaborate their own rules. Discipline will not be imposed, but discovered – discovered as the right, economical and harmonious way of action. We can avoid the competitive evils of the examination system, which merely serves to re-enforce the egocentrism inherent in the child: we can eliminate all ideas of rewards and punishments, substituting a sense of the collective good of the community, to which reparation for shortcomings and selfishness will be obviously due and freely given'.[60]

Education is a common preoccupation of anarchists, both theoretically and practically. Amongst the principal anarchist thinkers Godwin, Stirner and Tolstoy have all shared Read's concern, but only he went so far as to identify the school as the primary arena for anarchist action. What he originated was, in his words, 'a revolutionary policy', which would 'bring about a revolution in the structure of our society'.[61] Read's vision is an inspiring one and not, I consider, unrealistic – nor dependent on the ultimate validity of Jungian theory. There is, however, one major difficulty with it. All societies regard their educational systems as of central importance to social well-being, none more so than contemporary societies. The kind of intervention and social change that Read advocates would be far from uncontested – as is witnessed by the educational reforms of Thatcherite Britain, which to a significant degree have been directed at reversing the pedagogy and curriculum, especially in the primary school, which had been developed over the decades after 1944 and which the ideas of Read and the Society for Education through Art (of which he was President) had done much to influence. So we are necessarily returned to the struggle for social power, which is required in order to implement such far-reaching educational innovation.

After reading George Woodcock's study of Orwell, *The Crystal Spirit*, in 1966 Read wrote to him as follows:

'I haven't re-read any of Orwell's books recently, but they have always remained in my mind, and his personality, which remains so vivid after all these years, often rises like some ghost to admonish me. I suppose I have felt nearer to him than to any other English writer of our time, and though there were some aspects of his personality that irritated me – his proletarian pose in dress, his insensitivity to his physical environment, his comparatively narrow range of interests – yet who was, in general, nearer in ideals & even in eccentricities? You bring out his contradictions very well, & justify them. They didn't trouble me much, except when it came to the war but by then he was a sick man & I saw little of him.... If only he had lived a little longer he would have got rid of those "monumental imperfections" & would have become as great as any of the authors of the past he admired so much.'[62]

Read also had 'monumental imperfections' which prevented his very considerable gifts from being manifested, ultimately, in either original political and social theory, with the exception of his ideas about education, or creative writing of the first order (in poetry or prose).

Still, he wrote 'some of the finest prose of our time' as T.S. Eliot said. (At least I assume that it was Eliot who was responsible for the publisher's blurb on the dust-jacket of *The Contrary Experience*: 'Readers of the *Annals [of Innocence and Experience]* and of that strange romance *The Green Child* know that Sir Herbert Read has written some of the finest prose of our time; readers of *Moon's Farm* know that he has written some of the most moving poetry. And those who have read all these three books know that he is always inspired when he writes of his native Yorkshire.')[63] And he deserves to be continued to be read and studied by anarchists – particularly for his books on educational theory but also for the many perceptive and sometimes profound things to be found scattered throughout his political writings.

David Goodway

Notes

1. *Annals of Innocence and Experience* (London, 2nd edn., 1946), p. 127. All quotations are, where possible, from first or early editions of Read's works since he always extensively revised the texts of later editions, but not, as he himself emphasized, 'to give an air of caution to the impetuous voice of youth' (*Anarchy and Order: Essays in Politics* (London, 1954), p. 9).

2. The foregoing biographical summary is largely drawn from the authoritative 'Herbert Read – His Life and Work' (by Benedict Read) in *A Tribute to Herbert Read, 1893-1968* (catalogue of exhibition at The Manor House, Ilkley, 1975). It has been supplemented at points by *The Contrary Experience: Autobiographies* (London, 1963), Read's collected autobiographical writings; George Woodcock, *Herbert Read: The Stream and the Source* (London, 1972), chap. 1; and James King, *The Last Modern: A Life of Herbert Read* (London,

Introduction   23

1990). There is no satisfactory bibliography of Read's vast and confusing output but, to date, the most useful are Woodcock, pp. 293-7, Robin Skelton (ed.), *Herbert Read: A Memorial Symposium* (London, 1970), pp. 193-213, and Benedict Read and David Thistlewood (eds.), *Herbert Read: A British Vision of World Art* (Leeds and London, 1993), pp. 146-66.

3. *Poetry and Anarchism* (London, 1938), pp. 13-15.

4. Reprinted in *The Cult of Sincerity* (London, 1968), p. 76.

5. *Annals*, pp. 127-8.

6. *Ibid.*, pp. 129-30, 133-4.

7. Both were published by Stanley Nott Ltd of London, *Essential Communism* in the 'Pamphlets on the New Economics' series. John L. Finlay, *Social Credit: The English Origins* (Montreal and London, 1972), says that it was not until *Essential Communism* that Read made public his acceptance of Social Credit (p. 253) – and considers there is a natural affinity between it and anarchism.

8. *Annals*, p. 134.

9. Quoted by Jeffrey Meyers, *The Enemy: A Biography of Wyndham Lewis* (London and Henley, 1980), p. 310.

10. Wyndham Lewis, *The Demon of Progress in the Arts* (London, 1954), p. 53.

11. International Institute of Social History, Amsterdam: Goldman Archive, XXVII B, carbon of letter from Goldman to Read, 19 January 1938; letter from Read to Goldman, 20 January 1938. For an account of the activities of the English Section of the SIA see my forthcoming edition of the correspondence between Goldman and John Cowper Powys to be published by the Feminist Press at the City University of New York.

12. Letter from Goldman to Read, 5 June 1939, quoted by Alice Wexler, *Emma Goldman in Exile: From the Russian Revolution to the Spanish Civil War* (Boston, 1989), p. 214.

13. VR, '"A Man Born Free"', *Freedom*, 22 June 1968 (reprinted in *Anarchy*, no. 91 (September 1968), pp. 284-6).

14. George Woodcock, *Beyond the Blue Mountains: An Autobiography* (Markham, Ontario, 1987), p. 196.

15. *Tribute to Herbert Read*, p. 15.

16. King, pp. 263-6.

17. *Annals*, pp. 124-6.

18. *Poetry and Anarchism*, p. 16. Ben Read confirms that my interpretation unpacks what he was implying when he wrote 'perhaps the heart had its reasons.'

19. *Poetry and Anarchism*, pp. 71, 82.

20. Herbert Read (ed.), *Kropotkin: Selections from His Writings* (London, 1942), p.15.

21. 'Letters from China, 1959', in *Tribute to Herbert Read*, p. 47.

22. Woodcock, *Herbert Read*, p. 234.

23. It is worth observing that the 'remarkable' book, *A Chacun sa chance* (Paris, 1935), by this little-known writer, Hyacinthe Dubreuil, also deeply impressed Aldous Huxley in his contemporary libertarian treatise, *Ends and Means: An Enquiry into the Nature of Ideals and into the Methods Employed for Their Realization* (London, 1937), pp. 74-5, 83-5, 172.

24. *The Philosophy of Anarchism* (1940), reprinted in *Anarchy and Order*, pp. 51-3.

25. Murray Bookchin, 'Deep Ecology, Anarcho-syndicalism, and the Future of Anarchist Thought', in Murray Bookchin et al., *Deep Ecology and Anarchism: A Polemic* (London, 1993), p. 53.

26. *Poetry and Anarchism*, pp. 83-5.

27. *Ibid.*, pp. 86-7.

28. *Ibid.*, p. 87.

29. *Ibid.*, pp. 119-20. This passage is contained in the extract from *Poetry and Anarchism* that was Read's first contribution to the anarchist press: see below, pp. 27-9.

30. 'Introduction: Revolution and Reason,' *Anarchy and Order*, p. 26.

31. 'A note on policy submitted to the Meeting of the Committee of 100 to be held on December 17 1961,' printed in *Tribute to Herbert Read*, pp. 51-2. See also King, pp. 300-01; NW, 'Remembering Herbert Read', *Anarchy*, no. 91 (September 1968), pp. 287-8.

32. *Industry and Art: The Principles of Industrial Design* (London, 1934), p. 29, and repeated in *A Coat of Many Colours: Occasional Essays* (London, 1945), p. 77.

33. *Anarchy and Order*, p. 9.

34. University of Victoria, Victoria, BC: Read Archive, carbon of letter from Read to Hans W. Häusermann, 6 August 1937. For Read's shifting approach to the romanticism-classicism dichotomy, see David Thistlewood, *Herbert Read: Formlessness and Form: An Introduction to His Aesthetics* (London, 1984), esp. pp. 7-9, 38-49, 168-73; H.W. Häusermann, 'The Development of Herbert Read', in Henry Treece (ed.), *Herbert Read: An Introduction to His Work by Various Hands* (London, 1944), esp. pp. 53-5, 69-71, 79-80; also G. Wilson Knight, 'Herbert Read and Byron', in Skelton, p. 130.

35. 'Chains of Freedom' (1946-52), printed in *Anarchy and Order*, p. 171.

36. *Poetry and Anarchism*, pp. 96-7.

37. 'What is There Left to Say?' (1962), printed in *Cult of Sincerity*, pp. 55-6.

38. Henry Moore, 'Remembering Herbert Read', *Anarchy* no. 91 (September 1968), p. 287.

39. *The Education of Free Men* (London, 1944), reprinted below, p. 80. For Read as a romantic, see Herbert Read (ed.), 'Introduction', *Surrealism* (London, 1936), pp. 21-8, 87-91 [this essay was reprinted as 'Surrealism and the Romantic Principle' in *The Philosophy of Modern Art: Collected Essays* (London, 1952)]; *The Tenth Muse: Essays in Criticism* (London, 1957), p.4; E.H. Ramsden, 'Herbert Read's Philosophy of Art', in Treece, p. 45; Woodcock, *Herbert Read*, pp. 139-56.

40. George Orwell, review of *A Coat of Many Colours*, *Poetry Quarterly*, vol. 7, no. 4 (Winter 1945), reprinted in *The Collected Essays, Journalism and Letters of George Orwell* (Harmondsworth, 4 vols, 1970), IV, p. 69.

41. *The Politics of the Unpolitical* (London, 1943), p. 2.

42. *Ibid.*, p. 44; *Poetry and Anarchism*, pp. 16-17. For Read on Morris, see also *Art and Industry*, pp. 27-33; and 'William Morris', in *Coat of Many Colours*, pp. 76-9.

43. See, for example, *The Grass Roots of Art: Lectures on the Social Aspects of Art in an Industrial Age* (London, new edn., 1955), pp. 37, 49.

44. For Read on Ruskin see 'The Message of Ruskin', in *Coat of Many Colours*, pp. 231-7, and *Cult of Sincerity*, pp. 56-7. For Read on Gill see 'Eric Gill', in *Coat of Many Colours*, pp. 5-16, and below, pp. 57-60. When he reissued *The Politics of the Unpolitical* as *To Hell with Culture: and Other Essays on Art and Society* (London, 1963), Read dedicated it to Gill's memory. Robin Kinross, 'Herbert Read's *Art and Industry*: A History', *Journal of Design History*, vol. 1, no. 1 (1988), pp. 37-8, 44-5, provides a helpful discussion of the dialectical relationship between Gill and Read.

45. *The Grass Roots of Art* (London, 1947), p. 58.

46. *Ibid.*, pp. 63-5.

47. *Ibid.*, pp. 68-9.

48. *Ibid.*, pp. 71-2.

49. *Freedom*, 1 May 1948. The reviewer was Louis Adeane, author of *To the Crystal City*, a book on Read's writings that has, regrettably, remained unpublished (see George Woodcock, *Letter to the Past: An Autobiography* (Don Mills, Ontario, 1982), pp. 299-300; Read Archive, letters from Adeane to Read, 1949-52).

50. BBC Radio programme, *Recollections of Herbert Read*, 4 December 1977.

51. 'The Truth of a Few Simple Ideas' (1967), in *Cult of Sincerity*, pp. 43-5.

52. *Cult of Sincerity*, p. 90.

53. 'Education through Art', in Stefan Schimanski and Henry Treece (eds.), *Transformation Two* (London, 1944), p. 63.

54. King, p. 307.

55. *Cult of Sincerity*, pp. 44-5; *Education through Art* (London, 2nd edn., 1945), p. 187n ('Snake round the World and a Boat' is reproduced as Plate Ib, facing p. 96). David Thistlewood, 'Herbert Read: Education through Art', *Resurgence*, no. 154 (September/October 1992), gives a useful summary of this and Read's educational ideas in general. See also Thistlewood, *Herbert Read*, pp. 111-14; Michael P. Smith, *The Libertarians and Education* (London, 1983), pp. 118-22. In addition to *The Education of Free Men*, Read provides a clear and compact account of his views in 'The Aesthetic Method of Education', in *The Grass Roots of Art* (1954 edn.).

56. *Education through Art*, p. 5. For Read on Stirner see below, pp. 32, 38-9, 79, 106-111; *Cult of Sincerity*, pp. 84-92; *The Forms of Things Unknown: Essays towards an Aesthetic Philosophy* (London, 1960), pp. 173-6, 205.

57. *Education of Free Men*, reprinted below pp. 78, 93.

58. *Ibid.*, pp. 80-1.

59. See David Goodway (ed.), *Against Power and Death: The Anarchist Articles and Pamphlets of Alex Comfort* (London, 1994), pp. 19-20.
60. *Education of Free Men*, reprinted below pp. 86-7.
61. *Education through Art – A Revolutionary Policy* (London, 1955), p. 1. (This is a mimeographed pamphlet produced by the Society for Education through Art.) George Woodcock has been an eloquent expositor of this new anarchist strategy, which he compares to anarcho-syndicalism: see especially *Herbert Read*, chap. 8; but also *Anarchism: A History of Libertarian Ideas and Movements* (Harmondsworth, 2nd edn., 1986), p. 383, and *The Anarchist Reader* (Glasgow, 1977), pp. 48-9.
62. Read Archive, letter from Read to Woodcock, 3 August 1966 (reprinted in part in Woodcock, *Herbert Read*, p. 239). For Orwell's very penetrating assessment of Read see his review of *A Coat of Many Colours*, loc. cit.
63. Eliot, though, quite rightly considered that Wyndham Lewis was 'the greatest prose master of my generation – perhaps the only one to have invented a new style' (King, p.279).

1
The Prerequisite of Peace

WAR is a cancer that threatens to destroy the life of our civilisation, but I doubt if any direct surgery will remove it. Its symptoms are obvious, but its causes are secret, deeply buried in the history and habits of the body which bears it. The problem is not so easy to solve as most of our pacifists assume. It may be that there is an abstract ethical question, and that the answer is unequivocally in favour of universal peace. It may be that there is a concrete biological question, and that the answer is as unequivocally in favour of war. I doubt very much whether all the answers to all the questions that can be raised on this issue can be unanimous. There is not only a conflict of values involved, but also a hopeless confusion of motives. Some of the most aggressive and egotistical people I know are active pacifists; some of the gentlest and most sensitive men I have ever met were professional soldiers. They, too, hated war; but they accepted it.

I do not accept war. I consider that it is an insult to the life of reason; that it is cruel and senseless and wholly evil in its effects. Of its economic and social consequences I do not propose to speak: it is surely obvious enough to all who have lived in the post-war epoch that these have been disastrous. I seem to remember that Mr Douglas Jerrold once maintained that the Great War had been worth-while because it had achieved the westernisation of Turkey, but most of us find it hard to believe that the abolition of the harem and the fez was worth the sacrifice of twelve million lives.

In my opinion, the most convincing arguments for war are not logical at all, but based on certain obscure psychological motives. I do not mean that the arguments are convincing because they are obscure (a not unknown state of affairs). I mean that certain rationalisations of war persist because they are the expression of an emotional energy which would otherwise be repressed. When these rationalisations take a definite and elaborate form, the process of sublimation is obvious enough to anyone with a psychological training. But it is more difficult to explain a far more general attitude towards war and peace which is not active opposition or defence, but uncertainty and apathy. There may be two hundred thousand active pacifists in Great Britain; there are a few thousand active militarists; but the millions who will be decimated in the next war remain in the mass indifferent to the fate which threatens them, as sullen as gunpowder before it is fired.

I do not underestimate the important psychological factors which dispose the individual and the nation to a state of war-mindedness. But the psychology of mankind is not unalterable: it is on the contrary the most fluent and adaptable aspect of human life. We are at the mercy of unconscious forces, but what is unconscious now can be analysed and brought to the surface; we can discover the physical and material elements which cause or 'condition' these unconscious forces; and by controlling these basic elements we can eventually change the mental life of mankind. This mental life has changed often in the past, but only haphazardly and irrationally; we need the knowledge and resolution to change it deliberately and reasonably.

The only immediately realistic approach to the problem of war is economic. Economic imperialism is so demonstrably dependent on the support of armed force that only the most prejudiced capitalist can pretend to ignore its importance as a factor in the encouragement of warlike instincts. But the capitalist is quite logical (and for once he has the support of the psychologist) when he points out that warfare has a longer history than capitalism, and that the establishment of socialism in Russia, for example, has by no means been accompanied by a decline of the martial spirit. It may be argued that the militarism of the USSR is purely defensive; but it is militarism none the less, and there are few countries in the world where the pacifist is less free to preach his gospel of non-resistance. So long as nationalism persists as a sentiment, so long as collectivism masquerades as socialism, so long will socialist units be nothing more than capitalist units writ large.

War increases in intensity and effect as a society develops in group organisation. The greatest intensification of the horrors of war is a direct result of the democratisation of the State. So long as the army was a professional unit, the specialist function of a limited number of men, so long war remained a relatively harmless contest for power. But once it became everyman's duty to defend his home (or his political 'rights') warfare was free to range wherever that home might be, and to attack every form of life and property associated with that home.

The economic foundations of peace will never be secure so long as national boundaries exist; they will never be secure so long as collective units such as the nation exist. So long as it is possible to unite men in the name of an abstraction, war will exist; for the possibility of uniting the whole of mankind under the same abstraction is too remote to be worth considering, and so long as two or more abstractions exist with collective forces organised behind them, the possibility of war will exist.

The only pacifist peoples are certain so-called savage tribes living under a system of communal land tenure in a land of plenty: communities where the accumulation of capital and the power it gives has no purpose and therefore does not exist, and where there is no possibility of one man exploiting the labour of another. These conditions create not only the social and economic possibilities of peace, but also the much more important psychological possibilities. Such communities are, in the precise meaning of the word, *anarchist* communities.

There is no problem to which, during the last twenty years, I have given more thought than this problem of war and peace. There is no problem which leads so inevitably to anarchism. Peace is anarchy. Government is force; force is repression, and repression leads to reaction, to a psychosis of power, which in its turn involves the individual in destructive impulses and the nations in war. War, therefore, will exist so long as the State exists. Only a non-governmental society can offer those economic, ethical and psychological conditions under which the emergence of a pacifist mentality is possible. We fight because we are too tightly swathed in bonds – because we live in a condition of economic slavery and of moral inhibition. Not until these bonds are loosed will the desire to create finally triumph over the desire to destroy. We must be at peace with ourselves before we can be at peace with one another.

2
Berneri's Credo
(English translation by Herbert Read)

GRANT that my heart shall not harden; that it may continue always to love all men, just as they are, wilful as children that must be led from ways of wildness, weak as the sick that must be restored to health.

Grant that this heart may always hear the fall of tears, even through the luminous warmth of its moments of joy.

Grant that within this heart there shall be no hidden places which the golden light of the sun and the colours of its setting cannot reach.

Grant that the remoteness of the city of the sun shall not lead me to abandon the cities of the world. If I should shut myself in a tower of ivory, let it be only as a fervent worker in the field of thought and knowledge. But this lot only belongs to one whose light is the light of genius. Many, too many, are those who have no eyes, or do not open them wide enough to the truths of science and philosophy; too many slaves have need of a Brutus or a Spartacus; too many crowds cry to see Christ on Calvary that they may know that man becomes divine at the hour of sacrifice, that civilisation advances through the thorns, or perhaps retreats.

Grant that my heart shall not take pride in its beauties, and that my imagination shall not rest content with impossible deeds of heroism.

Grant that my will be steeped in trivial but continual endeavours and sacrifices.

* * *

Grant that my beloved may be as proud of me as I am of her.

Grant that I may be for ever tormented with discontent of myself and that I shall be ever anxious to make myself stronger and purer.

Grant that my daughters and friends in thinking of me may be impelled towards the good.

Grant that in dying I shall not be dissatisfied with my life.

Grant that I shall always be ready to die a death worthy of the life of a just man.

3

The Method of Revolution

ANARCHISM is a word of many meanings, many interpretations. Because of its vagueness, because of its associations with terrorism and with the pathetic actions of deluded individuals, it often seems advisable to abandon it. But no other word will do. Anarchy – *anarchia* – absence of government: it is an exact symbol of our meaning and is sanctioned by long historical usage. For these reasons I think we must retain the words anarchy and anarchism, infuse them with new thought and definite policies, so that reanimated and redeemed they will stand for a new way of living, a whole philosophy of life.

From its very earliest days the socialist movement included two opposed elements, which were philosophical rather than political in their essence. They perhaps derived, in the long history of European thought, from the old scholastic distinction between realism and nominalism. It is the distinction between those who believe in the real existence of universal qualities or ideas, and those who believe that all such ideas are abstractions derived from the world of experience. When Hegel raised the State to the level of an abstract entity, there was a part of humanity ready to follow him and to subordinate all variety and individualism to this conception. For if the State is given an absolute existence, it becomes the supreme end of all worldly activity: it is conceived as the perfect organisation of all our social activities, and no activities can be tolerated which interfere with its unity and order. But Hegel's conception of the State did not command general assent: another part of humanity refused to believe in the real existence of such an entity. The only reality, they said, is the individual: the individual with his sensations and desires, his weaknesses and grandeur, his folly and heroism. The State, they held, is only valuable in so far as it secures and promotes the happiness of the individual.

That statement already gives a relative value to the State: the State is valuable in so far as it promotes the well-being of the individual. The extreme egotism of Max Stirner, which asserts that only the individual and his desires have any validity, is not in question. That particular philosophy, which is not without its historical interest and importance, was effectively demolished by Karl Marx, and has only a remote connection with modern anarchism. What we have still to distinguish is, on the one hand, an attitude which values communal effort only in so far as it promotes the happiness of the individual; and, on the other hand, an attitude which is prepared to sacrifice that happiness to the wholeness, or perfection, or power of this abstraction called the State.

Naturally every politician and reformer will protest that his ultimate aim is the greatest happiness of the greatest number of individuals, and rationally it is difficult to see how any other doctrine can be held. But very few of the doctrines for which men organise themselves can be described as rational. The history of religion, the history of politics, the history of civilisation itself, is merely the passage from one form of obsession to another; and in the name of such an obsession – which is always called an ideal or a principle or simply 'the truth' or 'the faith' – men are enslaved, deprived of their freedom, and compelled by force to act against their individual interests.

Socialism has always been in this same danger. Properly regarded, socialism is the rational organisation of society to the end that men shall live together in freedom, security and plenty. There is nothing idealistic about such an aim. It is a question of the practical ordering of production and distribution, and though certain principles are involved, such as equality and justice, these are not so much abstract ideals as economic quantities. To equalise the burdens and benefits of production is a simple sum in division: it does not depend on the invocation of any articles of faith.

If we examine the principles of socialism as expressed, for example, in the *Communist Manifesto*, we do not find any arguments in favour of an idealistic conception of the State. Far from it. The State is everywhere recognised by the founders of modern socialism – by Marx, Engels and Lenin no less than by Proudhon, Bakunin and Kropotkin – as the product of social distinctions and an instrument of oppression. I could quote scores of texts to that effect, but let this summary from Engels' book on *The Origin of the Family*, quoted with approval by Lenin in his book, *The State and Revolution*, suffice:

'The State is therefore by no means a power imposed on society from the outside; just as little is it "the reality of the moral idea", "the image and reality of reason", as Hegel asserted. Rather, it is a product of society at a certain stage of development; it is the admission that this society has become entangled in an insoluble contradiction with itself, that it is cleft into irreconcilable antagonisms, classes with conflicting economic interests, may not consume themselves and society in sterile struggle, a power apparently standing above society becomes necessary, whose purpose is to moderate the conflict and keep it within the bounds of "order"; and this power arising out of society, but placing itself above it and increasingly separating itself from it, is the State.'

Modern anarchism – the consciousness that is growing up within the socialist movement and which cannot be stifled by any accusations of Trotskyism, liberalism, idealism, etc., is merely a reaffirmation of this view of the State. It expresses the conviction that, in the actual process of revolution, society has once more become entangled in an insoluble contradiction, has been cleft into irreconcilable antagonisms; and it asserts that these antagonisms have produced a form of State more absolute than ever.

Though I maintain that all the necessary principles of anarchism are to be found in the works of Marx, Engels and Lenin, nevertheless in examining the historical development of socialism during the last hundred years in search of the cause of this sad deviation, I think we are bound to discover that in certain questions of revolutionary tactics, Bakunin and not Marx was right.

The difference between Marx and Bakunin (apart from a difference of temperament) was really a difference in their conception of revolution. Marx conceived revolution as an historical process – a violent change, no doubt, but a change brought about by a trained and disciplined class-conscious proletariat.

Bakunin, on the other hand, conceived revolution as a spontaneous act – an explosion of forces that could no longer be repressed. Marx thought out a plan of campaign, with every step consolidated on an economic basis. Bakunin saw elemental passions directed to the immediate destruction of evil and to the equally immediate establishment of justice. This aspect of Bakunin's creed has since his time received a powerful reinforcement in Sorel's theory of direct action and the general strike.

But there is also this difference: Marx regarded the process of revolution as a process of inevitable evolution, comparable to the evolution of organic life. Capitalism contains within itself the seeds of its own destruction, and so revolution was held to be only possible in societies which had undergone a complete capitalist development and were ripe, as it were, for the change – ready for the fruit to fall. But Sorel saw nothing inevitable or organic about the process of revolution: according to him, the proletariat must hold itself completely aloof from all such gradualist concepts; it must 'build up institutions without any parallel in the history of the middle class'; it must 'form ideas which depend solely on its position as producer in industry'; and finally it must 'acquire habits of liberty with which the middle class nowadays are no longer acquainted'. The whole success of a revolution will depend on the proletariat having developed a new spirit, a new ethics, a new philosophy of life which breaks completely with all existing conceptions of society, and which is established with catastrophic violence.

It is obvious – more obvious now than it was in 1906 when Sorel published his *Reflections on Violence* – that a doctrine of violence can be used in more than one direction. Sorel's most effective disciple, in actual fact, has been Mussolini. But it is equally obvious that a doctrine of discipline and training and organic continuity with capitalism can be used in more than direction, and the National Socialist Party of Germany is there to prove it. But if we keep close to what we have regarded as the essential test of socialism – the disappearance of the State – then we shall be able to make the necessary distinctions.

The practical difference between the two methods of revolution is a difference in the time element. The Marxian revolution can only be achieved over a period of many years: the anarchist revolution is a question of hours. But this is too abstract a way of looking at the question: what is actually involved is human psychology. A revolutionary policy which needs a period of years for its accomplishment must work through the intellectual faculties – the passions are subordinated, or excluded altogether. But a violent revolution is achieved by passion, and the intellect is dormant. What is destroyed is destroyed in anger: what is created is created by instinct.

The word 'instinct' will be seized as evidence of an underlying mysticism, but I do not refuse that term, or rather what it implies. I am not a mystic, but my whole reading of history convinces me that nothing worthwhile is ever done that is not done in a spirit of fervour, of exaltation, of glory. In that spirit the Bastille fell, and the Commune was established; in that spirit the Russian Revolution triumphed and in that spirit the unarmed workers of the Spanish Republic threw themselves against the guns of the insurgent army and rendered the revolt abortive. But having achieved your end in righteous anger, there comes the task of consolidation. It is then that the calculators come forward, the men of craft and cunning, the doctrinaire economists and the dogmatic politicians. Men who are brave in battle are often humble in affairs, and easily surrender the position to these agents of efficiency. The position is then lost again.

> 'Politicians [says Sorel] argue about social conflicts in exactly the same manner as diplomats argue about international affairs; all the actual fighting apparatus interests them very little; they see in the combatants nothing but instruments. The proletariat is their army, which they love in the same way that a colonial administrator loves the troops which enable him to bring large numbers of negroes under his authority; they apply themselves to the task of training the proletariat, because they are in a hurry to win quickly the great battles which will deliver the State into their hands; they keep up the ardour of their men, as the ardour of troops of mercenaries has always been kept up, by promises of pillage, by appeals to hatred, and also by the small favours which their occupancy of a few political places enables them to distribute already. But the proletariat for them is so much cannon fodder ...
>
> The reinforcement of the power of the State is at the basis of all their conceptions; in the organisations which they at present control, the politicians are already preparing the framework of a strong, centralised and disciplined authority, which will not be hampered by the criticism of an opposition, which will be able to enforce silence, and which will give currency to its lies.'

These prophetic words, let me again remind you, were written more than thirty years ago.

The great necessity today is to study the causes of revolutionary failure. There is scarcely an honest socialist anywhere in the world who is not perturbed by this problem. Those who are orthodox attempt to explain it away on economic grounds: the survival of capitalist elements, the lack of adequate machinery for production, the necessity for evolving in logical historical phases, and so on. But these are precisely the reasons which do not convince the anarchist. In the course of history revolution has failed too often, and always we are given these same excuses. But look at the objective features of these failures, these reactions, these relapses, and what do you find? Always the same features! The establishment of a central governing body, the acquisition of privileges by this governing body, the creation of a new governing class, the re-division of society into rich and poor, master and servant, the powerful and the oppressed.

This process does not need an economic explanation. There is an explanation nearer home, nearer the truth, an explanation based on the limitations and weaknesses of the average human being. In short, the explanation is to be found in psychology rather than in economics.

Marx and Lenin repudiated one abstraction – the State. But in its place they put another – the dictatorship of the proletariat. They defined the proletariat as 'the class of modern wage-labourers who, having no means of production of their own, are reduced to selling their labour power in order to live' – a very clear and just definition. And we have seen that the revolution is to be effected by this class becoming conscious of itself, organising itself and forcibly overthrowing all existing social conditions. Having secured power, this class is to maintain a dictatorship until all injustices have been abolished and all class distinctions have disappeared. The nation will then be one vast community of producers organised for mutual benefit, and the proletariat as such will disappear and the State itself will wither away.

What actually happened in Russia, and what is now happening in Spain, is something very different. The proletariat in a sudden fervour committed its act of revolt; and out of the resulting chaos a minority emerged consisting mainly of intellectuals and professional politicians. This minority constituted a dictatorship in the name of the proletariat; but then almost their first act was to disarm the proletariat, to close the ranks of the party, establish a state army and a state police, and finally reduce the workers to a state of dependence far more absolute than before. There then ensues a series of intrigues among the politicians themselves whose sole purpose is to maintain a particular group in power and finally there emerges a single power within the group, a dictator or leader.

Socialism is in retreat. Everywhere in Europe it is being compelled to adopt the methods of its adversaries, to establish tyranny to resist tyranny; and in the process it is corrupted, defeated spiritually and materially. Socialism must retreat still further – to its first principles. It must recognise that a revolution will never be effected or maintained unless it is based on a complete and independent philosophy of life. The proletariat must have its own ethics and its own culture – something other than a watered version of bourgeois morality or a respectful imitation of academic learning. It must establish its ethics on the basis of its life and labour, and a new culture on fresh perceptions. Perhaps there are certain eternal verities in morality and art; but there is no reason to suppose that they are embodied in the manners and taste of a decadent civilisation. In any case, it is for the proletariat to choose, and not to be intimidated by the values established by the capitalist epoch. It is for the proletariat to discover its own values; and this it can only do in isolation. It must suspect every voice that addresses it from outside its own ranks (including the one that is addressing it now); it must reject every idea which it does not instinctively recognise as native to its own modes of feeling and perception. It must close its ranks and create its own clerisy. If it cannot achieve its own destiny, it has no destiny to achieve. Its dictators are projections of its own weakness: the shadow of its own death. Its only life is in the first principle of its faith: an organic community of free and equal individuals.

4

The Method of Revolution: An Answer

I welcome T. Michelson's very acute criticism of my article, and on some points I willingly accept his correction. In particular I admit that my contrast between a Marxian revolution which can only be achieved over a period of years and an anarchist revolution which is a question of hours is a metaphorical exaggeration. My main motive was to argue against 'the inevitability of gradualism'. A policy of revolution by planned stages leads to apathy in the revolutionary classes; the direction is left to leaders, whose only thought is to organise their followers in a well-disciplined army. We call it trade-union organisation, but what it becomes in effect is an industrial hierarchy which can be taken over by whatever power happens to direct the State. My point is that the control of the State must be seized violently, catastrophically; the reorganisation of society can then proceed according to programme. The alternative, for the anarchist, is not any other kind of revolution (there is no other kind), but rather a passive philosophical attitude which strives to direct all social movements towards the anarchist ideal.

Proletarian 'values'. I do not imply that the proletariat possesses any exceptional wisdom, or any special perceptions or sensibility. The true values are human values, or absolute values in relation to humanity. But it is the proletariat's special function to realise these values. It can only do so by remaining a coherent, independent force, and it can only maintain its coherence and independence by refusing to have anything to do with bourgeois culture and bourgeois 'society'. I grant that bourgeois culture contains many of the human values which we all desire to see established; and these will eventually be taken over by a new order of society. But to take them over on bourgeois terms (a seat in the stalls) – that is the beginning of the betrayal.

But much more important is the question of principle involved in the discussion of Stirner and Marx. On this point I must defend myself without reservation, for I believe the whole future of anarchism is bound up with this question. There is a type of anarchist, just as there is a type of Marxist, who is simply incapable of any progressive development of thought. They have their prophet and their dogmas, and no event in history, no advance in thought, can prevail against them.

When Stirner published his great book, he gave perfect expression to a logical thesis – the thesis of individualism. Marx, in his turn, gave perfect expression to a contrary thesis – the thesis of communism. That contradiction must be resolved, and by the very method of dialectics which Marx used to such good effect. I believe that to a great extent Marx resolved this fundamental contradiction, and that it is the Marxists, and not Marx, who, in Michelson's words, 'take society for their starting point and, by making the individual subservient to it, sacrifice light-heartedly its happiness to the entity – society'. Marx, I would still maintain, 'effectively demolished' Stirner (in *The German Ideology*), but he also profited by Stirner. He took the advice of Engels, which was: 'But what is true in his [Stirner's] principle, we, too, must accept. And what is true is that before we can be active in any cause we must make it our own egoistic cause – and that in this sense, quite aside from any material expectations, we are communists in virtue of our egoism, and that out of that egoism we want to be human beings and not merely individuals.' (letter of 19 November 1844, translated by Sidney Hook).

But if Marx could learn from Stirner, we can learn from Marx. I venture to think that I have passed through Marx to something nearer the truth; but in the process I have gained a tremendous respect for the genius of Marx, and until we anarchists have produced an economist and philosopher approaching his stature, it is simply futile to ignore his work. We have to build on the basis of that work; we have to conceive socialist thought as a dialectical development which includes Marx, Engels and Lenin no less than Stirner, Proudhon and Kropotkin. A practical anarchism for today must be directed towards the solution of immediate social and economic problems – that is to say, it must be revolutionary and communist. To insist upon individualistic anarchism is merely, in the circumstances, to condemn the whole doctrine to ineffectiveness.

5
The Open Fields System

The Open Fields by C.S. and C.S. Orwin.

THIS is a work of historical research which in the publisher's opinion could have no interest for readers of *Spain and the World*. Actually it is of great importance for anyone concerned with the practical realisation of anarchism. It does not describe an anarchist system of agriculture; nor a system which in any of its details we would like to revive. Nevertheless, it is a book from which the anarchist can derive considerable support for his theories.

Most people are aware that until a comparatively recent time much of the land of this country was common land – that is to say, communal land, cultivated by the community for the common benefit. They are aware that gradually, but for the most part during the eighteenth and nineteenth centuries, these common lands were enclosed and divided among individual owners. It is true that a considerable number have survived as 'open spaces' or 'recreation grounds', but the commons as agricultural units have virtually disappeared. They survive actively in only two or three places, one of which is the subject of this book.

The system of agriculture practised under this communal system of ownership is known as the Open Fields system – a system which lasted in this country for at least two thousand years, and which was only destroyed by the industrialisation or commercialisation of farming – by the introduction of the profit motive. The Open Fields were originally clearings made by settlers, who then proceeded to work the land in common for the common benefit. But these early settlers were not theorists; they were realists driven by practical and urgent needs to devise the most productive method of farming. This method was one which preserved individual initiative whilst submitting everything to common control. They divided the land into three parts. 'A large part... was kept under the plough to produce corn for man and straw for his beasts. Another part, much smaller, consisted still of the natural herbage though cleared of trees and bushes, and this was mown yearly to give hay for winter feed for livestock ... The third part comprised all that was left of the area under the control of the community, and it remained in its natural state of woodland or waste, except in so far as this was affected by grazing and by cutting timber and scrub for building and fuel.'

The extent of the arable land was determined by the number of ploughs in the community, and it was allotted amongst its members in strips representing a day's work with the plough, so that each man's strips alternated with those of his neighbours as day followed day. The strips varied in size and direction according to the nature of the land, and their position changed with the rotation of the crops. The fallow land was used for common grazing. The meadow land was divided in the same way as the ploughlands, each man getting his strip to mow for hay.

One of Mr and Mrs Orwin's objects is to show that this system, which at first sight looks so impracticable and uneconomic, was really the best system under the circumstances, and did incidentally result in giving everyone an equal share in the advantages and disadvantages of soils and situation. Inevitably it also involved a pooling of the common stock of knowledge which redounded to the general benefit of the community.

The greater part of the volume is taken up with a detailed examination of the only Open Fields still surviving in England as an economic unit, those at Laxton in the county of Nottingham. In addition to the actual survival of the system, an unusual quantity of documents and maps relating to the parish have survived which make it possible to trace the historical evolution of the Open Fields system with great accuracy. The whole community comes to life – their names, the extent of their holdings, the rents they paid and the daily and yearly round of their activities. But it is the community life itself, the way in which the parish lived as an economic unit, that has most interest and significance for us today. In particular, there are two points to emphasise.

In the first place, the government of the Open Fields was (and still is at Laxton) a pure democracy. The administration of the system was in the hands of the manor court, which consisted of all tenants and freeholders and appointed juries and officers to carry out its regulations. Every member of the community, therefore, had a direct responsibility, not only for the decisions of the court but for their enforcement. Or, in the words of the authors, 'both legislative and executive functions are vested in the people themselves'. Originally these functions had a far wider scope than the actual farming system. They included the relief of the poor, the repair of the highways and the keeping of the peace. At this point I would like to quote Mr and Mrs Orwin at some length:

> 'All these voluntary services, which everyone might have to perform, have now been merged in larger administrative units, but in the personal responsibility for the preservation of the general good, which still devolves, sooner or later, upon everyone, Laxton has retained something which has been lost everywhere else in the process of the enclosure of the Open Fields. Its people control their own affairs in the daily incidents of their work, by a scheme of voluntary administration maintained by public opinion without recourse to the law of the land and without the expenditure of a single penny. Encroachments upon the highway and upon the commons, trespass by straying stock, disputes as to boundaries, the cleansing of ditches and watercourses and the cutting of hedges – all of these things, together with the observance of the agreed system of husbandry, are settled here by the community at its own court. In other places recourse must now be had to the law, failing compliance with the instructions of paid officials in whom are now vested the powers once exercised by the community. In place of attendance at the court, of sharing in the responsibility for the regulations made thereat, of serving on a jury charged with the duty of securing the observance of such regulations, the dwellers in other parts of rural England can do no more than cast a vote for the election of someone to represent them on some local administrative body. After holding up his hand at a parish meeting or making a cross on his ballot paper, if, indeed, he do so much, the ordinary man thinks that his responsibility for local administration is fulfilled. Small wonder if his attitude towards it, thereafter, is one of complete detachment or of unconstructive criticism.'

We may therefore say that up to the beginning of the eighteenth century the agricultural system of this country, upon which the subsistence of the whole people depended, was carried on without any State interference, without legislature and without a bureaucracy. And this was a system which had endured for thousands of years. As a system it was destroyed by capitalism – by the substitution of farming for profit in place of farming for subsistence. Capitalism has introduced many improvements of a mechanical and technical nature, and there is no necessity to dispense with these. At Laxton the system has adapted itself to such improvements without any surrender of the communal principle. What exists at Laxton today could exist again in every parish; it does exist in the agricultural collectives established in Spain.

There is a second point to emphasise. The members of a village community such as Laxton not only have a direct personal responsibility for its social institutions, they have also an equal economic opportunity. Again I will quote the Orwins:

> 'Examples of ascent of the agricultural ladder from the bottom rung may be met with commonly enough all over the country, but nowhere else in England will there be found a village community nearly every member of which is at one stage or another in his progress from the bottom to the top. The rate of progress varies, of course, and not everyone reaches or expects to reach the top. But the opportunity is there, and it arises solely from the organisation of farming in the Open Fields. A man may have no more than an acre or two, but he gets the full extent of them laid out in long "lands" for ploughing, with no hedgerows to reduce the effective area and to occupy him in unprofitable labour... Moreover, he has his common rights which entitle him to graze stock over all the "lands", and these have a value the equivalent of which in pasture fields would cost far more than he could afford to pay.'

But however much such a man 'progresses' he still remains a responsible member of the community, enjoying exactly the same rights as the poorest cottager.

It is not claimed that the Open Fields system was ideal; poverty and hardship existed, and in the background was the feudal system, exacting service rents, payments in kind, tithes, etc. But at any rate the system demonstrates two facts so often denied: that a democracy does not necessarily imply a State or a bureaucracy; and that an industry can be administered by the workers themselves, without capital and without overseers. In short, the history of the Open Fields is a proof of the validity of the main principles of anarchism.

6
Lament for Spain

We are the victims of a trance that stay
In England's April bower this fateful year.
Our eyes are filled with drowsy light: a warm breath
Drifts gently over the withered fields. Upon the hills
The cherry-orchards lie like fallen clouds
Through which the sun has poured its tranquil gold.
Bright with firstling flowers my garden mocks

The dungeoned spirit brooding in its midst.
Among the birds that fill the virgin dusk
With plaintive songs, one voice that was not heard
Since love and longing ceased under the summer sun
Drops into the chilling air its vivid notes.
The nightingale is here again: he sits

On the same bough of the self-same tree
Where year by year with scarce a day's delay
He keeps his tryst. Down all the vale
Where oak trees rise above the ragged hedge
His fellow migrants take their stand, and as the stars
Throb into sight above the leafless elms,
Their songs, which faltered for a while,
Swell into a loud and sequent threnody.

Hither as he winged his way, this bird
Rested in some Iberian grove and saw
Tangled like the olive roots the limbs of men
Fallen that day defending Spain.
In the abandon of death they had embraced
Earth or sky: the silver light revealed
Cords of blood across their naked breasts.
They were a remnant band that stranded here
Fought till their last shot was gone,
Then met the armoured horde with lifted fist
And the cry of their faith: *No pasarán!*

    Their bodies stiffen in the upland air.
    The night is not still, guns and limbers
    Rumble on the distant road; a burning house
    Wounds with its ruddy glow the dove-soft sky
    And moaning women search the ruined fields.

Like the shadow of a falling leaf you flitted
Through the intricate thickets of death.
Your spirit was driven to seek
A cool nest in the north. You did not sing
Over these sombre men; but you caught as you passed
A sobbing note, and now when you sing
In an English valley, your passionate song
Is no longer serene. Symbol of love and life
It fills this April night with a wild lament.

7
Nearer to Reality

THE year has opened tragically for the true friends of Spain, but the disasters which have filled us with sorrow and apprehension can also serve to bring us nearer to reality. It is not that we have been living in a fool's paradise; there is nothing, either in the history of our movement or in the present alignment of forces, that could for a moment lead us to suppose that freedom and justice were easy to uphold. It is doubtful if our cause can ever be established by force of arms, because the arms we bear are dangerous, even to ourselves. The instruments of death are incompatible with freedom. We fervently desire the victory of the Spanish people and with victory we hope to carry forward our libertarian policy. A victory for Franco would mean, instead of an open campaign for freedom, for federalism and for workers' control, a return to the dark battle against tyranny. We do not fear that prospect. We know that though we are without wealth and opportunity to buy the weapons of modern warfare, we fight with the irresistible armament of our ideals. Against us is an embodiment of force and might – a power that must perish of its spiritual and intellectual poverty; with us is the immortal flame of humanity – the truth and love which penetrate all barriers and bring us, through centuries of oppression, nearer to the good life.

The mighty armaments which Franco has secured from his fascist allies may subdue the Spanish people, but they cannot extinguish the knowledge and enlightenment which have come into their lives. Indeed, the effect of this long strife is quite the contrary. It has illuminated, as never before, the misery of a people; it has thrown into sharp opposition the ideals of freedom and of force; it has caused millions of simple people, who never before dared to lift their minds above the dull routine of their slavish lives, to question the justice of their lot and to yearn for a fairer existence. The ideas which we had to instil by propaganda and education are now a common possession of all the people; and once a people is roused to a consciousness of its rights, once love replaces duty in their hearts, and mutual aid is seen as an alternative to moral and economic servitude, then no power of armaments and no alien mercenaries can for long withstand the spiritual power that is generated in their midst.

The Spanish tragedy brings us nearer to reality – above all to the realisation that the international solidarity of the working classes, which is the only force we can oppose to capitalism and fascism, does not yet exist. Do not let us disguise the ugly truth: the Spanish workers have been betrayed by their British, French and American comrades. History will record to our shame that in these very years which saw the destruction of the Spanish democracy for want of arms, our own workers were busily engaged on the rearmament of their capitalist masters.

We must create new bonds of international solidarity, free from the weaknesses inherent in parliamentary socialism. We must return to the foundations of our faith; for it is the head of this giant democracy, and not the feet, that has proved to be made of traitrous clay.

Our immediate duty is to alleviate our guilt with acts of solidarity. A people, homeless and persecuted because of the faith they share with us, must be rescued from death and despair. We must stir the conscience of our country, so that it gives shelter and food to those who are destitute because we have refused them arms for their self-defence.

8

Democratic Hospitality

THE illustrations which we reproduce in this number, and those which recently received wide publication in *Picture Post*, will bring home to people more vividly than any words can do, the conditions under which the Spanish refugees in France are living – and dying. The suffering which is being endured by hundreds of thousands of human beings distributed all over Europe and Asia begins to deaden the senses; like killing in war, persecution has become a normality which we accept without any qualms of conscience. Nevertheless, there are certain aspects of the Spanish tragedy which call for special comment.

If pity were inspired by anything but sentimental considerations – a weeping child, even a howling dog, is now more moving than a crucified man – the plight of the Spanish army which crossed into France early in March should have lit fires of indignation in every civilised land. Suffering from hunger and exhaustion, these men who for months had been fighting the rearguard action of European democracy were received in a democratic country not as heroes but as criminals. Indeed, as worse than criminals, for these are given at least decent shelter and adequate food. Our Spanish comrades were herded like animals in open compounds, surrounded by barbed-wire entanglements and armed guards, and deprived of the most elementary necessities of life. They were left to dig themselves holes in the sand, to dig futile shelters of sticks and rags, to scrounge for food like abandoned dogs. There was, at the beginning, some excuse for the Democratic Governments (it is not fair to put the whole blame on the French Government, in view of the 'close co-operation' which has marked the whole course of the non-interventionist policy of the democratic powers); they had not expected an invasion of such proportions and had no organisation ready to deal with it. But natural catastrophes like earthquakes and floods are even more unexpected, and yet they usually call into existence a prompt and efficient rescue service. In this case there was no sudden rush to help, only confusion and embarrassment. And meanwhile the refugees, many of them sick or wounded, perished by the hundreds – perished unnecessarily. A certain amount of aid was provided by the French trade unions, and by voluntary organisations. But even now, many weeks after the event, these brave soldiers of the Spanish Republic exist in conditions far worse than the concentration camps of Germany and Russia.

Why, then, do we continue to treat them like outcasts and criminals? We have declared our purpose: to oppose aggression wherever it appears in Europe; and these men have no other purpose. France still retains the gold reserves and the arms which rightly belong to these men, and there can be no practical difficulty in giving effect to such a policy. The only factor working against it is our inhuman treatment of these men on whom our security may depend. Their hearts are filling with bitterness and despair, and they might with justice refuse to trust those who have so repeatedly betrayed them. Even without the experience of these last few weeks, they might well ask themselves what there is to make them choose between the hypocrisy of the so-called democracies and the realism of the fascists. It is a question we are all asking ourselves. We are being called on to fight to defend a bankrupt institution – that parliamentary democracy which everywhere, most of all in Russia, is powerless to prevent the breakdown of the economic basis upon which the whole of our civilisation is built. The two forces which oppose each other in the world to-day are both negative forces – forces of despair and desperation. It was only in Spain that a new way of life, totally opposed to the economic assumptions of the modern world, seemed possible of realisation. For the moment that hope is defeated. We should not despise our Spanish comrades, therefore, if they elect to leave this scene of deception and in a new world, in Mexico for example, attempt once more to realise their great ideals. 'Arms for Spain' used to be our slogan. Let it now be 'Ships to Mexico'.

9

The Russian Terror

The Guillotine at Work: Twenty Years of Terror in Russia by G.P. Maximoff.

THIS is a formidable work of over six hundred pages, and is one of the most impressive indictments ever brought against a political regime. The author, a veteran revolutionist and active participant in the Russian Revolution, began with the intention of presenting a full picture of political persecution in the Russia during the past twenty years, but the material was so overwhelming in quantity that it was decided to confine the book exclusively to material dealing with the persecution of the Anarchists. The Social Revolutionists, the Social Democrats, Maximalists, Social Zionists, Tolstoyans, etc., all of whom have a similar tale to tell, must wait their turn. In view of the mass and complexity of the material, the author is to be congratulated on bringing such a difficult task to a successful conclusion, and the Berkman Fund and other groups which contributed to the cost of the publication on the magnificent use they have made of their meagre resources. At the same time the form of the book invites a word or two of criticism. The data and documents which give the volume its historical importance are preceded by a preliminary essay on 'The Sources of the Russian Terror'. This essay extends to 338 pages, more than half the book! Now admittedly the documents need some form of presentation, and it is important to show that the terror is not a recent development which we can label 'Stalinism', but was inherent in the ideas and methods of Lenin himself. This fact the author demonstrates conclusively, mainly by the quotation of Lenin's own words. But we cannot help feeling that this polemical argument would have been better as a separate volume, and that the data and documents which form the second part of the present work would have gained in impressiveness if they had been presented with a minimum of comment, something not much longer than the introductory essay on 'Anarchists in the Revolution', which does actually precede this second part.

This purely formal criticism seems trivial when we pass to a consideration of the contents of the book, which are of a terrifying actuality. Both in extent and intensity the Russian Terror has exceeded any previous political tyranny of which we have historical record: it reduces the terror which followed the French Revolution to insignificance and can only be matched by the exploits of Genghis Khan. At a conservative estimate the Russian Terror cost, in executions, epidemics and famine, from 20 to 22 million lives between the years 1917-34. The figures, as Maximoff says, numb one's brain, and the actuality is perhaps only to be grasped by focusing on individual cases. But what is demonstrated, by a consideration of the general features of the Terror, is that the ultimate cause was an idea, held on to with blind fanaticism. This idea expressed itself in the phrase 'the dictatorship of the proletariat', which was innocent enough when first used by Marx, but which became fatal through the intervention of two political expedients – the identification of the proletariat with the Bolshevik Party, and the use of the State as an instrument of revolution. Expedients and compromises may have been necessary for the effective defeat of the reactionary forces; but there is no doubt whatsoever that what took place was a progressive brutalisation of Lenin's own mind under the corrupting influence of the exercise of power. Some day, perhaps, we shall understand this process from a psychological point of view; meanwhile it has to be recorded as an historical tragedy involving the lives of millions of innocent people.

> 'Dictatorship leads to regression, to physical, social and moral decadence, toward slavery, toward complete, integral slavery, toward a sea of blood and an ocean of tears. It is natural, for dictatorship bases itself upon terror, upon the death penalty. But the death penalty, whoever uses it and wherever it is applied – on a large or small scale – results in moral corruption, brutalisation, loss of human values, stultification of individuality, lack of respect for the rights of others and consequently lack of respect for civil liberties, which in turn sooner or later leads, with the inevitability of a natural law, to the complete loss of all rights and liberties, to slavery, to a latent or expressly manifested dictatorship of a power-greedy and egoistic minority.'

Such is the lesson of the Russian Revolution.

It is impossible to review the second part of the volume in any detail. It consists of a year by year chronicle of arrests, persecutions and struggles of the Russian Anarchists, together with letters from prison and exile. There are many important manifestos and protests, extracts from newspapers and journals, and several 'human documents' which rise to the heights of tragic pathos. Ciliga, in the book reviewed in the last number of *War Commentary* [*The Russian Enigma*], has paid a disinterested tribute to the nobility of the Anarchists he met in Russian prisons and concentration camps. There are heroes in all sections of the revolutionary struggle, but in Russia, as more recently in Spain, the martyrdom of our comrades is an undying inspiration to all those who still work for a true socialism based on freedom, equality and brotherhood.

10

Use of Land

UNDER this title, on 1st October, Bernard Shaw opened a debate in *The Times* which, at the moment of writing, is still proceeding. It is an important subject, and one which will become desperately urgent in the years immediately ahead of us. Since *The Times* is not likely to give publicity to our views on the subject, let us begin our own debate. The subject has not been usefully considered by the anarchist movement since Kropotkin published his *Fields, Factories and Workshops*, and meanwhile the elements of the problem have been completely transformed. I am not forgetting the instructive experiments that took place in Spain during the brief existence of the Republic, but there the conditions were so different that they have little bearing on the agricultural policy of this country.

Shaw exhorts us to take a leaf out of Stalin's book and organise our agriculture on modern lines. In a few sentences which summarise the facts but do not recount the cost, he describes the stages by which Russia passed from a primitive agricultural community to one vast collective farm. He invites this country to follow the same steps, if not the same stages: he seems to imply that we might even take a short cut.

It is difficult to discuss the working of the present Russian agricultural system because the facts are obscure; there are no reliable reports from detached observers, and no statistics of any value. All we can be reasonably sure of is that the position is much better than it used to be, and that if Russia is not producing enough to give a square meal and a little over to every inhabitant, it is at least avoiding the famines of recent years.

By comparison our own system is hopelessly wasteful and antiquated – and 'antiquated' is perhaps not the appropriate word, for as Lord Bledisloe says (*The Times*, 14 October 1940): 'we have today (unlike a century ago) an agricultural community which, taken as a whole, is more deficient in up-to-date farming knowledge and less adequately equipped with personal supervision and personal guidance than that of any other civilised country, not excluding those whose claims to civilisation are temporarily blackened by insensate relapse into ethical and physical barbarity.' We cannot therefore claim that we have nothing to learn from the Russian experiments. We have, indeed, almost everything to learn from them, and the lesson is somewhat disingenuously hidden in a sentence of Mr Shaw's. Stalin, he says, 'found the solution in collective farming, State and co-operative, but mainly co-operative.' A truer statement of the facts would be: Stalin found the solution in a certain measure of collective farming, after he had failed to establish State farming. The orthodox Marxist scheme was a tragic failure, and merely resulted in famine and the deaths of untold millions of human beings. So State farming was abandoned and a compromise scheme of co-operative or collective farming quickly substituted, with much more success. In 1931, according to the official *History of the Communist Party of the Soviet Union* (Moscow, 1939) there were only 4,000 state farms as against 200,000 collective farms. Figures for later years are not given, but it is stated that by the end of 1934 the collective farms 'embraced about three-quarters of all the peasant households in the Soviet Union and about 90% of the total crop area' (*op. cit.*, p. 318). Trotsky (*The Revolution Betrayed*, 1936) states that '94% of the entire agricultural product is taken from the fields of the collective farms'.

What is a collective farm in the Soviet Union? It is officially defined as 'an agricultural artel in which only the *principal* means of production are collectivised'. This means, in effect, that 'the principal means of production, chiefly those used in grain growing, are collectivised, while household land, dwellings, part of the dairy cattle, small livestock, poultry, etc., are not collectivised' (*op. cit.*, p. 308). Now, though this departure from Marxist socialism is justified as good Leninism, that is to say, good opportunism, in so far as it departs from centralised state control of farming, it actually represents sound agricultural policy and sound anarchism. Its justification will be found in the works of Kropotkin rather than in those of Lenin. But let us leave polemics and turn to the English problem.

The solution of the agricultural problem in this country does not consist in expropriating the yeoman or tenant farmers, ploughing up the hedges and ditches and driving tractors over desolate stretches of open land – 'cultivating these isles by the million acres' as Mr Shaw puts it. It is true that the small farm of from fifty to five hundred acres is an anomaly – uneconomic in manpower and machine power and in all the problems of distribution. It is true that many farmers are scientifically incompetent and, what seems to distress Mr Shaw even more, incapable of making out their income-tax returns. But they have a good deal of traditional wisdom which is valuable, and they have an intimate knowledge of their land – and a good farmer must know the substance and texture of every square inch of his soil. All that knowledge goes down the drain if you simply expropriate these kulaks and replace them by a mechanic on a tractor.

The unrestricted application of mechanised methods to agriculture has not yet been proved an unquestioned benefit – any more than has the use of artificial manures. As the 'dust-bowls' of America prove, the land is apt to resent such 'inhuman' methods. Mr Shaw's state farms 'cultivating these isles by the million acres' would quickly bring about the same results here. Agriculture demands a certain minimum density of population, human beings and cattle, whose waste products feed the soil. But nobody but a medievalist or a mystic like Giono wants to abolish the tractor or to rely entirely on farmyard manure. What we want is a common-sense use of the power and products of modern science (and it is the scientists who have exposed the technical abuse of the soil), remembering that these should be used for the benefit of mankind, and not for the creation of profits or the provision of statistics for politicians.

What, then, is the solution of our land problem? I can best describe it in a series of practical proposals:

1. Abolish the private ownership of land.
2. Abolish rent.
3. Abolish all farms of more than fifty acres in extent.*
4. Group these smallholdings round 'open fields' – undivided land of several hundred (or even thousand) acres' extent.
5. Plan these collective farms on a regional basis for the provision of the principal means of production, 'chiefly those used in grain growing'.
6. Establish for each region a fully equipped agricultural research station where information and guidance will be freely available to all the collective farmers within the region.
7. In place of rent for smallholdings, exact a contribution of labour-units of work on the collective farm.

8. Let the workers on the collective farms elect councils whose duty it will be to appoint scientific managers, accountants, etc.
9. Abolish the Ministry of Agriculture.
10. In these, and many other subsidiary ways, preserve the essentials of sound farming, viz.:
    a) the interplay of individual and collective motives;
    b) a sufficiency of human beings and livestock on the land to maintain the organic life of the soil;
    c) the community life of the countryside.

Meanwhile another complementary process should be going on – the decentralisation of industry. This would distribute the population more evenly, help to solve problems of transport and distribution, and generally make for balanced, harmonious communities.

* Fifty acres – it might be less, but it would have to be something a good deal more than Jesse Collings' 'three acres and a cow'. It must provide not only for a man's family but for the daily needs of the workers on the collective, many of whom would normally belong to these family units.

11
Eric Gill: Anarchist

A FEW days before he died, in a letter he wrote to me about my pamphlet *The Philosophy of Anarchism*, Eric Gill said: 'I find it difficult to discover anything I don't agree with, and in spite of the appearance to the contrary I am really in complete agreement with you about the necessity of anarchism, the ultimate truth of it, and its immediate practicability as syndicalism.'

Any hesitation I might have had in publishing what was a privately expressed opinion is dispelled by the publication of Gill's *Autobiography*. In this sincere and noble book Gill makes quite clear that he was fundamentally an anarchist – that he was one of the many people who are anarchists in thought if not yet in name. That was already obvious in an essay on 'Ownership and Industrialism' which appeared in his book *Sacred and Secular*, published a year ago – an essay I would always recommend to people who want a first introduction to the principles of anarchism. In this latest and last book, Gill shows not only how he came to be an anarchist, but also how, with an integrity which I for one could only envy, he managed to live like one. As an exceptionally talented craftsman he was, perhaps, in an exceptionally favourable position: he had escaped from the capitalist treadmill, and could live more or less where he liked and how he liked. But that for him did not mean 'escapism': he did not retreat to the Côte d'Azur or California, but made his 'cell of good living' right here 'in the chaos of our world'. For those who had the privilege of knowing him, his example was an inspiration, his home a blazing light in the darkness. 'What I hope above all things is that I have done something towards re-integrating bed and board, the small farm and the workshop, the home and the school, earth and heaven'. So he writes towards the end of his autobiography. His whole life was directed to such a 're-integration' and it is his life, and the philosophy upon which it is based, that will endure even longer than his art.

'My socialism was from the beginning a revolt against the intellectual degradation of the factory hands and the damned ugliness of all that capitalist-industrialism produced, and it was not primarily a revolt against the cruelty and injustice of the possessing classes or against the misery of the poor. It was not so much the working *class* that concerned me as the working *man* – not so much what he got from working as what he did by working.' This shows the early direction of Gill's political ideas: he was what I have been accustomed to call an individualist, but in the letter already referred to he wrote: 'I think it would be good if you distinguished between the *individual*, as being the unit of a group whether of animate or inanimate nature, and the *person*. It is a primary doctrine of Christianity that men are unique persons. It is as persons that they are unique, whereas as individuals they may not be.' It is a distinction which I accept – it is, indeed, a distinction fundamental to anarchism, and the basic reason for our rejection of all forms of collectivism and state capitalism. When Gill first entered the socialist movement, through the Fabian Society, he found that no one respected this distinction – the socialist movement 'was not moved or led, still less could it be said to be inspired, by any ideas of man or man's life or of man's work other than those of the capitalist world against whose injustices and cruelties it was in revolt... Socialism as a political movement is hardly more than an attempt to re-order the distribution of factory products and factory profits.' The rest of Gill's political evolution should be followed in detail in his book, but in the end 'it began to be clear that the hateful world of the man of business and its hateful cruelties would never be abolished by those who profited by them and that "the mother of parliaments" was not an institution for righting wrongs (after all, it never had been) but one for the promotion and preservation of whatever seemed most profitable to owners of capital. And foreign politics was nothing but an extension of home politics on the same general principle.' As these things became clear to Gill, 'the hope of reform by parliamentary means began to recede proportionally.'

Gill then concluded that 'no merely political or economic rearrangement of the world was going to be effective to remove such horrors' – the horrors of capitalist society. The remedy, he felt, must lie in the sphere of religion and morals. He became a Christian, a Christian who was always a thorn in the side of the Church. The root of the social evil was a moral evil – the desire of money – and to Gill it was elementary that all Christians should condemn this evil or give up pretending to be followers of Christ. It seemed to him 'incomparably more horrible that men of business should rule us and impose their foul point of view on the world than it would be if the whole race of men and women should rot their bodies with lechery and drunkenness... What is truly monstrous and disruptive and corrupting to our life and virtue is that such persons should be our rulers – that they should have usurped the seats of kings, that their hideous teaching should have replaced the Gospel.' His final position is summed up in this paragraph:

> 'But one thing was clear: I must keep clear of politics – politics as the word is understood in our time and in what are called democratic countries. And I must keep clear of politicians – the gang of professional parliamentarians and town and county councillors. For in the first place politics is beyond me. Politics is like foreign languages – something outside my scope, something I can't do. Moreover, I do not believe political arrangements and re-arrangements are real. It is all a confused business of ramps and rackets – pretended quarrels and dishonest commercial schemings, having no relation to the real interests of peoples, neither to their spiritual nor their material welfare, and conducted upon no principles other than momentary self-interest. The prestige of parliament is an empty fraud and all its grandiose and clumsy procedure is more outworn and even less venerable than the ritual in Anglican Cathedrals. And politics is now a profession! Professionalism is a curse in any trade – the defence of anything, without due consideration of its goodness, on account of pecuniary interest or inertia. Public schools, the army, the law, architecture and, most frightful, the Church, all suffer from the curse of professionalism, though all these are served by trained and honestly devoted men. But politicians can make no such claim to our respect. It is not too much to say that they are trained to nothing but vote-catching, and that they are not and never have been anything but agents for the defence of monetary interests. Such was the origin of parliamentary representation, and such is its very soul. This is not the place for even the briefest outline of parliamentary history; it is only necessary to note that all its evils have been grossly augmented since the final and decisive victory of finance which the nineteenth century witnessed. There is now no hope of a reform of our society by parliamentary means.'

In this sense of the word, all anarchists are resolved to keep clear of politics. But politics in another sense – the politics of preaching and propaganda, of thought and work – the politics which consists of trying 'to make a cell of good living in the chaos of our world' – to such politics we must devote ourselves, and such is the politics which Gill practised with greater effect than he ever realised. He belonged to that rare company of *integral* socialists, whose lives are a consequence of their socialism, their socialism a consequence of their lives. He was the most honest man I have ever known, or am likely to know.

12
Bedlam Politics

SPEAKING at the Royal Institution yesterday, the Soviet Ambassador invited us never to forget that good English expression, *First things first*. An admirable sentiment which we can all approve.

But what are the first things which we should put first?

The first thing, according to Mr Maisky, is to crush Hitlerite Germany – not, be it observed, to crush *fascism* – that might bring the mailed fist down on the heads of some of our friends – on Admiral Darlan's head, on General Franco's head, on Comrade Stalin's head – and on heads still nearer home.

No! Our politicians no longer revile fascism; they have invented an historical abstraction called 'Hitlerite Germany', something which is neither Hitler nor Germany, neither fascism nor totalitarianism.

Is that putting first things first? Is it not rather an evasion of the real issue, which is now as it has always been the issue between freedom and tyranny.

When our leaders speak in unequivocal voices about political realities; when they admit that fascism is not confined to Italy or to Germany, but is a disease which has invaded every country in the world – Spain and France, Japan and the United States, Soviet Russia and the British Empire – then and then only shall we believe that they are putting first things first.

The reality is far otherwise. Our politicians are grotesque. They only need a bladder on the end of a stick to complete their clown-like appearance; an appearance which is nevertheless very deceptive; consider them:

Clown-politicians who hand out contracts with one hand and receive them with the other;

Clown-politicians who are patriotically inspired to defend their class interests with Swinton Committees and anti-comintern funds;

Clown-politicians who do their buying in the Black Market, and their cooking in Whitehall;

Clown-politicians who launch their chartered platitudes on the deep Atlantic of their hypocrisy.

Now the hypocrite is nearly related to the lunatic. The definition of one kind of lunatic is a man with a split mind.

Our leaders are mostly of this kind. With one half of their mind they admire this fellow Hitler. He has abolished unemployment, which they could never succeed in doing; he has created the most efficient army in the world, which they envy; he has liquidated those troublesome trade unions; above all, he is now doing the best job of all – ridding the world of the Bolshevik menace. One side of the mind of our leaders finds fascism very very attractive.

But the other side of this split mind realises that this fellow Hitler does not play the game. He is not a gentleman. He not only breaks all the rules of what is curiously called 'civilised' warfare, drops bombs on private property and on innocent civilians, he actually wants to pinch our markets, our shipping, our empire!

One could almost pity such tortured consciences, but then we realise that it is these idiots with a split mind who rule the demented world of today. A world in which the mad lead the mad.

For we have to admit that it is not our rulers alone who are mad. They have infected whole nations.

The extension of the war to Russia has achieved what the press calls the final unity of the British Nation. From the tory right to the communist left, we fight in one unbroken line.

Similarly, according to the same press, the virtual extension of the war to the United States has achieved a world-wide unity of the democratic nations: they fight in one unbroken line.

Now when you find such an appearance of unity in the world, history leads us to suspect the most complete form of suppression and persecution.

Man is various. He divides into various psychological types, and according to his type, his feelings and opinions will differ.

It is natural that men should suffer, and progress consists in the discussion and reconciliation of differences. That is the dialectical principle of life itself, and it is a process that has no finality. The only finality is death, or biological extinction.

When two men cannot reconcile their difference by reason and discussion, and cannot agree to differ, then they resort to fighting. Their neighbours pull them apart and the state of our civilisation or social morality is exalted enough to make such men feel ashamed of their behaviour.

When a few score men lose their reason and threaten to fight, then it is called a riot, and these men are restrained by their neighbours through professional keepers-of-the-peace called police. But the men who lost their reason are no longer so ashamed of themselves.

When a large part of a nation loses its reason and threatens to fight, then it is called a rebellion. Police are no longer adequate and the two halves of the nation must fight it out. Nowadays the side that can command the greatest number of tanks and aeroplanes suppresses the other side and that is called a victory for order and justice.

When two nations lose their reason and begin to fight, it is called a war, and there is now no longer the slightest trace of shame. To fight becomes a high moral duty, blessed by the churches. Each nation is united. It is a mass renunciation of reason, it is mass insanity. And there is no limit to what D.H. Lawrence called 'the abysmal insanity of the normal masses'.

This abysmal insanity is now world-wide. It engulfs Europe and Asia, Africa and Australia, and now spreads to America.

When Bedlam is universal it is the sane man who is accused of being abnormal. A sane man in an asylum has not much chance of being taken seriously. And if the lunatics are violent and break out of bounds, he is powerless to restrain them.

I wish this was a metaphor. I wish I were speaking to you in parables. But it is a strictly scientific description of the world we are now living in. We are living in a world seized with mass insanity. And it requires an almost superhuman effort to remain sane in such a world.

But assuming we retain our whole minds, our sanity, what then can we do?

Frankly, I do not think we can do anything spectacular. We are helpless. We have no tanks, we have no aeroplanes. We are a handful of peaceful men and women caught in the mad rush of millions of madmen.

Willy-nilly we are carried in the irresistible swirl of military and industrial conscription, of crushing taxation and poverty, of death and destruction. We are condemned to live in an epoch of physical misery and social degradation.

But one thing we retain, which all other people have lost: our spiritual calmness, the still voice of reason.

It is a precious possession which we have to carry through this dark age, and this we can do in the immemorial way in which truth has always survived tyranny, neglect and persecution.

The true believers in freedom are being driven to the catacombs again, and it was from the catacombs that a faith which was to transform the world once emerged.

That faith, in all its social and ethical implications, has long since been abandoned by the Church which is its official embodiment.

We here are nearer to the spirit of the catacombs than any other group of men in the world.

Let us act in the spirit of the catacombs, forming our cells, sending out our preachers, striving to throw out the evil spirits which possess the masses.

But the modern evangelist must work mainly through the printed word, and that is why we must establish and maintain a press, a press from which the Friends of Freedom can pour out an endless stream of pamphlets and periodicals, all testifying to this truth: *That man is born equal, to share equally the fruits of the earth, and to live in mutual friendship with all his kind.*

13

The Education of Free Men

WE stopped in the thicket beyond the threshing-floor at the very end of the village. Sämka picked up a dry stick from the snow and began striking it against the frosty trunk of a lime tree. Hoar frost fell from the branches onto our caps, and the noise of the blows resounded in the stillness of the wood.

'Lëv Nikolaevich,' said Fédka to me ... 'why does one learn singing? I often think, why, really, does one?'

What made him jump from the terror of the murder to this question, heaven only knows; yet by the tone of his voice, the seriousness with which he demanded an answer, and the attentive silence of the other two, one felt that there was some vital and legitimate connection between this question and our preceding talk.

Tolstoy
(translated by Aylmer Maude)

The social question will be decided by molecular processes in the life of the people which bring the tissue of society to a new birth. It will be decided from below, not from above, as an effect of freedom, not by the act of authority.

N. Berdyaev

1. What is the Purpose of Education?

'The true object of education', wrote William Godwin in the first sentence of his *Enquirer* (1797), 'like that of every other moral process, is the generation of happiness.' I know of no better definition of the aim of education, but like all definitions, it is regressive, throwing us back on the need for further definitions. What, for example, is meant by the word 'generation' – is it a natural process which only requires encouragement, or is it a regimen enforced by a special technique of teaching? And can happiness be defined in a way which would include the contradictory desires of any average group of men? More interesting perhaps than the definition itself is Godwin's parenthesis, which asserts without argument that education is 'a moral process.' A century and a half ago that might have been an obvious point of view, but it is a measure of our different outlook today that we would not immediately agree that morality enters into the question. The precept 'Be good, and let who will be wise,' would not nowadays find acceptance even in a Sunday school. Education – we do not say, but unconsciously assume – is an acquisitive process, directed to vocation. It is a collecting of means for a specific end, and most of the complaints about our educational system are directed against the adequacy of such means, or the failure to specify clearly enough the ends. Efficiency, progress, success – these are the aims of a competitive system from which all moral factors are necessarily excluded. In that respect, at least, our schools reflect truly enough our social order.

Happiness is an individual affair. It is ripeness in each fruit: the full degree of maturation, of sweetness, of fertility. But the fruit hangs on a tree, and though the fruits do not all ripen at exactly the same time, or in the same degree, the health of the tree is shown by its over-all ripeness. As Godwin went on to say, man is a social being. 'In society the interests of individuals are intertwisted with each other, and cannot be separated. Men should be taught to assist each other.' In other words, a factor in individual happiness is mutual aid, and these two aspects of man's existence are interdependent. Education is the process of their adjustment.

All the possible words we may use to express the purpose of education – tuition, instruction, upbringing, discipline, the acquisition of knowledge, the inculcation of manners or morality – all these reduce to two complementary processes, which we can best describe as 'individual growth' and 'social initiation.' In no respect do the educational systems characteristic of the various nations of today favour either of these processes. Either they force individual growth into a pattern which destroys its natural grace and vigour; or if a free and independent person does emerge from the process of education, it is only to find himself at odds with a society into whose concept of normality he does not fit.

The trouble about happiness, as Aristotle pointed out, is that it is a platitude: to give it as the aim of education, or of political science, seems somewhat superficial, especially to people with pretensions to wisdom, who are often animated by a desire to make men suffer before they enjoy. In Christian philosophy especially, there is always a premium attached to happiness. It is very necessary, of course, to deepen the concept of happiness, because we all soon discover how impermanent is the sense of well-being which comes from good nourishment, a pleasant environment, adequate means and perfect health. Happiness, in a word, is *psychological*, and all material riches are worthless unless we have peace of mind. This was realised by the ancient philosophers, by Confucius and Lao Tzu, by Socrates and Aristotle; and they therefore defined happiness in some such words as Aristotle's, who said that it is 'an activity of the soul in accordance with perfect virtue.' But that, again, is merely a definition which demands further definitions, and so Aristotle had to define what he meant by virtue. He came to the conclusion that there was no such thing as virtue, but only virtues, intellectual and moral. Wisdom and understanding, knowing how to act or behave in given circumstances, the science of life – that is one aspect of virtue; but a man may have all this knowledge but not be able to control his own impulses and desires. He may have perfect understanding, but be a creature of bad habits. Knowledge and self-discipline are therefore two different aspects of virtue, both essential to happiness, and both to be learned in the normal course of education.

The difference between these two aspects of virtue – let us follow the usual practice and call them intellectual and moral virtue – is that whilst the first can be made a subject of general agreement, the second depends on the temperament or disposition of the individual. Intellectual virtue can be codified and accepted as a system of beliefs and customs; but moral virtue is the interior function of each man's physiological and nervous make-up. Since a man deficient in moral virtue cannot be expected to appreciate properly the values of intellectual virtue, moral virtue has a fundamental priority in education. The first question in education, therefore, is how best to develop the moral virtues of children – that is to say, how best to train the physical senses with which each individual is endowed so that they mature to that state of temperance, harmony and skill which will enable the individual to pursue the intellectual virtues in freedom of will and singleness of mind.

Aristotle pointed out that moral virtue – the integrated personality, as modern psychologists would say – comes about as a result of habit. We are conditioned by nature to form habits, and the form our habits should take is inherent in nature. 'Neither by nature, then, nor contrary to nature do the virtues arise in us; rather we are adapted by nature to receive them and are made perfect by habit.'

The pattern of those habits which we are adapted to receive – i.e., to be taught – is found in nature: from nature we must take that pattern, and by habituating our children to that pattern, we shall perfect their moral virtue and enable them to achieve true happiness. That does not mean that we are slaves to nature, but that we can only discover freedom in nature. The free man is a man of nature, perfected in natural ways of behaviour.

Such is the theory of Aristotle: he derived it in a large measure from Plato, and to Plato we must turn for a detailed account of this natural pattern, and of the only effective method of adapting ourselves to it. But first let us note that the general tradition of education in Europe and America since the Renaissance has neglected or distorted this classical theory of education – first by blurring the clear distinction between intellectual and moral virtue, and then by ignoring the essential priority of moral virtue, by attempting to inculcate intellectual virtue into minds which have not received the necessary preparation. It is only onto a stock of goodness that knowledge can be safely grafted: by grafting it onto stocks that are unbalanced, undeveloped, neurotic, we merely give power to impulses that may in themselves be evil or corrupted.

2. The Pattern in Nature

To suggest that the pattern of moral virtue is to be found in nature seems immediately to involve us in a scientific approach to our subject. We have become so prejudiced by the claims put forward by certain scientists, that we have been content to leave 'nature' to science, and to let it be assumed that 'art' is something outside nature. Science implies measurement and classification – what is called 'scientific method' or analysis. But it is only one 'method' and wisdom, which includes science in its scope, implies also synthesis – the apprehension and understanding of wholes and relationships, the workings of the imagination and creative activity – in short, a subjective and sensational approach to reality; and this aspect of wisdom might be called the method of art, or 'aesthetic method'. As such, it must be regarded as an indispensable instrument of education; and since scientific method is not within the mental capacity of young children, and aesthetic method is natural to them, we must turn to art as the only method available for the first stages of education.

During the past fifty years a world-wide revolution has taken place in the appreciation of children's art; gradually we have come to realise that we have in art an instrument of education and not merely a subject to be taught. Children have an art, that is to say, a way of expressing themselves in visual and plastic images, appropriate to their stage of mental development and this pictorial language of theirs is something which exists in its own rights and which is not to be judged by adult standards. It is a means of communication possessed by every child, and one which can be used to give us an understanding of the child, and to give the child an understanding of its environment. Art is not now an 'extra': we no longer seek to pick out a few children with what used to be called an artistic temperament, and educate this minority to be artists. We recognise an artist of some kind in every child, and we maintain that the encouragement of a normal creative activity is one of the essentials of a full and balanced development of the personality.

This is a revolution to which many philosophers, psychologists and teachers have contributed, but it was John Ruskin who first suggested that the child's artistic activity should be entirely voluntary. It was an English psychologist, James Sully, who first made any considerable study of the characteristics of this voluntary activity. But great educationalists all over the world, following the lead of Froebel, were beginning to insist on the importance of spontaneity in all forms of education. The position we have now reached implies a claim that of all forms of spontaneous activity, a special educative value attaches to the artistic activity.

From this point of view, art is not to be treated as something external which has to be inserted into the general scheme of education. Nor, on the other hand, can education be regarded as something which can ever be complete without art. There is a certain way of life which we hold to be good, and the creative activity which we call art is essential to it. Education is nothing but an initiation into this way of life, and we believe that in no way is that initiation so successfully achieved as through the practice of art.

Art, that is to say, is a way of education; not so much a subject to be taught as a method of teaching any and all subjects. For this view of the educative role of art no originality can be claimed: we are but restating in modern terms the ideals which Plato expressed twenty-four centuries ago. And when we say we are restating these ideals in modern terms we do not mean that we are adapting Plato's ideas to modern needs. We are not distorting his meaning or intention in any one particular. When Plato uses abstract terms like harmony, grace and rhythm, and when we use the same abstract terms, we want to convey exactly the same meaning. It is only when we use more particular terms, like music or painting or architecture, that we diverge a little from Plato in that we illustrate our meaning from our richer store of experience. It does not follow that we are any nearer to the truth than Plato, but we are entitled to claim, if we have any faith at all in human evolution, that the use we can make of arts like music or painting or architecture is potentially much greater than it was for Plato. But only potentially. For what is the history of the modern world, a world so rich potentially, but one long record of unrealised potentialities, of missed opportunities? Not much is known about that obscure subject, Greek music; but not even our classical scholars have ventured to suggest that Greek music was anything but a primitive affair in comparison with the music of Bach, of Mozart, of Beethoven. But what proportional use have we ever made of this modern art in education? Our music, compared with Greek music, is a veritable extension of human sensibility. But what commensurate place does it occupy in our schools? We have eurhythmics, it is true, and let us pay all honour to Dalcroze who has in this one aspect of education set us on the right path. But even in those schools which have been wholly devoted to Dalcroze's ideals, it is to be doubted whether we have advanced even so far as the educational methods contemplated by Plato on the basis of the primitive music of Greece.

The claims made by Plato for an aesthetic mode of education are quite simply stated. Indeed, one cannot do better than translate Plato's own words. 'We attach such supreme importance to musical education' – he makes Socrates say in the *Republic* (III, 401-2) – 'because rhythm and harmony sink most deeply into the recesses of the soul, and take most powerful hold of it, bringing gracefulness in their train, and making a man graceful if he be rightly nurtured, but if not, the reverse.' Plato then describes in what we call considerable psychological detail, the exact effects of rhythm and harmony on the growing mind. But he does not, as is too often assumed in the discussions of his educational theories, ascribe these qualities to music only. He says that the same qualities 'enter largely into painting and all similar workmanship, into weaving and embroidery, into architecture, as well as the whole manufacture of utensils in general, nay, into the constitution of living bodies, and of all plants; for in all these things, gracefulness or ungracefulness finds place.' And he adds, for he has always the negative picture in mind, 'the absence of grace, rhythm, and harmony, is closely related to an evil style, and an evil character.'

There is something at once so simple and so comprehensive about this theory of Plato's that really we do not need to go beyond it. Music, painting, the making of useful objects, the proportions of the living body and of plants, these will, if made the basis of our educational methods, instil into the child a grace and harmony which will give it, not merely a noble bearing, but also a noble character; not only a graceful body, but also a sober mind. It will do this, says Plato, long before the child is able to reason, because it will inculcate what he calls, 'the instinct of relationship,'[1] and it is upon this instinct that reason itself depends. Possessing this instinct, the child will never do wrong in deed or in thought.

I ought perhaps to explain, at this point, what Plato meant by this 'instinct of relationship,' for it is the foundation of his theory of education, and one, moreover, which he never abandoned throughout the development of this thought. The theory as I have already given it comes from the *Republic*. This was a work of the philosopher's early maturity. Thirty years later, at the age of seventy, Plato wrote his *Laws*, which Professor Taylor has described as 'today the least generally known of Plato's major compositions,' and yet 'in some respects his most characteristic work.'[2] Here, in the second Book, we find his theory of education through art restated in unmistakable terms – 'handled,' as Professor Taylor says, 'with a psychological thoroughness to which the *Republic* affords no parallel.' The theory, I would maintain, is as simple as it is true. It is this: that the aim of education should be to associate feelings of pleasure with what is good and feelings of pain with what is evil. Now such feelings are aesthetic – a fact which would have been obvious to the Greeks. This word 'aesthetic' as we use it is cold and abstract, but it indicates a relationship which to the Greeks was very real and organic, a property of the physiological reactions which take place in the process of perception.

Now, says Plato, there exist in the physical universe, which we experience through our senses, certain rhythms, melodies, and abstract proportions which when perceived convey to the open mind a sensation of pleasure. For the moment we need not consider *why* these rhythms and proportions exist: they are simply part of the given universe. But if, says Plato, we can associate the concrete sensation of pleasure given by these rhythms and proportions with good, and the concrete sensation of pain given by the opposite qualities of disharmony and ugliness with evil; if we can do this systematically in the early years, while the infant mind is still open to such influences, then we shall have set up an association between natural and spontaneous feelings and graceful or noble behaviour. Lest it should be thought that I am reading into Plato more than is justified, let me quote his actual words, as translated by Professor Taylor:

> 'And therefore what I would say is this: a child's first infant consciousness is that of pleasure and pain, this is the domain wherein the soul first acquires virtue or vice... By education I mean goodness in the form in which it is first acquired by a child. In fact, if pleasure and liking, pain and dislike, are formed in the soul on right lines before the age of understanding is reached, and when that age is attained, these feelings are in concord with understanding, thanks to early discipline in appropriate habits – this concord, regarded as a whole, is virtue. But if you consider the one factor in it, the rightly disciplined state of pleasures and pains whereby a man, from his first beginnings on, will abhor what he should abhor and relish what he should relish – if you isolate this factor and call it education, you will be giving it its true name.'

Plato then illustrates his argument in this way: 'No young creature whatsoever... can keep its body or its voice still: they are all perpetually trying to make movements and noises. They leap and bound, they dance and frolic, as it were with glee, and again, they utter cries of all sorts. Now animals at large have no perception of order or disorder in these motions, no sense of what we call rhythm or melody.' But man, Plato goes on to point out, is distinguished from the rest of animal creation precisely by the fact that he possesses an aesthetic sense, which he defines as 'the power to perceive and enjoy rhythm and melody.' Link this power of aesthetic perception to the power of discriminating between good and evil and then the most fundamental aim of education has been achieved. Good is *spontaneously* associated with pleasure, evil with pain.

Such is Plato's theory of education, and it seems to me to be essentially simple and obviously true. Why, then, should it offer such difficulty and, indeed, incomprehensibility to the modern educator? Professor Taylor, in his Introduction to his translation of the *Laws*, offers this explanation:

> 'To Plato, as a true Greek, the ugliness of conduct which is morally out of place is the most immediately salient fact about it, and the beauty of holiness, if the scriptural phrase may be permitted, is something more than a metaphor. To judge by the tone of much of our literature, we are less sensitive on the point; we seem slow to perceive ugliness in wrong-

doing as such, or even ready to concede the "artistry" of great wickedness. It may be a wholesome discipline to consider carefully whether this dfference of feeling may not be due less to a confusion on Plato's part between the beautiful and the morally good than to a certain aesthetic imperceptiveness on ours.'

3. Art and Human Nature

Plato was an authoritarian. His political utopia has always been a model for exponents of the totalitarian state. It is therefore necessary to ask ourselves whether there does not lurk in this theory of education some denial of that freedom and integrity of the human personality which is the basis of our libertarian philosophy. Granted the prevalence of 'aesthetic imperceptiveness,' this danger would surely exist: the 'order of nature' would be interpreted in a systematic and insensitive manner, and the emergent faculties of the child would then be 'conditioned' to this rigid pattern. Plato's republic can undoubtedly be regarded as a rigid pattern of this kind: it is the creation of a poet, but its beauty is objective, calculated, classical: it is like a crystal of ice. But nature is a living growth, and human nature is warm and mobile. Between the form natural to growth, which is a creative achievement of the life force or whatever impulse animates organic matter, and the forms abstracted by the human intellect, there is this difference: the one is a continuing process of freedom or spontaneity, of growth and integration, whereas the other is an act of objectification, or externalisation and fixation, of cooling and petrification. Our criticism of Plato, if this were the place to pursue it, would charge him with abstracting from the natural process, making of it a measured pattern, and thereby destroying its quality of spontaneity, which in the human personality is the quality of spiritual freedom.

Two quite distinct developments during the past sixty years have made it possible for us to accept Plato's theory of the place of art in education without incurring the dangers which it would offer to imperceptive minds. One is the complete revolution which has taken place in our conception of art itself, and the other is the revolution in psychology.

The revolution in art is by no means complete, nor has a definite new standard or style yet been established. To some people it seems that the present state of art is merely confused and incoherent. But it must be obvious, even to the most bewildered spectator of the modern scene, that there is more essential similarity between a modern functional building and the Parthenon, than between the Parthenon and the classical buildings of our own time. The functional building and the Parthenon both exhibit the same fundamental features of good architecture – fitness for purpose, harmony of proportions, good manners: whereas a modern building in the classical style can only be described as a fantasy in architectural inappropriateness. As for modern painting, there again one need not accept all its confused manifestations as a progress towards the ideal of beauty which Plato had in mind. Nevertheless, those with an eye to see, and no censoring prejudice, will find among these confused manifestations of the modern spirit works of art which answer to the Platonic canon, and are symbols of the grace and rhythm and harmony which led Plato to make art the basis of his educational system. One can assert of all the arts that a spirit of enquiry and scientific understanding has, during the last thirty years or so, led us back to the basic principles, and that though we cannot yet point to the creative achievements of a great age, we are now in a position to understand the significance of art such as has not existed since Plato's time. That is a large claim to make for the modern philosophy of art; it is perhaps a conceited claim. But however humble and soberminded we may be, it is difficult to find any intermediate period which reached such an understanding. It is true that during the Renaissance there were great humanists like Alberti who owed much to the Platonic doctrine, and the art of that period was, of course, a much nearer approximation to Plato's ideals than anything we have so far produced in the modern period. But neither Alberti nor any of the later humanists, however far they went in the direction of identifying moral and aesthetic ideals, ever committed themselves to anything as radical as an aesthetic method of education. They were all grammarians at heart, and like Browning's hero,[3] had 'decided not to live but know,' a noble ideal for the few who are content to work 'dead from the waist down,' but not a principle for those who believe with Plato that the function of education is to promote the good life.

However much an increased understanding of the nature of art has enabled us to appreciate the truth and relevance of Plato's theory of education, we have been helped in an even larger measure by the increased understanding of human nature which we owe to modern psychology. Adequately to demonstrate this fact would lead us into a technical discussion which would not be appropriate now, but perhaps I might briefly indicate three directions in which modern psychology tends to support our claims.

The first relates to the significance of imagery in thought – imagery of all kinds, although it is simpler to discuss the subject in terms of visual imagery. We know, on the basis of many recent experiments, that the child begins life with a mind full of extremely vivid imagery. One school of psychologists even maintains that in the first years the child has difficulty in distinguishing between its perceptions of the external world and its secondary images, and that the normal memory-image is only gradually separated from these vivid eidetic images. Whatever may be the truth of this theory, we do know for certain that the next stage in development, the stage of conceptual thought, is only reached by the gradual suppression of imagery. Now the whole Aristotelian tradition in education is so committed to the superiority of conceptual or logical processes of thought that all means have been taken to drive images out of the child's mind and to make it an efficient thinking machine. It was accepted as axiomatic that logical methods of procedure were uniquely efficient, and the ambition of every pedagogue was to devise a logical scheme for every subject in the curriculum. It was experimentally established that images performed no useful function in abstract thought, and the more abstract the thought the more intelligent it was assumed to be. To quote a well-known educationalist,[4] 'those children of the most fertile imagery.. were by no means those of the highest school intelligence... the correlations between vivid and clear visual and auditory imagery and school intelligence are low, or it may be negative...' and so on.

I have no desire to question these established facts. But what we must question is the standard of 'school intelligence' implicit in all such tests. It is nothing but the logical bias in its most blatant form. We know the examinations and tests by means of which the standard is established. Most of us have suffered from their indignities. But now, with the support of other schools of psychology, we are in a position to challenge the whole of this logical or rationalistic tradition.We must not commit the mistake of putting forward another exclusive standard. Our science teaches us toleration. But we do assert, on evidence, that there is more than one standard of intelligence, and indeed, more than one mode of thought. The purpose of thought is to arrive at truth, and truth, we say, is not found exclusively in the possession of those with a high 'intelligence quotient'; it is just as likely to proceed out of the mouths of babes and sucklings, poets and artists, even madmen.

What has been established, by the particular school of psychology we are relying on, is that these babes and sucklings, poets and painters, visionaries of all kinds, have one thing in common – an imagination so vivid that it must be regarded as the use of the particular kind of imagery, that kind already referred to which has been called eidetic imagery. This imagery, which is natural to babes and sucklings, is in certain rare cases retained beyond adolescence, and among these rare cases are to be found our poets and painters and visionaries of all kinds. But more: when we come to investigate the nature of scientific thought, in so far as this thought is an inventive or creative activity, and not merely a logical arrangement of accepted facts, we find that it too relies on images. The whole of modern physics, for example, is studded with imagery, from Newton's falling apple to Eddington's man in a lift. Possibly there is more imagery in modern physics than in modern poetry.

With such facts in our hands we need not stop to defend the biological utility of the arts. We can turn on the scientists and convince them on the evidence of their own processes of thought. In so far as it is creative and biologically useful, their thought is imaginative. Yet the systems of education which they have devised, and the tests which they have imposed on children, give no marks to the imagination. Images, they say *and prove*, are not essential to efficient thought. So everything is done to suppress these inconvenient sprites, and to enthrone the absolute rule of the concept in the child's mind.

The second direction from which we receive psychological support for our claims is known as the Gestalt theory. It is hardly possible to express the significance of this theory in a few simple words, but the exponents of the theory would agree that it too is in the main a protest against a logical conception of knowledge and science. What they say, in effect, is that there are no facts apart from the act or process of experiencing them, that the 'facts of a case' are not grasped by enumeration, but must be felt as a coherent pattern. The word 'felt' must be emphasised, for this factor of feeling in perception is aesthetic. It is not only the perception of a particular pattern, but also a discrimination in favour of that particular pattern. That is to say, out of all possible patterns of behaviour, one is chosen as being particularly fit or appropriate. It feels right – one feels at once the ease with which this particular pattern is apprehended, and the appropriateness of the action that ensues. And then, since this particular pattern of behaviour feels right, it tends to be repeated, and other modes of behaviour tend to become assimilated to it.

What the psychologists call the acquisition of a pattern of behaviour is nothing but the process of learning – learning, that is to say, in the sense of acquiring skill in the doing of anything – walking, skating, weaving, painting, assembling an engine. 'Grace and skill,' says one of the Gestalt psychologists, 'go hand in hand; their achievement is never the result of combining acts which themselves are awkward and unskilful. In order to do anything gracefully and skillfully one must first hit upon the "fortunate variation" in behaviour which is most suitable to the conditions.'

This has led us back to Plato again. In that part of the *Republic* which precedes the theory of education already referred to, Plato analyses the nature of form and rhythm, and what he says in effect is that the laws of form and rhythm are not given *a priori*, but are to be discovered in the best and most efficient actions. The following passage is from the *Republic*, and not from the work of a modern Gestalt psychologist. In studying the law of rhythms, Plato says, 'we must not aim at a variety of them, or study all movements indiscriminately, but observe what are the natural rhythms of a well regulated and manly life, and when we have discovered these we must compel the foot and the music to suit themselves to the sense of such life, and not the sense itself to the foot and the music.' In other words, in modern words, aesthetic laws are inherent in the biological processes of life itself; they are the laws which guide life along the path of ease and efficiency; and it is our business as educationalists to discover these laws in nature or experience, and make them the principles of our teaching. Balance and symmetry, proportion and rhythm, are basic factors in experience: indeed, they are the only elements by means of which experience can be organised into persisting patterns, and it is of their nature that they imply grace, economy and efficiency. What feels right works right, and the result, as measured by the consciousness of the individual, is a heightened sense of aesthetic enjoyment.

We now come to the final aspect of the psychological evidence. It is even more difficult to summarise than the last-mentioned aspect, but for a different reason. The evidence is not complete. We have indeed, got out of our depths and we flounder in a stormy sea. The theory of the unconscious is still disputed, and we must be careful not to claim too high a therapeutic value for those forms of free expression which we wish to encourage as part of our educational methods. That the young child – the very young child – has its repressions and its complexes no less than its parents and teachers is now sufficiently evident, but the treatment of psychoses and neuroses in the child presents quite exceptional difficulties to the psychiatrist. It is not, of course, for the teacher to meddle in such matters without training, but the psychiatrist might well ask the teachers to co-operate with him. Apart from any other aspect of the question, a child's drawings, produced as a result of spontaneous activity, are direct evidence of the child's physiological and psychological disposition, and in the opinion of some professional psychoanalysts, these drawings have more clinical value than any other form of evidence. But that is an aspect of the matter for which we must seek expert guidance. There is, however, a simpler aspect which is well within our lay competence. We know that a child absorbed in drawing or in any other creative activity is a happy child. We know just as a matter of everyday experience that self-expression is self-improvement. For that reason we must claim a large portion of the child's time for artistic activities, simply on the grounds that these activities are, as it were, a safety valve, a path to equableness. That is a practical reason which might convince the reluctant logicians, but of course, it is not our main reason for claiming a large portion of the child's time. We cannot hope to overcome the ramparts of the rationalist tradition with our real reason, for that would seem too impracticable, too idealistic. For our real claim has no limits. We do not claim an hour or a day of the child's time: we claim the whole child. We believe that we have within our grasp a method of education of absolutely universal validity. We believe that the grace we can instil by means of music, poetry and the plastic arts is not a superficial acquirement, but the key to all knowledge and all noble behaviour. We suspect that much, if not all, of the misery in the world today is due to the suppression of imagination and feeling in the child, to the prevalence of logical and rationalistic modes of thought that do violence to those principles of grace and rhythm and fair proportion which are implicit in the order of the universe. We believe that our function, not merely as artists and art teachers, but as teachers and examplars in general, is, as Plato said in one of his most visionary flights,

> 'to be guided by our instinct for whatever is lovely and gracious, so that our young men, dwelling in a wholesome climate, may drink in good from every quarter, whence, like a breeze bearing health from happy regions, some influence from noble works constantly falls upon eye and ear from childhood upward, and imperceptibly draws them into sympathy and harmony with the beauty of reason, whose impress they take.'[5]

4. The Uniqueness of the Person

These influences of which Plato speaks fall upon the organs of a unique sensibility. Uniqueness is a natural fact. It is a result of the infinite permutations and combinations of the *genes* which are the agents of life transmitted and united in the process of conception. Identical twins, by the uniqueness of their identity, give us a measure of the enormous diversity of persons in general.

This diversity is not a biological accident. It is the dialectical basis of natural selection, of human evolution. Any attempt, therefore, whether by education or coercion, to eliminate the differences between persons would frustrate the natural dissemination and growth of the human race. It is possible and even 'scientific' to hold that we should attempt to control this growth, just as we have controlled the growth of species like the horse and the sheep. But such control could only be effectively exercised if we had an agreed aim in view. We breed horses for strength or speed, sheep for a finer fleece. But it is a godlike assumption to breed the human race for any predetermined quality, and the idea has only entered the minds of totalitarian philosophers like Plato and Hegel, or been the policy of extreme fanatics who have attempted to put the ideals of such philosophers into practice.

Opposed to this point of view is another equally extreme – it received its fanatical expression in the philosophy of Max Stirner, to which Marx and Engels devoted some of their most destructive criticism. This philosophy asserts, with a logical consistency which some of its opponents might emulate, that all values can only be received and judged through the instrumentality of a unique sensational system, and that everything exterior to the wishes and desires of this ego is either a false rationalisation of these instinctive drives, or a form of self-deception which leads to frustration and eventually to aggression and self-destruction. Altruism, that is to say, is an illusion, and only by recognising that fact can we achieve individual happiness.

The truth, as it is manifested in events, lies somewhere between these two extremes. 'History,' wrote Engels, 'makes itself in such a way that the final result always arises from conflicts between many individual wills, of which each again has been made what it is by a host of particular conditions of life. Thus there are innumerable intersecting forces, and infinite series of parallelograms of forces which give rise to one resultant – the historical event. This again may itself be viewed as the product of a power which, taken as a whole, works *unconsciously* and without volition. For what each individual wills is obstructed by everyone else, and what emerges is something that no one willed.'⁶

It is not the purpose of education to eliminate this conflict between individual wills – the attempt would be foredoomed to failure because the conflict is inherent in our biological nature. But obviously 'the historical event' would be very different if, instead of a blind clash of individual wills, we could substitute some form of willing accommodation.

Two necessary processes are involved. One we shall call *initiation;* the other *reciprocity.* Before we can give effective direction to these processes, we must give precision to the units involved. A game cannot be played to a conclusion unless the counters have a fixed value; trade cannot be carried on without specific tokens of exchange; and in the same way society can only function harmoniously if the individuals composing it are integrated persons, that is to say, people whose physical and mental growth has been completed, so that they are whole and healthy, and by that very reason competent to render mutual aid.

We shall deal with the processes of initiation and reciprocity presently: but first we must fully recognise the biological significance of uniqueness. It is true that we come into the world trailing clouds of glory; a Heaven which is universal and impersonal lies about us in our infancy, and though the shades of the social prison-house begin to close on the growing boy, he is still, in Wordsworth's exact phrase, 'Nature's Priest.' Each infant mind is endowed with his share of a racial consciousness (an 'archaic heritage,' as Freud calls it). But this is but one component in a system of perceptions and instincts, a 'vision splendid,' which is unique. Why we affirm this uniqueness, and do not want it to 'die away, and fade into the light of common day,' why we do not want it to be 'ironed out' by impersonal powers, is explained by our reading of the biological evidence. At the heart of life is what is sometimes called a *dialectic,* but which is quite simply a strife between positive and negative forces, between Love and Death; and it is out of the tension created by this strife that further vitality, or what is optimistically called progress, arises. We can even venture to say, that the more definite the terms of this opposition – the sharper the conflict – the more vigorous will be the life. The first charge on the educator, therefore, is to bring the uniqueness of the individual into focus, to the end that a more vital interplay of forces takes place within each organic grouping of individuals – within the family, within the school, within society itself. The possibilities are at first evenly weighed between *hatred,* leading to crime, unhappiness and social antagonism, and *love,* which ensures mutual aid, individual happiness and social peace. What is certain is that the more desirable outcome is not ensured simply by the forcible suppression of the less desirable instincts: the whole meaning of education is that we seek to avoid hate by *positive* means, that is to say, by encouraging the stronger growth of love, which is indeed that grain of mustard seed, 'which a man took, and sowed in his field, which is indeed the least of all seeds, but when it is grown, it is the greatest among herbs, and becometh a tree, so that the birds of the air come to lodge in the branches thereof.'

5. The Parent and the Child

The first and most fundamental stage of education is carried on in the family circle. This fact, which in all its potentialities has always been realised by the Catholic Church, has only recently been given 'scientific' demonstration through the practice of psychoanalysis. Only a tradition of education which for centuries has cultivated intellectual virtue at the expense of moral virtue could have ignored so vital a consideration. The exponents of that tradition, who have not usually seized on children before the age of seven or eight, have then tried and often tried in vain to 'mould the character' of those committed to their care; but the truth is that 'the little human being is frequently a finished product in his fourth or fifth year, and only gradually reveals in later years what lies buried in him.'[7]

It is not possible to study the implications of psychoanalysis for education without becoming convinced that they are of overwhelming importance, and that it is futile to discuss theories of education for the later stages of the child's life until we have made some reasonable provision for the first phase, during which the child is still physically dependent on its parents, and largely abandoned to their care. That this care is often inspired by loving-kindness is not a sufficient guarantee of its efficiency. Children, psychologically speaking, can be killed by kindness, or 'spoilt.' In our present civilisation we have to deal with a situation which has become a systematic hypocrisy, organised by neurotics, and into this system the child enters, not armed with powers of resistance, but doomed to conformity.

He is doomed by his impulse to imitate, or identify himself with, some adult in the family circle – usually the mother or father. But this emotional tie is not a simple choice for the child. The boy may wish to be as big and strong as his father; but at the same time he is in love (and in a very real sense) with his mother. Gradually this boy begins to feel that his father stands in his way with his mother. His identification with his father then takes on what Freud calls 'a hostile colouring' and becomes identical with 'the wish to replace his father in regard to his mother.' The child is therefore in its earliest years caught up in a crisscross of instinctive reactions which involve love and hate even towards the same object. This naturally leads to a mental state of insecurity or anxiety, and since the basic instinct in life is to protect one's own life – to live securely and full of contentment – there is an equally natural instinct to repress those reactions of hate which we find lead to discontent and unhappiness. But psychoanalysis has shown that an instinct is never repressed without seeking unconscious compensation. We cannot, in this short treatise on a general subject, go into the details of all the psychological processes involved: it is sufficient to say that psychoanalysis finds in this universal situation of the infant a sufficient explanation of all those aggressive impulses, jealousies, tempers, bad manners and selfishness which it is the particular purpose of moral education to restrain or transform.

The educator must therefore ask, to what extent can this situation itself be dealt with, so that the development of these aggressive impulses is foreseen and controlled. To that question the psychoanalysts have given no very definite answer. Freud himself seems to deprecate analysis of normal children. 'Such a prophylactic against nervous disease,' he wrote, 'which would probably be very effective, *presupposes an entirely different structure of society*. The application of psychoanalysis to education must be looked for today in quite a different direction.' And he then goes on to give a definition of education which to some of his followers has seemed somewhat reactionary.

> 'Let us get a clear idea of what the primary business of education is. The child has to learn to control its instincts. To grant it complete freedom, so that it obeys all its impulses without any restriction, is impossible... The function of education... is to inhibit, forbid and suppress, and it has at all times carried out this function to admiration. But we have learnt from analysis that it is this very suppression of instinct that involves the danger of neurotic illness... Education has... to steer its way between the Scylla of giving the instincts free play and the Charybdis of frustrating them. Unless the problem is altogether insoluble, an optimum of education must be discoverable, which will do the most good and the least harm. It is a matter of finding out how much one may forbid, at which times *and by what methods*. And then it must be further considered that the children have very different constitutional dispositions, so that the

same educational procedure cannot possibly be good for all children.'[8]

Later in this same paragraph Freud enumerates the task of the educator as:
(a) to recognise the characteristic constitution of each child;
(b) to guess from small indications what is going on in its unformed mind;
(c) to give him the right amount of love, and at the same time
(d) to preserve an effective degree of authority.

This approach to the first phase of the child's life has carried us beyond the family circle into the general field of education. But it should be obvious from this very brief consideration of the problem that the relationship first established between the child and its parents, and then extended to the family circle, is fundamental. Joined to the innate disposition of the child (its physically determined temperament), this first stage of growth and initiation controls all the later stages. If the behaviour of parents towards their children were dependent on learning a technique (as the behaviour of the teacher is held to be) the situation of mankind would be desperate. Luckily in this respect healthy parents are guided by healthy instincts, and mutual love between parents and children can prevent and heal the wounds to which we are liable. But more often than not in the modern world parents are not healthy: they participate in a vast social neurosis, which has many causes and many aspects, but which is essentially due to that drastic suppression of the sexual impulses demanded by our modern civilisation. It follows from this that the reform of education can never be a departmental affair: it is the whole man that is spiritually sick, and we cannot make him well by repressing this or that aspect of his daily existence. At the same time it is too optimistic to assume that a particular social revolution will carry all the necessary reforms in its sweep. It is man's relationship to society itself that is wrong, and none of the forms of society which at present prevails, or is in prospect, attempts to change that relationship. We change the name but not the form of that relationship. Parents, family, school, workshop, local environment – all that is still a *physical* or biological reality to which the child can be emotionally and morally related; beyond are the abstractions of church, state and nation to which only the mind responds, a mind open to all the ambiguity of words, symbols and ideals, the ground of all our misunderstandings, an unreal world which bears no correspondence to the pattern of nature.

6. The Teacher and the Child

Neither in the passage I have quoted, nor elsewhere in his writings, does Freud venture to suggest even the outlines of a successful *method* of education. But it will be seen that he tends to throw the burden on the individual educator: that is to say, there is no single psychologically correct system of education, but only the possibility of developing a right relationship between the particular teacher and his pupil. This is in line with the general doctrine of psychoanalysis, which is a psychology of individuals. (The psychology of the group must seek some other name, such as phyloanalysis). The assumption is, of course, a realistic one, for however much a child may be influenced by the environment of a particular school or the general aspects of a particular discipline, the funnel through which this experience is poured into his mind is always the individual teacher. This is due, not only to the fact that it is the obvious function of the teacher to mediate between his pupil and the outer world, but even more to that process of identification to which I have already referred and which is one of the psychological mechanisms whose existence and scope have been revealed by psychoanalysis. This 'earliest expression of an emotional tie with another person' (the boy with his father, for example) soon takes on complexities due to what we would normally call subjective and objective attitudes (e.g., the boy's desire to *be like* his father and the boy's desire at the same time to *have* his father). Without going into all the further complexities which ensue in the family circle, it should be obvious that a new situation arises when the child leaves the family circle for the school and finds there another adult with whom he must develop an emotional tie. The result in most cases is a transference – partial or complete – of the symptoms of identification from the parent to the teacher. Incidentally, other children are experiencing the same transference, from *different* parents to the *same* teacher, and this mutual tie is the nucleus of the first *group* in whose unity the child is likely to participate.[9] This is the situation of which the teacher has to take advantage and it is one which requires infinite tact and charity. It easily degenerates, on his part, into an attitude of dominance, and on the part of the child, into a state of hypnotic dependence. (The parallel in the wider sphere of politics will be obvious.)

During the course of this change from absolute dependence on and ideal identification with the parent, there is established in the mind of the individual what Freud has called the 'super-ego.' The 'ideal' element is, as it were, separated from the physical parent, and becomes the growing child's conscience, his faculty of self-observation and moral purpose. Freud himself has observed that 'during the course of its growth, the super-ego also takes over the influence of those persons who have taken the place of the parents, that is to say, of persons who have been concerned in the child's upbringing, and whom it has regarded as ideal models.'[10] This gives the teacher his only possibility for what is called 'character-formation.' Unfortunately, as Freud also pointed out, parents and teachers are seldom disinterested in this situation. Instead of teaching children a rational morality, they 'follow the dictates of their own super-ego.' '...In the education of the child they are severe and exacting. They have forgotten the difficulties of their own childhood, and are glad to be able to identify themselves fully at last with their own parents, who in their day subjected them to such severe restraints.'[11]

In this way, not merely the sins, but also the prejudices and psychological abnormalities of the parents are passed on to the children from generation unto generation.

The good teacher is one who is able to break out of this vicious circle, and establish a wholly personal relationship with his pupil, one which is based on love and understanding for the unique personality which has been entrusted to his care. Such a teacher will not attempt to impose on his pupil arbitrary conceptions of 'good' and 'bad', which the child is unable to feel or understand (and which therefore lead to a state of tension or disunity which is one origin of neurosis). He will ignore the whole system of 'make-believe' with its rewards and punishments, its constraints and inhibitions. He will try instead to establish a relationship of reciprocity and trust between himself and his pupil, and one of co-operation and mutual aid between all the individuals within his care. The teacher should identify himself with the pupil in the same degree that the pupil identifies himself with the teacher, and he should probably endeavour to make this process, on the pupil's part, more conscious than it would normally be. What is required is the give and take of a mutual relationship. The child is likely to develop his side of the relationship in the natural course of his development: from the teacher a more deliberate approach will be necessary, for he must really identify himself with the other person, and feel and do as he does. The teacher sees the situation from both ends, the pupil from one only. In this way the teacher gradually learns to distinguish and anticipate the real needs of his pupil, and only in this way is it possible for him to accomplish those tasks which Freud assigns to the teacher –

to recognise the child's disposition, to understand his mind, to love him and to preserve effective authority over him.[12]

7. The Person and the Group

If this right relationship is developed between the teacher and his pupil, and the teacher thus becomes the focus of a group of pupils who love him and trust him, it is then easy to establish the precepts of mutual aid within that group. This means that within the group – the class, the house, the school – a relationship of reciprocity has been formed which can take the place of those relationships of constraint which are normal in traditional methods of education. If this feeling of trust in the teacher were the only psychological motive active within such a group, it is possible that complications due to envy and rivalry would ensue. But actually the group develops spontaneously a social life and cohesion which is independent of the teacher. The spontaneous emergence of groups among children has been studied by educationalists like Jean Piaget and Susan Isaacs, and a social experiment on a large scale which covers the whole development of the individual is being conducted at the Peckham Health Centre,[13] with results which fully support this thesis.

The importance of this development, in the life of the child, is that it leads the child *by natural stages* from a self-centred state of egotism to an attitude of social co-operation. There is then no question of forcing the child to recognise and accept a moral code whose justice it cannot appreciate. That abstract 'sense of duty' is wholly outside the child's mental range: the child can only be coerced into its observance. But that sense of 'playing the game' which emerges when children evolve their own activities is a real thing: it is a felt relationship between little human beings who must co-operate to achieve their common aim. And to achieve this aim they must create a pattern – the rules of the game which give coherence and form to their activities. In such spontaneously evolved patterns, giving pleasures and satisfaction to the growing animal instincts and desires, lies hidden the pattern of a society in which all persons are free, but freely consenting to a common purpose.

It is impossible to exaggerate the fundamental nature of this aspect of education, which I have called *initiation*. At this stage of life a choice must be made which inevitably dictates the form which our society will take. In one direction we can institute objective codes of conduct and morality to which our children are introduced before the age of understanding and to which they are compelled to conform by a system of rewards and punishments. That way conducts us to an authoritarian society, governed by laws and sanctioned by military power. It is the kind of society in which most of the world now lives, ridden by neuroses, full of envy and avarice, ravaged by war and disease.

In the other direction we can avoid all coercive codes of morality, all formal conceptions of 'right' and 'wrong'. For a morality of obedience we can substitute a morality of attachment or reciprocity, that living together in perfect charity which was once the ideal of Christianity. Believing that the spontaneous life developed by children among themselves gives rise to a discipline infinitely nearer to that inner accord or harmony which is the mark of the virtuous man, we can aim at making our teachers the friends rather than the masters of their pupils; as teachers they will not lay down ready-made rules, but will encourage their children to carry out their own co-operative activities, and thus spontaneously to elaborate their own rules. Discipline will not be imposed, but discovered – discovered as the right economical and harmonious way of action. We can avoid the competitive evils of the examination system, which merely serves to re-enforce the egocentrism inherent in the child: we can eliminate all ideas of rewards and punishments, substituting a sense of the collective good of the community to which reparation for shortcomings and selfishness will be obviously due and freely given. In all things, moral and intellectual, we should act on the belief that we really possess only what we have conquered ourselves – that we are made perfect by natural habits, but slaves by social conventions and that until we have become accustomed to beauty we are not capable of truth and goodness, for by beauty we mean the principle of harmony which is the given order of the physical universe, to which we conform and live, or which we reject and die.

8. The Freedom of the School

The reader who has followed me with agreement so far must now be prepared for some logical consequences which are at variance with the general trend of progressive thought. Progress in education throughout the civilised world has been for the most part conceived in terms of 'national systems,' and all our endeavours have been to make such systems more and more inclusive, and more and more standardised. If only the system is perfect, we have argued, the products will be as good as possible.

We might have proceeded in other ways: we might, for example, have concentrated on the training of teachers, and having made that perfect, said to them: Go out into the world, and wherever there are children to listen to you, in village halls and at street corners, in highways and byways, gather little children round you and teach them as once Christ taught them. We might, that is to say, have thought of teachers as missionaries rather than as masters; and who would venture to say that the state of the world would then have been worse than it is?

There are still other possibilities. Instead of entrusting the education of children to bureaucratic organisations divorced from the main business of life, we might have developed the apprenticeship system, and made education a preparation for vocation – the doctors educating some children, the lawyers others, the engineers others, the weavers and the miners still others. Each guild or trade would have taken in its future apprentices from the beginning, much as, even now, some religious orders supervise the education from early years of those children destined to become novices. Instead of these and other possibilities, we have established *national* or *state* systems of education. In some countries, England among them, a few schools still manage to exist outside the official orbit, but unless, like some of the so-called 'public' schools, they are richly endowed, they fight a losing battle against the increasing ubiquity and efficiency of the state schools.

There is no need to describe this system, because we all have experience of it. But few people are conscious of its dangers. These are of two distinct kinds.

The first of these dangers was anticipated by Godwin, and I cannot do better than repeat his warning:

> 'The project of a national education ought uniformly to be discouraged on account of its obvious alliance with national government. This is an alliance of a more formidable nature than the old and much contested alliance of church and state. Before we put so powerful a machine under the direction of so ambiguous an agent, it behoves us to consider well what it is that we do. Government will not fail to employ it to strengthen its hands and perpetuate its institutions. If we could even suppose the agents of government not to propose to themselves an object which will be apt to appear in their eyes not merely innocent but meritorious, the evil would not the less happen. Their views as institutors of a system of education will not fail to be analogous to their views in their political capacity: the data upon which their conduct as statesmen is vindicated will be the data upon which their instructions are founded. It is not true that our youth ought to be instructed to venerate the constitution, however excellent; they should be instructed to

venerate truth, and the constitution only so far as it corresponded with their independent deductions of truth. Had the scheme of a national education been adopted when despotism was most triumphant, it is not to be believed that it could have forever stifled the voice of truth. But it would have been the most formidable and profound contrivance for that purpose that imagination can suggest. Still, in the countries where liberty chiefly prevails, it is reasonably to be assumed that there are important errors, and a national education has the most direct tendency to perpetuate those errors and to form all minds upon one model.'[14]

It is difficult to realise that this passage was written more than 150 years ago, before the growth of national states like France and Germany, and before the institution of totalitarian regimes which make this very use which Godwin feared of their educational system. We in Great Britain have attempted to impose certain safeguards, such as school managers and local educational authorities, but these bodies are gradually losing their independence, and the new Education Act virtually abolishes their powers. Here as elsewhere a system of national education has become potentially a system of national propaganda, designed to inculcate certain attitudes and beliefs which *may* not correspond with our independent deductions of truth. National Socialism in Germany, with its wild distortions of scientific truth and of historical fact, would not have survived so long had not the government utilised the national system of education for the dissemination of the party's doctrines. The same is true of the national communism established in Russia. To regularise and nationalise the instruments of education is merely to convert these instruments into weapons of dictatorship.

A second objection to a national system of education is psychological rather than political. Mankind is naturally differentiated into many types, and to press all these types into the same mould must inevitably lead to distortions and repressions. Schools should be of many kinds, following different methods and catering for different dispositions. It might be argued that even a totalitarian state must recognise this principle but the truth is that differentiation is an organic process, the spontaneous and roving association of individuals for particular purposes. To divide and segregate is not the same as to join and aggregate – it is just the opposite process. The whole structure of education, as the natural process we have envisaged, falls to pieces if we attempt to make that structure rational or artificial.[15] Like life itself, animal as well as human, education must follow a principle of organic consistency: we must *feel our way* to the right units, and out of the natural grouping of these units round the biological actualities and practical activities of man, free and healthy institutions will emerge. Among these we shall find institutions in which children can mature the principle of growth innate in each one of them while at the same time they are initiated into the fellowship of their familiars.

9. A Community of Individuals

Freud was never tired of warning us of the thinness and brittleness of the shell we call civilisation. 'Civilised society,' he writes in one place,

> 'which exacts good conduct and does not trouble about the impulses underlying it, has thus won over to obedience a great many people who are not thereby following the dictates of their own nature. Encouraged by this success, society has suffered itself to be led into straining the normal standard to the highest possible point, and thus it has forced its members into a yet greater estrangement from their instinctual dispositions. They are consequently subjected to an unceasing suppression of instincts, the resulting strain of which betrays itself in the most remarkable phenomena of reaction and compensation formations... Anyone thus compelled to act continually in the sense of precepts which are not the expression of instinctual inclinations, is living, psychologically speaking, beyond his means, and might objectively be designated a hypocrite, whether this difference is clearly known to him or not. It is undeniable that our contemporary civilisation is extraordinarily favourable to the production of this form of hypocrisy. One might venture to say that it is based upon such hypocrisy and that it should have to submit to far-reaching modifications if people were to undertake to live in accordance with the psychological truth.'[16]

Freud himself never ventured to outline those 'far-reaching modifications' which society would have to undergo for the sake of psychological truth, which I think we may assume is the same thing as psychological happiness. But he did indicate in unmistakable terms that he did not consider such necessary modifications to have been achieved under the collectivist systems of Russia and Germany.[17] For this reason Marxists have often condemned this great scientist as a reactionary, and it is true that by their insistence on the integrity of the family, for example, psychoanalysts find themselves in the company of conservative forces such as the Catholic Church. But they will not for this reason be deterred from stating the psychological truth as they see it. That scientific obligation will also lead them to side with those political forces which oppose the state as such. Already certain followers of Freud set drastic limits to the beneficial effects of state interference. For example Dr Edward Glover, the director of the Psychoanalytical Institute of Great Britain, does not hesitate to declare that 'state worship is a form of fetishism derived from the displacement of family dependence,' and suggested further that 'however useful the state may be in the regulation of material things it is nevertheless a backward and superstitious organisation'.[18] Its true function is 'to promote and strengthen in every possible way the status of the family within which civilisation is born and maintained and by which it is transmitted.'

It is important to realise that these psychologists are not recommending a particular policy on ideological grounds; they are dealing with the psychological and the physiological health of the human organism, and they assert that this health cannot be maintained unless certain conflicts which are the product of modern civilisation are avoided. These conflicts arise when in the course of his childhood and youth man finds that he has to adjust himself to unreal systems of law, morality and convention – systems which are unreal because they are remote and abstract, not necessarily in conformity with his biological needs nor with the general pattern of nature. Man is born free; and everywhere he is in *mental* chains. Neurosis, crime, insanity – these are but so many symptoms of a disorder which is basic to our form of society. Man is ill-adjusted from the nursery up, and this ill-adjustment and consequent unhappiness is not something which can be prevented or removed by individual analysis – it is a group disorder and can only be removed by 'far-reaching modifications' of our contemporary civilisation.

We who demand freedom in education, autonomy in the school and self-government in industry are not inspired by any vague ideal of liberation. What we preach is really a discipline and a morality as formal and as fixed as any preached by church or state. But our law is given in nature, is discoverable by scientific method, and, as Aristotle points out, human beings are adapted by nature to receive this law. Because we are so adapted, freedom, which is a vague concept to so many people, becomes a perfectly real and vivid principle, because it is a habit to which we are pre-conditioned by biological elements in our physical frame and nervous constitution.

Education, from this point of view, is an undeveloped science. To discover, for example, the degree of poise and co-ordination in the muscular system of the body is an art which has never yet been defined and practised. Harmony within the family, harmony within the social group, harmony within and among nations – these are no less psycho-physiological problems, questions of pattern and practice, of adjustment to natural proportions and conformity to natural harmonies.

Each individual begins life as a dynamic unity. Into that original unity tensions and distortions are introduced by an unconscious and largely alien environment. It is alien because it is unconscious. Unless we were motivated by hatred towards the human race, we could not consciously introduce those abstract systems of law and morality on which the evolving body and soul of the person, born to potential unity and beauty, are disastrously stretched and deformed.

I do not pretend to know what are the exact precepts of a morality of love and mutual aid: I doubt if they can be formulated more explicitly than they were long ago in tbe Sermon on the Mount. But life, which is an organic growth, cannot be lived according to an abstract formula of words, but only to a pattern, and not to a pattern in the abstract sense of a defined form, but only to a living, evolving form, which obeys rules not in stasis, but in growth. Life is movement: we cannot halt it for a moment without killing it. The pattern is only visible in time. We can give pattern to our span of years, but we cannot, without death or distortion give life to a pattern of law, to any 'purely verbal, symbolic system of behaviour.'[19] The basis of a living community, the basis of individual happiness, is physiological: it is only in so far as this physiological basis has unity with nature (*physis* = nature) that society itself can have harmony and health. It is in small units – in the family circle, in the classroom and in the school, that this harmony and health must be first achieved. In so far as some abstraction called the state interferes with the integrity of these groups – and by their integrity we mean their capacity for spontaneous growth – in that degree the state is denying life and health to its citizens. Freedom is simply space for spontaneous action: men live in communities solely to secure that space.

10. Summary

I hope I may now expect from my reader a clearer understanding of what is meant by 'freedom in education.' We can now see that it is more exact to speak of 'education for freedom.' But this is a misleading slogan unless we remember the means, which is the discipline of art, the only discipline to which the senses naturally submit. Art, as we have seen, is a discipline which the senses seek in their intuitive perception of form, of harmony, of proportion, of the integrity or wholeness of any experience. It is also the discipline of the tool and the material – the discipline imposed by pencil or pen, by the loom or the potter's wheel, by the physical nature of paint, textiles, wood, stone or clay.

But the point about such discipline is that it is innate: it is part of our physiological constitution, and is there to be encouraged and matured. It does not have to be imposed by the schoolmaster or the drill sergeant: it is not a kind of physical torture. It is a faculty within the child which responds to sympathy and love, to the intelligent anticipation of impulses and trends in the individuality of the child. For this reason the teacher must be primarily a person and not a pedagogue, a friend rather than a master or mistress, an infinitely patient collaborator. Put in a drier and more pedantic way, the aim of education is to discover the child's psychological type, and to allow each type its natural line of development, its natural form of integration. That is the real meaning of freedom in education.

The art of children is supremely important for this very reason: it is the earliest and the most exact index to the child's individual psychology. Once the psychological tendency or trend of a child is known, its own individuality can be developed by the discipline of art, till it has its own form and beauty, which is its unique contribution to the beauties of human nature. This, of course, is the antithesis of those totalitarian doctrines of education (not confined to totalitarian countries) which strive to impose a unique concept of human nature on the infinite variety of human persons.

A child's art, therefore, is its passport to freedom, to the full fruition of all its gifts and talents, to its true and stable happiness in adult life. Art leads the child out of itself. It may begin as a lonely individual activity, as the self-absorbed scribbling of a baby on a piece of paper. But the child scribbles in order to communicate its inner world to a sympathetic spectator, to the parent from whom it expects a sympathetic response.

Too often, alas, it receives only indifference or ridicule. Nothing is more crushing to the infant spirit than a parent's or a teacher's contempt for those creative efforts of expression. That is one aspect of a crime which disgraces the whole of our intellectual civilisation and which, in my opinion, is the root cause of our social disintegration. We sow the seeds of disunity in the nursery and the classroom, with our superior adult conceit. We divide the intelligence from the sensibility of our children, create split-men (schizophrenics, to give them a psychological name), and then discover that we have no social unity.

We begin our life in unity – the physical unity of the mother and child, to which corresponds the emotional unity of love. We should build on that original unity, extending it first to the family, where the seeds of hatred are so easily and so often sown, and then to the school, and so by stages to the farm, the workshop, the village and the whole community. But the basis of unity at each successive stage, as at the first stage, is creativity. We unite to create, and the pattern of creation is in nature, and we discover and conform to this pattern by all the methods of artistic activity – by music, by dancing and drama, but also by working together and living together, for, in a sane civilisation, these too are arts of the same natural pattern.

Notes

1 This is, of course, a translator's phrase (Davies and Vaughan) and not always adopted by other translators. But it represents accurately enough Plato's general meaning.

2 *The Laws of Plato*, trans. by A. E. Taylor (London: J. M. Dent & Sons, 1934).

3 *The Grammarian's Funeral*.

4 Charles Fox, *Educational Psychology* (London, 1930), p.86.

5 Trans. by F. S. Cornford (Oxford University Press, 1941).

6 Tolstoy expressed a similar view of history in *War and Peace*.

7 Freud, *Introductory Lectures on Psycho-analysis* (1922), p. 298.

8 *New Introductory Lectures* (1933), pp. 191-2. (My italics.)

9 'A primary group of this kind is a number of individuals who have substituted one and the same object for their ego ideal and have consequently identified themselves with one another in their ego' (Freud, *Group Psychology and Analysis of Ego*, p. 80).

10 *New Introductory Lectures*, p. 87.

11 *Ibid.*, p. 90.

12 Godwin, in an essay 'Of the Obtaining of Confidence', long ago expressed this truth in words which have lost none of their relevance to this discussion:

'If any man desire to possess himself of the most powerful engine that can be applied to the purpose of education, if he would find the ground upon which he must stand to enable himself to move the whole substance of the mind, he will probably find it in sympathy. Great power is not necessarily a subject of abuse. A wise preceptor would probably desire to be in possession of great power over the mind of his pupil, though he would use it with economy and diffidence. He would therefore seek by all honest arts to be admitted into his confidence, that so the points of contact between them may be more extensively multiplied, that he may not be regarded by the pupil as a stranger of the outer court of the temple, but that his image may mix itself with his pleasures, and be made the companion of his recreations' (*Enquirer*, pp. 124-5).

13 '"Community" is not formed merely by the aggregation of persons assembled for the convenience of sustaining some ulterior purpose, as in a housing estate connected with a single industry; not by the aggregation of individuals kept in contiguity by the compulsion of necessity, as in "special areas" wrecked by unemployment; nor held together, as in some social settlements, by the doubtful adhesive of persuasion; nor indeed meeting the needs of war time as in "Communal Feeding", "Communal Nurseries". Its characteristic is that it is the result of a *natural functional organisation in society*, which brings *its own* intrinsic impetus to ordered growth and development. In our understanding, "community" is built up of *homes* linked with *society* through a functional zone of mutuality. As it grows in mutuality of synthesis it *determines its own* anatomy and physiology, according to biological law. A community is thus a specific "organ" of the body of society and is formed of living and growing cells – the homes of which it is composed' (Innis H. Pearse and Lucy H. Crocker, *The Peckham Experiment: A Study in the Living Structure of Society* (London: Allen & Unwin, 1943), pp. 291-2.

14 *Political Justice*, VI, 8.

15 Such a 'rational' organisation is attempted in the new Education Act. The division of secondary schools into three types, grammar, technical and modern, represents artificial categories based on 'aptitudes' determined by a cursory examination held at the immature age of 10-11. Subsequent interchange between these categories is legally possible, but administratively difficult and therefore unlikely. The articulation proposed here is regional or local, the smallest units being nursery schools, several of which feed a primary school, of which in turn several feed a secondary school – the schools increasing in size as they cater for higher age groups and wider areas but always remaining 'multilateral' in their curricula. Only in this way can we hope to retain that dialectical interplay between diverse dispositions which is the basis of a natural character-formation. The vocational segregation of 'like-minded' children from the age of eleven onward can only lead to intellectual dullness and social apathy. Birds of a feather flock together, but what is now proposed by our rulers is that they should be caged together.

16 'Thoughts for the Times on War and Death', *Collected Papers*, Vol. IV. Schiller said very much the same in his *Letters upon the Aesthetical Education of Man*: 'In this way individual concrete life is gradually extinguished, in order that the abstract whole may prolong its miserable existence, and the state remains for ever a stranger to its citizens, because it is nowhere present to their feelings. Compelled to reduce to some order the multiplicity of its citizens by classifying them, and only to know humanity through representation at second hand, the governing classes end by altogether losing sight of their citizens, reducing them to some figment of the mind. Meanwhile the subject classes cannot but welcome coldly laws which are so little addressed to them personally. In the end, tired of a bondage which the state does so little to lighten, positive society disintegrates – a fate which has long overcome most European states. It dissolves into a moral state of nature, in which the public authority is nothing more than a class, hated and betrayed by those who make its existence necessary, respected only by those who can do without it.'

17 Cf. especially *New Introductory Letters*, Lecture XXXV, 'A Philosophy of Life'.

18 'State Parentalism', *New English Weekly*, March 23, 1944.

19 Dr Trigant Burrow.

Two Speeches

14
Before the Trial

WE are met at a very significant moment in history. We are told that the end of the war in Europe is in sight – a matter of a few days, even of a few hours. The embattled forces of the Allies are closing in from all sides – dancing round the gigantic crater of ruin which is Germany.

Our statesmen have made a chaos and call it victory. Millions of men are dead, and their silence is called peace. Millions of slaves and prisoners stream eastward and westward – to the North and to the South – anywhere from the centre of this ghastly compass of war. As they travel along the dusty roads, they lose their marks of identity, their uniforms and badges – they resume their human shape and appearance: the grey mass of the unemployed. From unemployment they were snatched by the Conscriptors. The war began in Unemployment: the war will end in Unemployment.

A few days ago Eisenhower reported that he had taken two million prisoners since D Day. 'Not enough,' replied Sir James Grigg, 'I want two million *and four*.' At this stage in the unfolding of the European tragedy, four people have been arrested, here in this Land of Liberty. We have met here to ask *Why*?

Why at this final stage of the universal butchery are these four comrades arrested? Is it to be seriously contended that at this twelfth hour any words of theirs could so disaffect members of His Majesty's Forces that the outcome of the war would be in doubt? I hope that that will be the argument, for it would be the biggest compliment ever paid to the philosophy of anarchism. What other charge, in relation to the war - and remember that 39A is a wartime regulation – what other charge is conceivable? I see none, and therefore I conclude that 39A is being used for other than its intended purpose. If I am asked what other purpose is conceivable, I would point to the singular fact that whilst in all other European countries (the so-called neutrals excepted) the fascists or collaborationists have been incautious enough to come out into the open, and have been caught there, *here* they have never emerged from their hiding-places – have never taken off their masks.

There was a time – back in 1940 – when I thought that here too the war would inevitably lead to revolution – that it would be neither won nor lost without a social upheaval. I was wrong. We won the Battle of Britain, but lost the chance of a British Revolution. The fascists – I do not refer to a poor prematurely-born homunculus like Mosley – the fascists kept on their masks, stayed in their hide-outs. There were regulations and controls – lots of them – but the new controller was the old boss writ large. There was no essential change. We were, and in all essentials we have remained, a fascist plutocracy.

Against this crypto-fascism in our midst, only an insignificant minority has hitherto fought openly. Some have fought in a roundabout way – by collaborating with Badoglio in Italy, with King George in Greece, with General de Gaulle in France – I am too naive to appreciate the tactics of our communist friends. But a few people, and prominent among them our four arrested comrades, have fought our home-based fascism openly and directly. They have fought with increasing vigour and growing success. A certain weight of opinion has formed behind them, particularly among members of the younger generation. It seems possible that our fascists in high places have become aware of this small but brilliant band – have seen this small but bright red-light, and have resolved to extinguish it before it becomes a glowing beacon. How else explain a move which on every other interpretation is patently ridiculous?

Comrades, the time for doubts and hesitations is past. Those who waited for the war to bring about a revolution must now repent their mistake. The situation is unequivocal. There will be no revolution – just yet. But from this moment we move into active resistance. The front line of the Resistance Movement is now here, in England, and we, *alone* if necessary, will continue the fight against fascism. We have French comrades, Dutch comrades, Polish comrades, comrades whose underground struggle we have admired. But from now on we must treat them as heroes of another day. We have supported them in their struggle against fascism. We do not now expect them to fraternise with the friends of fascism here. In the moment of their victory we expect them to continue the fight by our side.

That fight will not be conducted in the hills or on the beaches or in any such romantic places – it will be carried into the streets and docks, into slums and factories. Nor shall we fight with block-busters and tanks, not even with tommy-guns and bombs. Our weapons are words, and all we need for success is freedom of speech and expression – 'everywhere in the world.' That is the first of the four freedoms, but what cynical mockery is this which in the moment of victory falls on our comrades on no other charge than the exercise of that freedom. But we shall not suffer their persecution. We do not challenge any law that is natural, any trial that is just. But we stand firm in asserting the traditional rights which free men in this country have fought for throughout the centuries and we challenge that State which, with arbitrary authority and ignoble instruments – I refer to our political police – has dared to abrogate those traditional rights: we challenge that State to an unrelenting strife. It is a small group of anarchists whose freedom is threatened, but, comrades, I do not speak to you now as an anarchist: I speak to you as an Englishman, as one proud to follow in the tradition of Milton and Shelley – the tradition of all those poets and philosophers who have given us the proud right to claim freedom of speech and the liberty of unlicensed printing. For that, comrades, is the issue, and in that issue we shall engage our personal liberty and if necessary our lives.

We could give our comrades many inspiring words to remember as they stand in the dock next week, but most of all I would like them to remember those words which an American Quaker addressed to an American jury during the last war, when he was facing a similar charge. That Quaker's name was Eugene V. Debs, and here are the beautiful words he used on that occasion:

> 'Gentlemen of the Jury, I am accused of having obstructed the war. I admit it. Gentlemen, I abhor war. I would oppose the war if I stood alone. I believe that nations have been pitted against nations long enough in hatred....
>
> 'I am opposed to war. I am perfectly willing on that account to be branded as a traitor. And if it is a crime under the American law to be opposed to human bloodshed, I am perfectly willing to be branded as a criminal and to end my days in a prison cell...
>
> 'And now, Gentlemen of the Jury, I am prepared for the sentence. I will accept your verdict. What you will do to me does not matter much. Years ago I recognised my kinship with all living beings, and I made up my mind that I was not one whit better than the meanest of earth. I said

then, and I say now, that while there is a lower class I am in it: while there is a criminal element I am of it: while there is a soul in prison, I am not free.'

Like Eugene Debs, our four comrades have dared to stand firm in the cause of humanity. What they have said, all lovers of peace and freedom have said and will continue to say. Our comrades go to trial as our representatives. In the hour of their trial, and after their trial, whatever its outcome, we shall not fail them. If the four are imprisoned, forty will step into the breach and carry on. If forty are imprisoned, four hundred will be there to take their place. We have been challenged: we accept the challenge. We will fight: fight the Defence Regulations and that foul and un-English institution, the political police. We will fight tyranny and oppression in every shape and form, everywhere in the world, until freedom is finally a reality, and justice a natural right.

15
After the Trial

AT our last meeting I said that if our comrades were imprisoned, we who remained free would continue the struggle against the forces of repression now active in this country, against the political police, against every enemy of freedom. That struggle is now on. The weapons with which we can fight are limited: they are the very weapons which our authoritarian government is attempting to take away from us – our printing press, our pamphlets, our right to speak and publish the truth that is within us. Limited as they are, these are nevertheless the only weapons we need to create such a volume of protest that press and parliament, the public at large will be compelled to listen to us. We shall not rest until our comrades are released, and even then we shall go on, to create such a consciousness of the existing danger to our common liberty, that the cause of it is for ever eliminated from our society.

It will not be an easy campaign. Among the many lessons which this episode has taught us, the most surprising to me has been the indifference of the so-called liberal press. There have been exceptions, and in particular I would like to mention the *Manchester Guardian*. But for the most part, once they had exhausted the 'news value' of the case in a sentence or two, the rest has been silence. Here was a clear threat to the liberty of the Press. Did the Press rise in righteous indignation? We have not heard a single note of complaint. This institution which boasts that it is the guardian of our national liberties was perhaps a little drunk with the prospects of a military victory: at any rate, it slept whilst the very liberties which they thought were being secured in Europe, were filched from us here in the Old Bailey.

Then there is Parliament. We anarchists have never placed much faith in the dim inmates of that opium den, but we note that many of them talk frequently of liberty, inside the House and out. But what has Parliament done to defend our liberty in this case? We know well enough that all that gang talk endlessly about freedom, it is a nice inspiring word – but they uphold its reality only so long as it does not threaten their private interests.

In these last few weeks more hypocrisy has been smeared over our daily and weekly papers than ever before in our history. If you can bring yourself to read the leading articles and commentaries in these periodicals, you will find the word 'freedom' in almost every paragraph. You are told that we have just won the greatest war in history – for 'freedom'. You are asked to celebrate this glorious victory – 'in the cause of freedom.' You are even encouraged to get drunk for 'freedom.' We are not deceived. So long as our three comrades remain in prison, victory is an illusion, and the man who celebrates it is nothing but a mug.

We have met here tonight not to celebrate a victory, but to take counsel after a defeat. In the face of that defeat, I propose now briefly to reaffirm the beliefs for which our comrades have been persecuted and imprisoned. It would give me great pleasure to do this if only to show that we are by no means intimidated by what has happened. The penalties of the Courts are only justified on the assumption that they deter others from repeating the alleged offence. We are not moved one inch from our course. All that legal pantomime at the Old Bailey was from every point of view a futile and costly farce. It has cost our side quite a lot: it must have cost the State more – several thousand pounds. There are the salaries of Inspector Whitehead and his agents for the three or four months they devoted to the case: there are the still larger salaries of the Attorney General and his assistants for the many days they devoted to the reading of *War Commentary*: the still larger salary of his lordship the Judge for the four days he spent listening to the case: and then the more modest wages of the ushers who tried to keep us out of the Court and of all the various clerks and bailiffs who filled the benches in the Court. Nor must we forget the wages of the policemen who inspected all our identity cards one day. That makes a pretty total which might have been justified if the prisoners on trial had been gangsters or profiteers, murderers or swindlers.

But what in actual fact were the prisoners in the dock? They were men who held a certain belief, a theory of society, an ideal of civilisation, and all they had done, the only crime with which they could be charged, was that they had incidentally taken steps to bring their beliefs to the attention of members of His Majesty's Forces.

What is this belief whose mere propagation constitutes a crime? I am going to tell you, in simple direct words, and what I shall say will amount to no more and no less than the substance of the beliefs for which our comrades are now suffering a sentence of imprisonment.

We begin with the central fact of WAR. We say that if our civilisation is to survive – not this country nor that country, but the whole civilisation of which we are members – war must be eliminated. War has now reached a stage of technical development which in future will involve, not merely the deaths of millions of human beings – men, women and children – but also the complete destruction of the material necessities of life: food, housing, communications, health. War will henceforth mean annihilation, not merely for the vanquished, but for all who engage in it.

We then analyse the causes of war, and this is where we begin to differ from other people who would also like to get rid of war. We say that modern war cannot be explained in terms of capitalism, of imperialism, of economics or of populations: it is a disease of civilisation itself, something inherent in the very structure of modern society. In order to get rid of war, we must alter the structure of society.

But 'to alter the structure of society' is merely a polite way of saying that a revolution will be essential, and it is for using this word 'revolution' that our comrades are in prison. They would not have been put in prison if they had expressed a wish to alter 'the structure of society' – which only shows what power is attributed to *words* when they become *weapons*.

But whatever we call the process, the choice before our civilisation is clear: either revolution or annihilation. That is the unescapable conclusion which we anarchists have reached, and we claim that it is a rational, indeed a logical conclusion.

But what then does revolution imply? We say that the structural fault in our civilisation which leads to war lies in the doctrine of national sovereignty, which requires for its expression and propagation the social organ known as the State. Modern wars are conducted by States, through their paid servants – the politicians, civil servants and armed forces. Wars do not, in our stage of development, break out naturally between *peoples*, and in spite of all the powers of persuasion which States can command and direct, the peoples remain largely indifferent to the issues involved in State wars. Put in another way, we might say that modern wars are essentially ideological, and ideologies belong to classes, not to peoples. The peoples have no ideologies anywhere. They have interests and prejudices, customs and superstitions: they may be selfish and egotistic, but everywhere and at all time their main purpose is to secure a living from the soil, or from the labours of their hands or brains: and they know that such a purpose is not furthered, but frustrated, by war. Lives, houses, cattle, tillage, material possessions of every kind – these are the common wealth of the people, however unevenly distributed that wealth may be. That kind of wealth is destroyed by war. What is not destroyed by war is another kind of wealth – gold, bonds, credits and other goods not made by labour: these may escape war, just as German Bonds will survive this war, or as Russian Imperial Bonds have escaped 'the greatest revolution in history': but this kind of wealth does not belong to the people, but to the State and its servants, and, one must add, to its dupes.

Under defeat, a particular State may disintegrate. We have seen several States disintegrate during the past few years – France, Belgium, Italy, Greece, and now Germany. This, we say, provides a golden opportunity to make the necessary structural alterations in our social system. It is, in fact, a revolutionary situation, and in such a situation, when the State has revealed all its insubstantiality, and has vanished overnight, we must not let any body of gangsters or looters step out of the ruins and organise another State. That will only lead inevitably to another war and a worse war. In such a revolutionary situation, our comrades said, and I repeat, the armed forces have ceased to exist as instruments of a State: for the moment the nations have become peoples, people in arms. Let the nation remain a people in arms – stick to your arms, we say to such a people, rather than deliver them up to any gang which takes on itself to speak in the name of a new State. If we are a people, all equal and all equally armed or disarmed, then we can get together and agree on a new form of society, a non-governmental society, in which nation will no longer be opposed to nation, State to State, but a society in which people will work together for the common good. When that reform has been accomplished, everywhere in the world, we can all throw away our arms, and live in peace ever after.

That is the doctrine which our comrades preached, for which they have been persecuted and imprisoned. You may not agree with it – you may not agree with Buddhism or Christianity, with communism or conservatism, but we do not, in this country, imprison people for being Buddhists or Christians, conservatives or communists. Why, then, in the name of all that is just and equitable, are these three anarchists deprived of their liberty?

Well, it is perhaps a simple miscarriage of justice, an anomaly of the law, some bad kind of joke played by the State jesters. That would be the most agreeable explanation to offer. But if that is not the right explanation, if our comrades have been imprisoned in the pursuance of a ruthless and determined policy, then the rights we believe we possess as citizens of this democratic country are at an end. There is no longer in this land such a thing as the liberty of unlicensed printing for which Milton made his immortal and unanswerable plea: there is no longer any such thing as freedom of expression which ten generations of Englishmen have jealously guarded. These words are now a mockery, and either we have been duped slaves to accept such a breach of our traditional rights, or we resolve never to rest until they are restored. I cannot imagine what perfidy of mind has spread among our judiciary that it has so far forgotten its trust as to allow so great an abuse of justice under the excuse of wartime regulations – regulations which peace has now made obsolete. Some of these Regulations have just been abolished – the fascists have been set free, but our comrades remain in prison. These Regulations which were admitted under protest at the time of their enactment, and only accepted in view of their temporary force, were designed, however illogically, to secure a victory in the cause of freedom. By all accounts, that victory has been won. But we are here to assert that the war which has been won on the Continent of Europe has been lost in this island of Britain, and we can have no joy in victory, nor ease from strife, until our comrades once more stand beside us as free men.

16

Amnesty Campaign

WE reproduce below a statement which has been issued to the press by the Freedom Defence Committee in connection with their campaign for an amnesty for all people held in British prisons under wartime regulations and laws. The campaign was initiated by the display of posters calling upon the people to demand such an amnesty, and we reproduce the photograph of these posters. Already there have been many signatures to the demand for an amnesty, and the activities of the committee have received the support of many people, of various opinions, who realise the danger at the present time of the complete loss of our elementary civil liberties unless some really vigorous body exists for resisting the progress of reaction and regimentation, even when it appears under the guise of a Labour government.

The Committee intends shortly to start a second campaign against the continuance of military and industrial conscription.

Although the war in Europe has ended, and the fascist internees have been released from their confinement, thousands of men and women are still in prison under wartime laws. These prisoners are not offenders against the common law, and the regulations under which they were incarcerated are admitted to be extraordinary measures necessitated only by the emergency of a major war.

They include political prisoners (whom the law chooses to class as felons), conscientious objectors, deserters, absentees and offenders under many bureaucratic regulations. The civil prisons are overcrowded with them, and many more are held under appalling conditions in military concentration camps, often undergoing long sentences for trifling offences.

Whatever excuse may have been given during the past few years for such imprisonments is surely invalidated now that the war in Europe is ended and we are told that the nation will gradually return to peacetime conditions. The most important task of a return to peace, more urgent even than housing or food, would appear to be a rectification of those injustices which were committed during wartime when the fundamental rights of the citizen were suspended under the pretext of an emergency situation. It is to be hoped that the new Labour government will take early action to alter this situation.

The Freedom Defence Committee intends to begin an immediate campaign for an amnesty for all civilian and military offenders against wartime laws, and would welcome the support of all who are anxious for the liberation of the British prisoners of war in British prisons. A demand for such an amnesty will be presented to the Home Secretary, and signature forms are available from the offices of the Committee, 17 St George Street, Hanover Square, London W1.

The Freedom Defence Committee was originated in February of this year, under the name of the Freedom Press Defence Committee, to assist the four anarchists who were being tried under Regulation 39A. At that time it became evident that there was a need for a permanent vigilance body to fight for the preservation of elementary civil liberties, and the Freedom Defence Committeee, consisting of individuals of many different shades of liberal, socialist and libertarian opinion, was formed for that purpose.

Herbert Read, Chairman
Freedom Defence Committee

17

The Centenary of
The Ego and His Own

THERE are several reasons why the centenary of Max Stirner's *The Ego and His Own* should not pass without commemoration, the least important being the merely historical fact that it played a decisive part in the philosophical discussions out of which emerged Marxism. Marx devoted three-quarters of *Die Deutsche Ideologie*, an immense work, to a refutation of Stirner's philosophy, and Marx was not given to wasting his time on trivialities. Marx triumphed over Stirner as he triumphed over Feuerbach and Bakunin: he had the last word and it is still echoing in the political events of the present day. But after a sleep of a hundred years the giants whom Marx thought he had slain show signs of coming to life again. 'The issues which Stirner raised and Marx met,' Sidney Hook observes in a brilliant book which he devoted to the intellectual strife of this period,[1] 'have a definite relevance to the conflict of ideas and attitudes in the contemporary world in Europe and America today. Indeed, we might even say that this is due to the fact that Stirner and Marx are here discussing the fundamental problems of any possible system of ethics or public morality.' That was written ten years ago, and now, after a world war which has brought all these fundamental problems into sharper focus, the relevance of Stirner's philosophy is all the more apparent.

The clash of altruism and egoism is one of the commonplaces of ethics, and the issue is never in doubt. Stirner is usually dismissed as the most extreme representative of the philosophy of egoism known to history, and students in our academies of learning only hear of him as a lost soul condemned to the lowest regions of limbo. His famous book was originally published in Leipzig, ironically enough by the same publisher who a few months later published Engels' *Condition of the Working Class in England in 1844*. *Der Einzige und sein Eigentum*, as Stirner's book was called, hardly survived Marx's onslaught, but some mention of it is made in two books which played a great part in the development of thought during the second half of the nineteenth century – Lange's *History of Materialism* (1866) and Eduard von Hartmann's *Philosophy of the Unconscious* (1869). The references in Lange's book aroused the curiosity of John Henry Mackay, the German poet with a Scottish name, who then read *Der Einzige und sein Eigentum* and was so moved by it that he devoted a considerable part of his life to a rehabilitation of Stirner's name and work. His biography of the philosopher was published in Berlin in 1898. Later Victor Basch, who held the chair of aesthetics at the Sorbonne until quite recently, published an appreciative study of Stirner's philosophy. George Brandes also saw the importance of Stirner, and when, at the turn of the century, Nietzsche's philosophy became the vogue, Stirner was presented as one of his precursors. An English translation of Stirner's book was sponsored by the American anarchist, Benjamin Tucker, and excellently carried out by Steven T. Byington. This translation, with an Introduction by Dr James L. Walker, another American anarchist, was published by A. C. Fifield in London in 1913. I bought my copy in 1915, and it is a book which I have never lost sight of – it is a book which once read is persistently recalled to memory. In America it has been re-issued as a popular classic in the Modern Library, but here in England it remains unknown and unsolicited.

I have not read Stirner's original text, but its vitality survives translation, and it is easy to detect the influence it had on Nietzsche's *style* (its influence on his thought is still more obvious). Read the following passage (appropriate enough today for its content) and you hear the very voice of Zarathustra:

> 'Listen, even as I am writing this, the bells begin to sound, that they may jingle in for tomorrow the festival of the thousand years' existence of our dear Germany. Sound, sound its knell ! You do sound solemn enough, as if your tongue was moved by the presentiment that it is giving convoy to a corpse. The German people and German peoples have behind them a history of a thousand years: what a long life! O, go to rest, never to rise again – that all may become free whom you so long have held in fetters. The *people* is dead. Up with *me*!
>
> 'O thou my much-tormented German people – what was thy torment? It was the torment of a thought that cannot create itself a body, the torment of a walking spirit that dissolves into nothing at every cock-crow and yet pines for deliverance and fulfilment. In me too thou hast lived long, thou dear – thought, thou dear – spook. Already I almost fancied I

had found the word of thy deliverance, discovered flesh and bones for the wandering spirit; then I hear them sound, the bells that usher thee into eternal rest! Then the last hope fades out, then the notes of the last love die away, then I depart from the desolate house of those who now are dead and enter at the door of the – living one:

"For only he who is alive is in the right".

Farewell, thou dream of so many millions! farewell, thou who has tyrannised over thy children for a thousand years !
'Tomorrow they carry thee to the grave! Soon thy sisters, the peoples, will follow thee. But when they have all followed, then – mankind is buried, and I am my own, I am the laughing heir !'

The whole of *The Ego and His Own* is not written in this exalted style – indeed, Stirner's style, for a German style, is unusually direct and clear, and he completely eschews the symbolism so characteristic of Nietzsche. Some of his terminology presents extraordinary difficulty for the English translator, for we have no exact equivalents for words like *Einzige, Eigner, Einzigkeit, Eigenheit* and *Eigentum*, but with the help of some footnotes Steven Byington successfully overcame these problems.

Stirner wrote his book at a decisive moment in the history of European thought – at a moment when the traditional dogmas of religion, politics and philosophy were being discarded, and people everywhere were adopting the new dogmas of socialism, communism, Hegelianism, materialism and many other 'isms.' It might be said that the whole purpose of Stirner was to show that these revolutionaries were merely jumping out of the frying-pan into the fire, throwing off one set of shackles merely to adopt another set. A man is only free, Stirner maintained, if he gets rid of *all* dogmas, renounces *all* 'isms,' and confronts the world as an *Eigner*, a unique person existing in his own rights, self-determined and self-directed. 'I am my own only when I am master of myself, instead of being mastered either by sensuality or by anything else (God, man, authority, law, State, Church, etc.); what is of use to me, this self-owned or self-appertaining one, *my selfishness* pursues.'

In so far as this doctrine was applied to absolutism, to nationalism, to religious dogmatism, it was (and still is) acceptable enough to a large number of people (it is the basic assumption of those people who at the moment are organising a Society of Individualists). But Stirner carried his relentless analysis into the revolutionary camp, and showed that their ideals, called humanism, liberalism, communism or what not, were merely traps for the unwary.

'The HUMAN *religion* is only the last metamorphosis of the Christian religion. For liberalism is a religion because it separates my essence from me and sets it above me, because it exalts "Man" to the same extent as any other religion does its God or idol, because it makes what is mine into something other-worldly, because in general it makes out of what is mine, out of my qualities and my property, something alien – to wit, an "essence"; in short, because it sets me beneath Man, and thereby creates for me a "vocation." But liberalism declares itself a religion in form too when it demands for this supreme being, Man, a zeal of faith, "a faith that some day will at last prove its fiery zeal too, a zeal that will be invincible".'

That last phrase is quoted from Bruno Bauer, whose uncritical idealism had been too much for Marx. When he comes to Stirner, Marx has to take a very different stand. Engels had already warned him (in a letter of November 19, 1844, quoted by Hook, p. 173n.) that 'what is true in his principle, we, too, must accept. And what is true is that before we can be active in any cause we must make it our own, egoistic cause – and that in this sense, quite aside from any material expectations, we are communists in virtue of our egoism, and that out of egoism we want to be human beings and not merely individuals'. That acute observation has been enormously reinforced since Engels' time by psychoanalysis, which has shown to what great extent our ideals, even when apparently most disinterested, are but rationalisations or sublimations of egotistic impulses or expressions of unconscious and yet selfish motives. Marx's criticism of Stirner's subjectivism would need drastic revision to be convincing today. But where Marx is on stronger ground is in showing that Stirner's 'own' or 'unique one' is a philosophical abstraction which one can divorce only in theory from the environmental influences which determine the nature of the individual personality.

At this point Stirner becomes relevant to the philosophy of personalism, and indeed Berdyaev has admitted that

> 'in Max Stirner, in spite of the falsity of his philosophy, true personalism is to be found, but in a distorted form. In him a dialectic of the self-affirmation of the ego comes to light. The "unique one" is not personality because personality disappears in the infinity of self-affirmation, in unwillingness to know an other, and to achieve transcendence to the utmost. But in the "unique one" there is a modicum of truth, for personality is a universe, a microcosm, and in a certain sense the whole world is its property and belongs to it; personality is not partial nor a particular nor subordinate to the whole and the common.'[2]

Stirner would have had his answer to Berdyaev – he would have found his surrender to 'suprapersonal values' but the old slavery in a new form, and no freedom at all in his mystical transcendentalism.

The most pertinent criticism of Stirner is that which is directed against his doctrine that freedom implies power, though it is not a criticism which Marxism can make with any sincerity. Certainly some of Stirner's statements can be construed as a defence of the competitive spirit, and therefore as a defence of capitalism. But Stirner was really only concerned, as Erich Fromm has been in our time, to insist that freedom is a very ambiguous term – that there is all the difference between freedom *from* and freedom *for* something. 'My freedom,' wrote Stirner, 'becomes complete only when it is my – *might*; but by this I cease to be a merely free man, and become an own man. Why is the freedom of the peoples a "hollow word"? Because the peoples have no might! With a breath of the living ego I blow peoples over, be it the breath of a Nero, a Chinese emperor, or a poor writer.' Marx, if not his followers, would have subscribed to this. And I think that most modern psychologists – certainly Jung, Burrow, Reich and Fromm – would subscribe to what is the essence of Stirner's claim – that freedom, 'in the full amplitude of the word' is 'essentially self-liberation – i.e., that I can only have so much freedom as I procure for myself by my ownness.' Stirner's doctrine is, in fact, a plea for the integration of the personality, and on that basis the charge of 'selfishness' becomes somewhat naive. As Fromm says, if an individual can 'love' only others, he cannot love at all. 'Selfishness is rooted in this very lack of fondness for oneself. The person who is not fond of himself, who does not approve of himself, is in constant anxiety concerning his own self. He has not the inner security which can exist only on the basis of genuine fondness and affirmation.' But Stirner had said the same thing: 'I love men too – not merely individuals, but every one. But I love them with the consciousness of egoism; I love them because love makes *me* happy, I love because loving is natural to me, because it pleases me. I know no "commandment of love." I have a *fellow-feeling* with every feeling being, and their torment torments, their refreshment refreshes me too; I can kill them, not torture them.' Like Mencius and Chuang Tzu, Stirner realised that 'the feeling for right, virtue, etc., makes people hard-hearted and intolerant.' The whole of Stirner's treatment of the subject of love is of great subtlety and profundity, and Marxian criticism does not touch it at all. So far as I know only Martin Buber, himself the most profound of modern philosophers of the self, has appreciated this aspect of Stirner's work and given some discussion of it.[3]

Buber is critical of Stirner, but he does give him the same kind of importance in the history of human thought which he (and many others) now give to Kierkegaard.

'What Stirner with his destructive power successfully attacks is the substitute for a reality that is no longer believed: the fictitious responsibility in face of reason, of an idea, a nature, an institution, of all manner of illustrious ghosts, all that in its essence is not a person and hence cannot really, like father, and mother, prince and master, husband and friend, like God, make you answerable. He wishes to show the nothingness of the word which has decayed into a phrase; he has never known the living word, he unveils what he knows. Ignorant of the reality whose appearance is appearance, he proves its nature to be appearance. Stirner dissolves the dissolution. "What you call responsibility is a lie", he cries, and he is right: it is a lie. But there is a truth. And the way to it lies freer after the lie has been seen through.'

Finally I would like to suggest that the fashionable doctrine of existentialism must owe something to Stirner – the resemblances are too many and too close to be accidental. Sartre's philosophy is said to derive from Heidegger, a philosopher of whose work I have read very little, and Heidegger is said to derive from Kierkegaard, of whose work I have read a good deal. But I see no resemblance at all between the end-links of this chain, between Kierkegaard and Sartre. But the characters in Sartre's plays and novels are constructed round a philosophy which seems to me to be identical with Stirner's (plus a little American pragmatism). They are all busy discovering the illusory nature of freedom, the tyranny of 'isms': they are all resorting to a non-metaphysical, anti-hypothetical view of reality. Every Sartrean hero concludes much in the concluding words of *The Ego and His Own*:

'In the *unique one* the owner himself returns into his creative nothing, out of which he is born. Every higher essence above me, be it God, be it man, weakens the feeling of my uniqueness, and pales only before the sun of his consciousness. If I concern myself for myself, the unique one, then my concern rests on its transitory, mortal creator, who consumes himself, and I may say:
"All things are nothing to me".'

Notes

1 *From Hegel to Marx* (London, 1936), p.163.
2 *Slavery and Freedom* (London, 1943), p.34.
3 *Between Man and Man*, trans. by Ronald Gregor Smith (London 1947).

18

Neither Communism nor Liberalism

THE contemplative sentry in *Iolanthe* described himself as 'an intellectual chap', so perhaps his well-known ditty may be quoted in the Third Programme. He marvelled, you will remember,

> How Nature always does contrive
> That ev'ry boy and ev'ry gal
> That's born into the world alive
> Is either a little Liberal
> Or else a little Conservative.

This I had always considered to be a peculiarly English doctrine. It is reflected in our two-party system of government, of which we are inordinately proud – a centre party, it has always seemed to us, is an eccentricity indulged in by foreigners. God gave us two hands only – a left and a right, and on this analogy we divide our politics into left and right, our morals into good and evil, our conduct into right and wrong, and we like to see things in black and white – we distrust all intermediate shades.

But the recognition of intermediate shades – in politics or anything else – is not what I am going to speak about tonight. I would like to persuade you of the existence of colours or categories which are completely different.

When that great humanist, Salvador de Madariaga, spoke to you a few weeks ago on 'The Crisis of Liberalism', I was surprised to find that he too, a Spaniard, was singing the sentry's song from *Iolanthe*. He reduced the variegated spectrum of Continental politics, first to three parties, and then to two exclusive attitudes. He suggested that the whole of our existence is ruled by an antithesis – he called it *the statistical* and *the psychological* aspects of human nature. I am not going to quarrel with these categories, nor with the distinction between communism and liberalism which they so clearly illuminated. But I would say that only by oversimplifying the obstinate complexity of things can such general descriptions of historical tendencies be reduced to the particular programmes of the liberal and communist parties. We live in a pluralistic universe – or so I hold – and there is not one truth, nor even two alternative interpretations of the one truth. There are a certain number of facts proved probable, and then a vast empire where nescience rules, into whose secrets we can only reach with the groping antennae of imagination and myth.

To return to our political problems. If we analyse the press, the pronouncements of parties, and popular assumptions generally, then I agree with Señor de Madariaga; it looks as though there are only two policies offered as alternative solutions of our political crisis. Conservatives are really liberals, and liberals sometimes call themselves radicals and in effect are socialists or communists. These vague abstract words do not, however, indicate precisely the nature of the alternative social orders. What liberalism offers us is a system of laissez-faire, of open markets, of free enterprise based on the accumulation of capital. What communism offers us is controlled production and controlled consumption, the control being in the hands of the centralised authority of the State. Both systems claim to be based on democratic principles, though, as Señor de Madariaga pointed out, there is a vast difference in the interpretation given to these principles by communists and liberals.

I believe that both systems lead inevitably to totalitarianism, by which I mean the control of all our affairs by a central authority. I do not think I need elaborate this point in relation to communism. Communism, as it has developed in Russia, openly proclaims its authoritarianism. It suppresses all dissident opinion, directs from a central bureau all economic activities, all education and training, all scientific research and cultural expression. Even in the less developed form of democratic socialism, such as we now experience in this country, we already have the nationalisation of certain industries, the central control of production and consumption, the direction of labour and the closed shop.

But liberalism, it will be said, opposes such a conception of social order. Liberalism believes in the freedom of the individual, in government in accordance with the will of the majority: in open covenants openly arrived at, and so on.

Nevertheless liberalism leads inevitably into the same totalitarian trap as communism or socialism.

This is not an original view of mine: it has been expressed very forcibly by some of the world's greatest political philosophers – by Proudhon, by Lord Acton, by Alexis de Tocqueville. These political philosophers have realised that an inevitable tendency towards centralisation exists in the very principle of democracy and this constitutes a mortal danger. I admit that I am here making an identification between liberalism and democracy which is not strictly logical. Integral liberalism, as we might call it, does not ally itself with any specific system of government: it is primarily a doctrine of individual liberty, which it regards as a natural right to be preserved by the most reasonable system of government. But nowadays liberals always assume that the most reasonable system of government is a democracy. And that is how they come to surrender their integrity.

De Tocqueville put the matter in the form of a maxim: 'A democratic people,' he said, 'tends towards centralisation, as it were by instinct. It arrives at provincial institutions only by reflection.' He thought that this tendency towards centralisation is inherent in the democratic system, but inherent or not, it became inevitable with the growth during the nineteenth century of the concept of national sovereignty. He confessed that he could not conceive how a nation in this modern sense could live and prosper without a powerful centralisation of government, but he went on to say (in his book on *Democracy in America*) that 'a centralised administration is fit only to enervate the nation in which it exists, by incessantly diminishing their local spirit. Although such an administration can bring together at a given moment, on a given point, all the disposable resources of a people, it injures the renewal of these resources. It may ensure a victory in the hour of strife, but it gradually relaxes the sinews of strength'.

Acton, who also gave much thought to this problem, came to the conclusion that 'Liberty depends on the division of power. Democracy tends to unity of power'. And as a safeguard he suggested: 'To keep asunder the agents (of power), one must divide the sources, that is, one must maintain, or create, separate administrative bodies. In view of increasing democracy, a restricted federalism is the one possible check upon concentration and centralism.'

It has always been recognized since the time of the Greek philosophers that the practicability of a free democracy was somehow bound up with the question of size – that democracy would only work within some restricted unit such as the city-state. This was the conclusion of Plato and Aristotle in the ancient world, and their view has been supported in modern times by great political philosophers like Rousseau, Proudhon, Burckhardt and Kropotkin.

Based on this realisation, a political philosophy has arisen which opposes the whole conception of the State. This theory, which would abolish the State, or reduce it to insignificance, is sometimes known as distributivism, sometimes as syndicalism, sometimes as guild socialism, but in its purest and most intransigent form it is called anarchism. Anarchism, as the Greek roots of the word indicate, is a political philosophy based on the idea that a social order is possible without rule, without dictation – even the dictation of a majority. Señor de Madariaga in his broadcast used the word as an antithesis to order, which is a common misuse of the word. Anarchism, indeed, seeks a very positive form of social order, but it is order reached by mutual agreement, not order imposed by unilateral dictation.

Though anarchism as a political doctrine has a respectable ancestry, and has numbered great poets and philosophers like Godwin and Shelley, Tolstoy and Kropotkin among its adherents: though even now it is the professed faith of millions of people in Spain, in Italy, and, alas, in Siberia: though it is the unformulated faith of millions more throughout the world – though, that is to say, it is one of the fundamental political doctrines of all time, it has never been given a place in our insular discussions of the political problems of our time.

Why this conspiracy of silence? I shall not spend any time on that interesting speculation, but I shall try, in the few minutes left to me, to give you the main principles of this distinct political theory.

Believing that an expanding democracy leads to the delegation of authority, to the creation of a governing class of politicians and bureaucrats – believing, in Acton's words, that democracy tends to unity of power, and inevitably to the abuse of power by power-corrupted politicians, we who are anarchists seek to divide power, to decentralise government down to the localities in which it is exercised, so that every man has a sense of social responsibility and participates immediately in the conduct of his social order.

That is the political aspect of the theory. But it is equally in the economic field that democracy tends to unity of power – either the power of the capitalist monopoly or the power of the nationalised industry. We believe in the decentralisation of industry and in the deproletarisation of labour, in the radical transformation and fragmentation of industry, so that in place of a few powerful trade combines and trade unions, we should have many small co-operative farms and workshops, administered directly by the workers themselves.

We believe, that is to say, in a federal or co-operative commonwealth, and we believe that this represents an ideal which is distinct from any offered by liberalism or communism. You may be inclined to dismiss it as an impracticable ideal, but within limits we can prove that it does work, in spite of unfavourable economic conditions and in the face of ruthless opposition from capitalists or communists. There have been many failures and many false starts, but these have been studied by the sociologists of the movement, and we know pretty accurately why certain co-operative communities have failed. We think we know for what reasons others have survived for a century or more – the Hutterites, a religious community, was founded in Moravia in the 16th century and has carried out these principles successfully ever since. More remarkable, because operating within the economic structure of a modern society, are the highly successful co-operative agricultural communities established in Palestine, in Mexico and under the Farm Security Administration in the USA. At Valence in France a very successful experiment is taking place. In this case the co-operative community combines a highly skilled industry (the manufacture of watch-cases) with agriculture. I do not pretend that these experiments prove the case for an anarchist society. But they are highly significant tests of the human capacity for co-operative living – experiments which give us every confidence in the social and economic soundness of our wider proposals.

I am old enough to remember the days, before 1917, when people would say: Oh, socialism is all right in theory, but it could never be put into practice. Against such an argument socialists of that time could only put their faith – a faith which, we must admit, has been amply justified. Now on every side we meet the same argument against anarchism, against the co-operative commonwealth. No feudal baron could have believed in a world ruled by merchants and money-lenders; and in their turn these merchants and money-lenders refused for a long time to believe in the possibility of a world ruled by bureaucrats. I do not expect that many of my listeners can believe in a world in which the very idea of rule is abolished, in which we live by mutual aid, in which all thought of profit, all aggressive impulses, the concept of national sovereignty and the practice of armed imperialism, are forever absent. But when you consider the world in all its moral and economic chaos, when you see humanity fearfully transfixed by the threat of atomic warfare, can you for a moment believe that our civilisation will be saved by any change less profound than that which I have described tonight?

19

Anarchism: Past and Future

WHAT I have to say on this occasion is addressed to anarchists – to all those who feel an intellectual or emotional sympathy for the political tradition denoted by the word 'anarchism'. I am not concerned for the moment with propaganda or persuasion – rather, with self-criticism and what might be described as 'a call to order'.

I begin with this challenge: no fundamental thought has been devoted to the principles of anarchism for half a century. The last important contribution to anarchism was Kropotkin's *Mutual Aid*, written fifty years ago.

It might be argued that Kropotkin, and others before his time, Tolstoy, Bakunin, Proudhon or Godwin, had formulated a political philosophy which was good for all time – a sacred text which only needed the exegesis of later commentators to bring it up-to-date. Apart from the fact that deep contradictions exist between the writers I have mentioned, whose reconcilement would call for a synthetising work of genius, there are certain historical events of the past fifty years which have fundamentally affected all systems of thought. There have been two world wars – symptomatic of some deep social disorder; there has been a revolution in Russia which has undergone some very significant transformations; there has been a drift in the distribution of world power which has brought the United States into the periphery of our affairs; there have been changes in methods of production and means of communication which have transformed the economic basis of society; and finally, a new weapon, the atom bomb, has been invented which has decisive implications for revolutionary strategy. These are but the most dramatic of the changes which have affected our life since the writing of *Mutual Aid*: there are many advances in scientific research and philosophical thought which are no less significant for the future of anarchism.

Naturally, I believe that there are certain universal truths which determine our anarchist attitude, and which will always differentiate us from the socialist, the liberal, the capitalist or the fascist. But these so-called universal truths are few in number and very general in expression; they are abstractions, intellectual concepts, emotional attitudes. We are probably compelled to adopt them, not so much by reason, as by temperamental disposition. They are beliefs which have to be translated into acts.

The fundamental beliefs or attitudes underlying anarchism can, in my opinion, be reduced to three – three principles which we must accept if we are to continue to call ourselves anarchists.

The first is the belief in *personal freedom* – not merely a belief in individual liberty, but in a state of mental equilibrium in which thought is calm and life is harmonious. It is no good being politically free if we remain psychologically obsessed.

The second belief is in the social principle of *mutual aid*. We anarchists do not accept either the individualistic philosophy of the liberals and capitalists, or the totalitarian philosophy of the socialists and communists – we believe that society can be organised on a co-operative and federal basis, free from exploitation and from dictation.

About the third belief we may not be so unanimous, but I personally think that it follows originally from the first and second beliefs, and that it is now forced on us by the logic of events. It is the belief in *non-violence* – in non-violent resistance to oppression, and in non-violent methods of attaining our ends.

These beliefs are not self-evident to the majority of people, and it follows that we have to use our powers of reasoning and persuasion to secure the agreement of our fellow-men. My contention is that we are not at present doing this in any scientific or consistent manner. We are divided among ourselves, open to accusations of vague idealism and muddle-headedness, and of being fundamentally lazy or reactionary.

I shall now indicate some of the specific fields of knowledge which call for interpretation in the light of our fundamental principles.

There is first of all the field of *history*. We are advocating a certain form of social organisation – the co-operative community. Such communities have been tried as experiments in the past and are being tried as experiments in various parts of the world today. Some of these experiments date back to the Roman Empire; others begin in the Middle Ages; others are of recent origin. It is true that Kropotkin has devoted a brilliant chapter or two to the most significant of these historical types; and

Rudolf Rocker has given us a general survey of the history of civilisation which brings out clearly the values of the federal principle. But a much more detailed examination of the historical evidence is needed; and apart from specific research into the history of co-operative communities, there is need for an analysis of history in general in the light of our principles. The history of law and criminology, for example, should provide evidence of immense value; the history of land tenure, or of trade organisations are other examples. I am not suggesting a tendentious interpretation of history: I think we have everything to gain from the objective truth. But let us get at the facts which support our beliefs, and weigh them against the facts which are held to support other beliefs.

The next field of necessary research is *anthropological*. Kropotkin, again, was a pioneer in this field, but since his day an immense amount of fresh material has been published, and from my own superficial and incomplete knowledge of this subject, I know that much of the evidence collected and published by anthropologists like Margaret Mead, Malinowski, Verrier Elwin, and scores of obscurer field-workers, has direct bearing on the co-operative organisation of production and the subtler problems of collective integrity.

Anthropology would soon lead us to the wider field of *sociology*. Sociology is a very wide and indeed amorphous subject, but almost every aspect of it has some bearing on the issues raised by anarchism. It sometimes seems to me that the many problems investigated by the sociologist converge on the discussion of one point – the nature of the incentives which maintain the vitality and well-being of societies. Certainly, unless the structure of a society includes what might quite simply be called 'a stimulus to work', that society will decay. The formidable attack on totalitarian forms of socialism delivered by economists like von Mises, Röpke and Hayek concentrates on this weak spot in the socialist State. It is an attack which is supported from day to day by events. Not only in this country, not only in France and Scandinavia, but by their own confessions in the USSR also, and perhaps there most decisively the incentives to work have declined. Almost everywhere – in spite of increased wages and an improved standard of living – the rate of production per man-hour has declined catastrophically during the past fifty years.

There is evidence which shows that this is not entirely an economic question. When all due weight has been given to factors like wages and housing, standard of living and conditions of work, an unknown factor remains which we can only call *zest*: a certain positive attitude towards society and the future which shows itself, not only in rates of production, but also in the birth-rate. The same factors seem to govern the two processes of production. These factors are *psychological*, and psychology is the next sphere which demands our patient investigation.

Psychology may be either individual or social. That individual psychology has some bearing on our problems should be obvious enough, but to show how nearly it touches them, let me quote a few sentences from a forthcoming work by C. G. Jung:

> 'The psychologist firmly believes in the individual as the sole carrier of mind and life. Society or the State derive their quality from the individual's mental condition, for they are constituted by individuals and their organisations. No matter how obvious this fact is, it has not yet permeated collective opinion sufficiently for people to refrain from using the term "State" as if it referred to a sort of super-individual endowed with inexhaustible power and resourcefulness. The State is expected nowadays to accomplish easily what nobody would expect from an individual. The dangerous incline leading down to mass psychology begins with this plausible thinking in big numbers and powerful organisations, where the individual dwindles away to mere nothingness. Yet everything that exceeds a certain human size evokes equally inhuman powers in Man's unconsciousness, totalitarian demons are called forth, instead of the realisation that all which can really be accomplished is an infinitesimal step forward in the individual's moral nature.'
>
> (*Essays on Contemporary Events*, p. xvii)

'When people are thrown together in huge masses and considered only as a herd, it has the most devastating moral and psychical effect upon the individual. The foundation for collective crime is laid by just such a state of things; and then it is really a miracle if the crime is not actually committed. Do we seriously believe that *we* would have been proof against it? We, who have so many traitors and political psychopaths in our midst? It has filled us with horror to realise all that man is capable of, and of which we are consequently also capable; and since then a terrible doubt regarding humanity – in which we also are included – nags at us.

'Nevertheless – and there should be no mistake about this – such a state of degradation can only be brought about by certain conditions. First and foremost among these is the accumulation of urban, industrialised masses; i.e., of people whose abilities are only partially mobilised, owing to the unnatural, one-sided character of employment in factories, shops, and so on. They have been uprooted from their natural soil and have lost every kind of healthy instinct, even that of *self-preservation*. For dependence on the State can be measured in terms of loss of the instinct of self-preservation, which is a deplorable symptom. Dependence on the State means that one relies on everybody else (= State) instead of on oneself. Every person hangs on to the next, with a false feeling of security; for one is still swinging in the air even when hanging in the company of 10,000 other people – the only difference being that one is no longer aware of one's own insecurity. The increasing dependence on the State is anything but a healthy symptom, for it means that the people are on a fair way to become a herd of sheep, always relying on a shepherd to drive them on to good pastures. The shepherd's staff soon becomes a rod of iron, and the shepherds turn into wolves.'

(*Essays on Contemporary Events*, pp. 52-3)

But it is in the wider field of social psychology that the most pertinent work remains to be done. Social psychology, which is sometimes called group psychology or phylo-analysis, is, properly understood, the foundation of our whole attitude. We might say that all other political attitudes – capitalist, labour, communist – are attitudes without a sound psychological basis. Some Marxists, aware of this deficiency in their own philosophy, attack psychology as a pseudo-science, or as a bourgeois science, but that is only an indication of their own limitations. Psychology has its charlatans, like every other science, but its scientific achievements, particularly in the field of mental therapy, cannot be disputed.

The main problems of social psychology revolve round the relationships which exist, or should exist, between the individuals and the group. Most mental illnesses, unless due to constitutional defects, are the result of maladjustment, and can often be cured by the 'integration of the personality' – by which phrase we mean the effective restoration to the individual of a sense of community with others. Repressions which result in an unconscious sense of frustration are the root cause of individual maladaptations and of most aggressive impulses. But obviously the problem is not entirely an affair of the individual: there are two terms to the process of integration, and most maladjusted individuals might complain with some justification that it is not themselves, but the group which needs readjustment. And any psychologist who has worked outside his consulting-room is bound to admit the justice of this complaint. From the family to the State, the group in modern society is a flabby, inchoate, uneasy organism, and until we have discovered what is wrong with these organisms, we shall fail to effect any widespread readjustment of individual neurosis.

I believe, myself, that the pioneer work in this field has already been done by a group of American psychologists under the leadership of Dr Trigant Burrow, but until the final results of their research have been published, it is difficult to substantiate this belief. We can already see from works like *The Biology of Human Conflict* and *The Social Basis of Consciousness*, that a new level of psychological research has been reached and that it has a direct bearing on the problems of social organisation. I believe myself that the conclusions will be a direct and powerful vindication of the political philosophy of anarchism. I am prepared to admit that other psychological theories, particularly those of Wilhelm Reich, are equally relevant. I am not insisting that any particular system of psychology should be adopted by anarchists: I am only suggesting that psychology has a direct bearing on all social issues, and that our political philosophy must be grounded in psychological truth.

When we have got hold of the right principles of social relations, there will then be the problem of putting them into practice. The idea that this can be done by some kind of revolutionary *coup d'état* is really very childish. You cannot readjust individuals to society, or society to individuals, by purely external measures of control. The necessary changes are not so much political as biological – not structural, but organismic. The only way a biological or organismic change can be induced is by training or education. The word *revolution* should largely disappear from our propaganda, to be replaced by the word *education*. It is only in so far as we liberate the growing shoots of mankind, shoots not yet stunted or distorted by an environment of hatred and injustice, that we can expect to make any enduring change in society. Revolutions fail because they are built on the bogs and volcanoes of vast social neuroses; the few sane and enlightened pioneers who may lead a revolution are almost immediately swamped by the forces of the collective unconscious which the violence of the revolutionary event releases. It is not the enemy confronting the barricades which defeats a revolution, but the forces coming up from the rear.

We may have to act in a revolutionary spirit in a given situation – I shall discuss revolutionary tactics presently – but a new order of society such as we desire can only be given a firm and enduring foundation within the physique and disposition of the human being, and education in its widest sense is the only means we have of securing such fundamental changes in the whole social group.

About the type of education likely to bring about such fundamental changes, there may be legitimate differences of opinion. I have my own ideas about it which I call 'education through art', and I have given a summary of them in the Freedom Press pamphlet called *The Education of Free Men* [reprinted above, pp. 65-95]. In general, what is necessary is some form of moral or ethical education. The declining influence of the churches has left an enormous gap in the process of education. The education given in primary and secondary schools, in universities and in technical colleges, is an almost exclusively *intellectual* education: it trains the mind and memory of the growing child, but neglects the emotions and sensibility.

Some of you may look askance at words like 'ethics' and 'morality' and fear that they may be a cloak under which some escapist form of religious mysticism would be gradually introduced. But that is really a very narrow-minded and timorous attitude. You have only to consider the psychological make-up of the human being, and to compare this structure with the normal methods of education, to realize that fundamental constituent elements of the human psyche are either completely ignored, or ruthlessly suppressed, by present practices in the schools. Everything personal, everything which is the expression of individual perceptions and feelings, is either neglected, or subordinated to some conception of normality, of social convention, of correctness. I am not suggesting that we should educate for a world of eccentrics, of wilful egoists. Far from it. I am really suggesting that these forces which we call feelings, instincts and emotions, should be used creatively, and communally – that we should substitute, for our neurotic separateness and discordant relationships, disciplines of harmony and of art. The end of moral education is the creation of group discipline, of group unity or unanimity, a living-together in brotherhood. Brotherhood is an instinctive social unity – a unity in love. But it does not grow without care, without a united will and a discipline. Just as the family can be an epitome of hell if it is based on discordant wills, on parental disharmony, on ignorant suppression of natural instincts, so society is hell let loose when it is one vast neurosis due to social inequalities and social disintegration. Moral education is simply education for social unity, and as such it hardly exists to-day. But it is the only guarantee of the endurance, of the lastingness, of the social revolution. It is for this reason that towards the end of his life Kropotkin turned his attention to the subject of ethics. He lived to publish only the first part of his work, which was a clearing made in the tangle which has grown up round the subject. But he intended to build in the clearing he had made, and was working on a positive system of ethics when he died in Russia. I always hope that this last work of his may have survived, and will in some happier time be published. But we cannot wait for that chance. We have to go on from the point where Kropotkin left off, and give to the world a conception of morality or ethics which is an expression of our fundamental beliefs.

Finally, we have to develop and give a more perfect expression to our philosophy of freedom. Our philosophy is our faith. We believe that it is firmly based on empirical evidence – on the evidence of the natural order of the universe, on the evidence of biology and history. But we have to give systematic order to that evidence and eloquent expression to the general concepts which arise from the evidence. We shall find some support in ancient philosophy – in Indian, Chinese and Greek philosophy; but virtually we have to build on new foundations – the scientific foundations which I have already described.

What I have outlined is a coherent plan of research and work – a sevenfold system of study and creative activity, leading step by step from the facts as we find them in history and existing societies, through the basic facts of human psychology and social economy, to the methods of education and the philosophical formulation of our ideals. Perhaps it sounds all too systematic to you, but it is far from my intention to suggest the rigid structure of a universal philosophy on the lines of Comte or Herbert Spencer. Humanity is diverse; evolution is creative. A philosophy of freedom is a philosophy which allows for growth, for variation, for the possibility of new dimensions of personal development and social consciousness.

How does this programme which I have sketched for the future of anarchism differ from our previous conceptions of anarchism? Well, obviously, it is less political. I will not admit for a moment that it is less revolutionary. But the revolution envisaged is a humane one, and not a political one. But if we can secure a revolution in the mental and emotional attitudes of men, the rest follows. This is fundamental anarchism – anarchist fundamentalism. It discards for ever the romantic conception of anarchism – conspiracy, assassination, citizen armies, the barricades. All that kind of futile agitation has long been obsolete: but it was finally blown into oblivion by the atomic bomb. The power of the State, of our enemy, is now absolute. We cannot struggle against it *on the plane of force*, on the material plane. Our action must be piecemeal, non-violent, insidious and universally pervasive.

But this does not mean that we should retire to some sort of monastic life and lead a purely spiritual existence. On the contrary, we must study various forms of non-violent action, and above all the strategy and tactics of the strike weapon. Passive resistance to all forms of injustice must be organised, and must be made effective. Our most immediate aim is resistance to military conscription and the preparation of some co-ordinated policy of universal resistance to all forms of military action wherever and for whatever reason used. That aim alone is sufficient to absorb the energies of all those comrades whose temperaments are extraverted and energetic. But however much we become engaged in such revolutionary activities, do not let us forget that the real revolution is internal, that the most effective action is molecular, and that only in so far as we change the actual disposition of men do we guarantee the enduring success of the social revolution we all desire.

20

The Problem of War and Peace

Science, Liberty and Peace by Aldous Huxley.
War, Sadism and Pacifism by Edward Glover.

THE fear of war continues to be the pre-occupation of the whole world, and a great deal of our time and money is spent, either on efforts to establish and preserve peace, or on preparations for still another war. But do we really understand the nature of the problem of war and peace? How is it conceivable that we, who are gifted with rational faculties, and are citizens of a common world, will presently proceed to destroy each other with the terrible weapons which modern science has put in our hands, and for reasons which are merely economic, or political, or ideological. We all know that the atomic warfare of the future will exceed even the last war in horror, terror, and the destruction of life and civilisation. Why, then do we not merely contemplate the possibility of such a war, but even despairingly admit its inevitability? Why cannot mankind be sane when its very existence is threatened by causes which *should* be within the control of reason, of science, of pity?

The two authors whose books we are considering have different answers to these questions. Mr Huxley, in spite of the mysticism which to an increasing extent dominates his writings, is really an optimistic rationalist. The 'Inner Light' does, it is true, make its fitful appearance in this new tract for the times. He says that if only 'ministers of the various sects and religions would abandon sentimentality and superstition, and devote themselves to teaching their flocks that the Final End of man is not in the unknowable Utopian future, but in the timeless eternity of the Inner Light, which every human being is capable, if he so desires, of realising here and now, then the myth of progress would lose its harmfulness as a justifier of present tyranny and wrongdoing.' But, alas, sighs

Mr Huxley, the average human being will never attain this timeless eternity of Inner Light because he is fascinated by a will o' wisp which he calls science, and which, far from leading him to Utopia, is creating round him a social and economic hell of which war, in all its scientific efficiency, is merely one aspect.

Mr Huxley's pamphlet is really a frontal attack on the amoral scientific mind of to-day. It is the scientist who, without any sense of moral values, and overriding conception of goodness or beauty, has created social tendencies which inevitably lead to the concentration of power in irresponsible hands, to a centralisation of industry in amorphous inhuman cities, to a world-wide condition of economic insecurity which can only be resolved by war. The ideals of science are always in the direction of more and more power, more and more production, greater speed and completer mechanisation, and along with these materialistic ideals goes a mental attitude which accepts such quantitative achievements as progress, and believes that such progress is the only object in life.

No one, I think, can question this diagnosis of the materialistic trends of our civilisation, nor deny their connection with man's insane proneness to war. But what we must question is the assumption which Mr Huxley then makes, that we have only to redirect these scientific trends in order to secure peace. 'Let us suppose,' he says, 'that those who make it their business to apply the results of pure science to economic ends should elect to do so, not primarily for the benefit of big business, big cities and big government, but with the conscious aim of providing individuals with the means of doing profitable and intrinsically significant work, of helping men and women to achieve independence from bosses, so that they may become their own employers, or members of a self-governing, co-operative group working for subsistence and a local market.' Suppose, repeats Mr Huxley, 'that this were henceforward to become the acknowledged purpose guiding the labours of inventors and engineers.' Why, then, cries Mr Huxley, a progressive decentralisation of population, of ownership of the means of production, of political and economic power, would become possible. We could increase the local sources of food supply by improving insect controls and multiplying refrigerator units; we could develop entirely new foods such as edible yeasts; we could synthetise chlorophyll; and as for fuel (which at present causes so much international tension) we could revive windmills and construct paraboloid mirrors of large size which would be capable of superheating steam and even of melting iron by direct action of the sun's rays.

O brave new world! But Mr Huxley does not tell us how the chemist and the biologist, the physicist and the engineer are to be persuaded to see the Inner Light, and redirect their energies towards such eminently reasonable ends as decentralisation and regional co-operation.

A change of heart such as Mr Huxley requires is a psychological process, so let us turn to Dr Glover, one of the leading psychoanalysts in this country. He has just published a new edition of a book he wrote fourteen years ago, but the new volume is more than twice the size of the old one, and its argument has been greatly strengthened by the material evidence provided by another world war. If I say that I regard this book as the most important contribution ever made to the solution of the problem of war and peace, I shall be accused of exaggeration and defeat my aim, which is to persuade you to read *War, Sadism and Pacifism*. But what, in the whole range of science and politics, could be more important than a solution of this problem? If a scientist has put his finger on the real cause of war, and has indicated methods by means of which war might be prevented, then not even the invention of anaesthetics or antiseptics, the cure of cancer or tuberculosis, could claim to be more important. Diseases ravage our lives, but war destroys civilisation itself, and all that makes life worth living. So please listen to what Dr Glover has to say.

Dr Glover is a scientist and he is using a scientific language which cannot wholly, or accurately, be translated into the language of everyday life. But I shall try to restate his thesis in simple words. He begins with the fact that we are all creatures compounded of love and hate. We are born into a world of harsh reality, and from the very first days of our lives we have to struggle against forces which threaten our inborn selfish instincts. We have to fight for food, for air, for freedom of movement, and in that struggle we turn against the very objects of our love – our mothers, our fathers, our brothers and sisters. But for one reason or another we do not, or we cannot, express this hatred: we are *frustrated* and therefore bury or *repress* those unsocial, disloyal, ungrateful feelings. We are then no longer conscious of their existence, but psychoanalysis has proved beyond any doubt that such feelings continue to exist, in a deep and inaccessible region of the mind: that they are bottled up, as it were, under pressure, and continually seek objects upon which they can vent their hateful force.

Opportunities for such a discharge of hatred do not normally occur in the orderly conventional life we lead in peacetime, so the energy accumulates until we find an excuse for war, and there occurs a catastrophic purgation of our overcharged emotional system.

What we have to do, in order to prevent war, is to make sure that our aggressive instincts are not frustrated and repressed, especially during the period of infancy. We cannot get rid of the primary instincts of hatred – they are part of our human heritage, the curse with which we are all born. But we can hope to reduce the mental strains which cause outbreaks of irrational violence, delinquency, crime and war. 'Reduce unconscious anxieties,' says Dr Glover, 'and hostile reactions begin to disappear.' In the individual this can be done by a short-term policy of psychoanalysis and mental therapy or healing. But you cannot, in this way, treat all the millions of individuals that constitute the warring nations. So a long-term policy of social analysis and social therapy is needed. That policy, to be effective, must be carried out in the formative stages of the disease: it is a preventive therapy, or prophylactic, and it must take place in the nursery, in the home, in the school. 'I do not believe,' says Dr Glover, 'that war between civilised nations will ever be prevented until we learn how to bring up children in a more reasonable and understanding way than we do at present.' But a more reasonable and understanding way implies measures which will shock the conventional citizen and parent. For – it is no use disguising the fact – our impulses of hatred are closely related to our sexual impulses, and one of the first things we must do is to try and reduce what Dr Glover calls 'the tangled mass of superstitions and conventions that obstruct all rational adaptation to sexual life.' 'It is difficult,' he says, 'to over-estimate the reduction in emotional friction that could be secured if more rational codes were applied to sexual problems from infancy onwards.' But the essence of any such reform is that it should be carried out in an atmosphere of love and intimacy. 'The really shocking thing about Western Civilization,' Dr Glover thinks, 'is that it permits and approves, on both cultural and economic grounds, the delegation of upbringing from the family to every conceivable form of substitute parent or training institution. To my mind it is much more shocking that Anglo-Indian parents should board out their little three or four years old children in Bognor than that a native mother should go to work with her baby slung over her back, or that little tribal children should carry on their sexual play before the indulgent and amused eyes of their parents. Indeed, I would go so far as to say that the successful upbringing of children requires a Renaissance of Family Culture. The family must somehow or other win back from the State the rights it has lost; and it must re-establish a scale of values in which the place of honour is given, not to social achievement, but to transmission of humane family culture.'

There is no time to enter into any further detail of the diagnosis which Dr Glover makes, or of the preventive measures which he prescribes. Many of his practical recommendations are the same as Mr Huxley's – he agrees, for example, that the centralisation of power and production and the worship of the State are the symptoms of our social neurosis: that the main problem is 'how to extend the cultural authority of the family and to curtail the spurious cultural authority assumed by the State.' But he knows that we cannot rely on anything so uncertain as a change of heart. He believes that the problem is a scientific one, but he fears that unless scientists know how to manipulate the forces of love and hate they will make a greater mess of government than any laymen. For our politicians he has nothing but contempt: 'undaunted by an endless and humiliating story of absolute failure, they continue their labours with an unruffled faith in the rule of thumb.' Some entirely new method of approach to the problem is essential, and that method is suggested by the theory and practice of psychoanalysis.

On the basis of that theory and practice we can at least be sure that 'any investigation of the subject which neglects to correlate war phenomena with primitive infantile phases of unconscious mental development can only end in futility and frustration' – a difficult sentence which means that the war to end war must be fought long before our children reach the playing-fields of Eton or of any other school.

We need a new science of upbringing, and for a few of the millions now spent on UNO, UNESCO and the armaments of a fear-ridden world, we could have it.

21

The End of an Age

Essays from Tula by Leo Tolstoy. With an Introduction by Nicolas Berdyaev.

THESE essays were well worth reprinting, but one could wish that a little consideration had been given to their editing. A bundle of pamphlets seems to have been thrown together and sent to the printer without more ado. They appear in no logical or chronological order, and in most cases no information is given about the date of their composition or first publication. One essay is dated May 1914, four years after Tolstoy's death. As no trouble has been taken with the texts, footnotes which might have been informative in 1900 are reprinted in a misleading manner – for example, on page 95, we are told that Moscow has a very defective system of drainage, which may still be true, though it is not likely that the cesspools are now emptied into barrels every night. On page 83 another footnote informs us that 'in Russia... the greater part of the agricultural work still is done by peasants working their own land on their own account'. It would not have taken an editor half-an-hour to give these footnotes a retrospective sense. A brief preface states that the essays included are either 'little known or not easily obtainable in England today', but four of the nine essays reprinted appear in the later volumes of the Oxford University Press edition and are at any rate easily accessible.

Nevertheless, the volume is very welcome, for some of the essays are otherwise unobtainable and are among the best social criticism ever written by Tolstoy. *The Slavery of our Times*, which was recently reissued by the Porcupine Press, is included and is welcome in this context since it gives a comprehensive summary in about seventy pages of Tolstoy's political creed. It is the most uncompromising statement he ever made of his anti-governmental position. More interesting, perhaps, to readers of *Freedom* is the next essay, 'An Appeal to Social Reformers'. I believe this pamphlet was first issued by the Free Age Press, Christchurch, in

1900. In it, Tolstoy clearly defines his views on anarchism. After reviewing the theories of Godwin, Proudhon, Bakunin, Kropotkin, Max Stirner and Tucker, Tolstoy proceeds:

> 'So that whilst correctly recognising spiritual weapons as the only means of abolishing power, the Anarchist teaching, holding an irreligious materialistic life conception, does not possess this spiritual weapon, and is confined to conjectures and fancies which give the advocates of coercion the possibility of denying its true foundations, owing to the inefficiency of the suggested means of realising this teaching.
>
> 'This spiritual message is simply the one long ago known to men, which has always destroyed power and always given to those who used it complete and inalienable freedom. This weapon is but this, a devout understanding of life, according to which man regards his earthly existence as only a fragmentary manifestation of the complete life, and connecting his life with infinite life, and recognising his highest welfare in the laws of this infinite life, regards the fulfilment of these laws as more binding upon himself than the fulfilment of any human laws whatsoever.
>
> 'Only such a religious conception, uniting all men in the same understanding of life, incompatible with subordination to power and participation in it, can truly destroy power.'

Elsewhere Tolstoy identifies this vague religiosity with Christianity, but with a Christianity deprived of all ecclesiastical organisations, all ritual and superstition, in short, with the ethics of the Sermon on the Mount. He nowhere, so far as I know, gives a very clear definition of 'infinite life', and it is doubtful if he believed in personal survival after death. His positive belief was in the sanctity of human life, and in love:

> 'It is so simple, so clear. You live; that is, are born, mature, grow old, and then you die. Is it possible that the aim of your life can be in yourself? Certainly not. How then? man asks himself. What then am I? The only answer is: I am something that loves; at first it seems something loving only itself; but one need only live a little to see that to love the self which passes through life and dies, is impossible and purposeless. I feel that I ought to love, and I love myself. But, loving myself, I cannot but feel that the object of my love is unworthy of it; yet not to love is impossible to me. In my love is life. What is to happen? To love others: one's neighbours, friends, and those who love us? At first it seems that this will satisfy the demands of love; but all these people are in the first place imperfect, and, secondly, they change, and, above all, they die. What is one to love? The only answer is: love all, love the source of love, love love,

love God. Love, not for the sake of the loved one, nor for oneself, but for love's sake. It is only necessary to understand this, and at once all the evil human life disappears, and its meaning becomes clear and joyful.'

That quotation comes from an address delivered to a group of peasants during the summer of 1907: it is one of the last and the most moving of Tolstoy's declarations of faith. But it would be a mistake to assume from words like these that Tolstoy was unaware of the grim nature of the social struggle that awaited the oppressed masses. He could not believe in 'the spread of the unrealisable teaching of socialism, dreadful in its despotism and wonderful in its superficiality' – he anticipated very clearly the inevitable tendency of socialism to develop into totalitarianism. He saw perfectly clearly that the State was the enemy of Man, and his most forceful pages are directed against this growing danger. Against the State he realised that the only weapon was non-obedience, passive resistance, and he carried his policy in this direction to a fearless and uncompromising extreme. The best expression he ever gave to this revolutionary *policy* is found in an essay originally published by William Heinemann in 1906, and reprinted here – 'The End of the Age'. From his clear-sighted vision of the apocalyptic nature of the revolution then revealing itself he derived only one hope of deliverance: the cessation of obedience to governments.

> 'For this great revulsion to take place it is only necessary that men should understand that the State, the fatherland, is a fiction, and that life and true liberty are realities; and that therefore it is not life and liberty that should be sacrificed for the artificial combination called the State, but that men ought in the name of true life and liberty to free themselves from the superstition of the State and from its outcome– criminal obedience to men.'

Tolstoy's message has not grown out-of-date. In the present 'end of an age', when fear and anxiety and collective crime have expanded beyond even Tolstoy's conception of the possibilities, these essays come to us with prophetic force and urgency. He strides like a giant over all the pettifogging economists and politicians and confronts us with his unanswerable accusations, his scorn, and his overwhelming love of life and humanity.

22

Jankel Adler: The Artist

IN Jankel Adler, who died suddenly in Aldbourne (Wiltshire) on April 25th, Europe has lost one of its leading artists and the libertarian movement one of its most devoted friends. A man of great personal charm, of profound mind, and of restless energy, his death at the height of his powers, and just when full recognition had at last been given to his genius, is a sad tragedy.

Adler was born on July 26th, 1895, at Lodz in Poland. He studied in Germany, and used to acknowledge, as the only master from whom he had learned anything useful, a certain Professor Wiethüchter. I must leave to others who knew him in Germany to place on record his movements in the years between the two wars. All I know is that in 1925 he was in Düsseldorf painting murals for the Planetarium. In 1931 he was invited to paint frescoes for the Bauausstellung (Building Exhibition) in Berlin, and during these years he painted murals in association with several modern architects. He was then best known as a mural painter, but canvases of his were acquired by several German museums (Berlin National Gallery, Essen, Düsseldorf, Frankfurt, Mannheim, Saarbrücken, Barmen and Cologne); others by his native city of Lodz, by Tel Aviv and Moscow. He travelled considerably – to Spain, Italy, Yugoslavia, Russia, Czechoslovakia and Rumania. The outbreak of the last war found him in France. On the collapse of France in 1940 he succeeded in escaping to Scotland and eventually found his way to London. No 'master', during the past seven or eight years, has had such a profound influence on the younger generation of British painters. Colquhoun, MacBryde, Le Brocquy, Keith Vaughan, Craxton – most of these artists would, I assume, gladly acknowledge Adler's inspiring influence. These artists represent the most vital tendencies in contemporary British art, and Adler's coming to England will have to be reckoned, in any future history of British art, as a decisive event.

It was decisive in more than one sense – not only as a personal influence, but also as constituting a break with the influence of the School of Paris, which English painters for many years had slavishly followed. On this question I had some comments to make in a Preface I contributed to the catalogue of the first exhibition held by Jankel Adler in London (Redfern Gallery, June-July 1943), and it may be of interest to repeat them here:

> 'Some historian of the future will surely point out, as one of the significant features of the interwar period, the almost complete divorce which existed between the art of the countries east and west of the Rhine. If he is a superficial historian, he will probably see in this divorce some reflection of the ideological conflict which came to a head in the present war. But art is not so easy as politics. If we seek for the origins of Eastern European art, we shall find them in Scandinavia (Munch) and Russia (Malevich, Kandinsky, Gabo, Chagall) rather than in Germany itself; and those of Western European art in Spain (Picasso, Miró, Dali) or Greece (Chirico) rather than in France itself. Again, the characteristically modern movement in Germany (Expressionism) was explicitly repudiated, and indeed exterminated, by the Nazi regime. At first it found no open welcome in the democratic countries. In fact, cultural trends during the past twenty-five years have shown a baffling independence of national, racial and economic factors, and we may extend our sympathy to the dialectical materialist who attempts to sort it all out in accordance with his theories.
>
> 'Art, like women's clothes, is to a large extent controlled by the most powerful of all dictators – fashion. In both spheres we in England used to take the lead from Paris, and Paris ignored everything east of the Rhine. As a result, a great artist like Paul Klee has only recently been given due recognition in this country, and other great artists, such as Emil Nolde, are still unknown here. It is thus possible for us, in the year 1943, to discover for the first time an artist born in 1895 in Poland and long since established in his own country and in Germany.
>
> 'It will be readily admitted that these works are impressive: the quality which they, in common with Eastern European art in general, may be said to lack is something which we in the West would probably call intimacy. We have admitted Klee, alone of trans-Rhenish artists, because he is "intimate". That preference, or prejudice, is a cult with us: our sensibilities are conditioned to it by the whole of the Western tradition with its search for "quality", by which we mean the nuances and delicacies, the subtleties and privacies, of the Impressionist and Post-Impressionist

formulae. The Eastern tradition, like the Byzantine tradition from which it ultimately derives, has other values. They are at once more metaphysical and more social. They are expressive of ideas rather than of personalities, and they are addressed to a congregation rather than to an individual. It is significant that Jankel Adler, for example, has painted many murals.

'The scale and character of such paintings do not imply any corresponding coarseness of technique. We are at once struck by the virtuosity of these canvases: the immense range of effect which the medium is made to yield, the infinite resonance of the colour harmonies. The formal invention, again, is extremely rich: there is no tendency, as in so much modern art, to adopt a convention or cliché and endlessly repeat it.

'As for the content of these pictures, it is obvious that they represent something more than an organisation of abstract relationships. They have a metaphysical content – something less "innocent" than the child-like vision of Klee, something not so sophisticated as the inventions of Picasso. It is not surprising to learn that Adler is a friend of the great Jewish mystic, Martin Buber. I do not suggest that it is possible to find a key to Adler's paintings in Buber's writings. The art is self-sufficient. But the painter and mystic belong to the same world of thought, and distinguish from things and events a realm of being where, in Buber's words, "measure and comparison have disappeared: it lies with yourself how much of the immeasurable becomes reality for you." And further: the intuition of such a world-order "does not help to sustain you in life, it only helps you to glimpse eternity".'

I hope Adler has left some record of his philosophical ideas. I regret now that I did not see more of him, to entice him into those realms of thought with which he was so familiar. He was devoted to the great Chinese teachers – Lao Tzu and Chuang Tzu – and I think also to Meister Eckhart. In social theory he acknowledged Proudhon, Tolstoy and Kropotkin, but I do not know with what relative degree of enthusiasm. But he was proud to call himself an anarchist – he was convinced that anarchism is the only philosophy compatible with the creative spirit of the artist.

23
Culture and Religion

Notes towards the Definition of Culture by T.S. Eliot.
The Dilemma of the Arts by Wladimir Weidlé.

THE two books I propose to talk about tonight, although they have somewhat different titles, deal with what is essentially the same theme – it might be called the crisis of our western civilisation.

Both authors are Christians, and Christians with a highly-developed sense of tradition. Both assert that culture is in some sense dependent on religion. For Mr Eliot culture is the incarnation of religion. Professor Weidlé puts it the other way round – religion is the life-giving element in culture. Both authors assert, as an incontrovertible fact, the decline of culture since the Renaissance, and both seek to associate this decline with a disintegration of European art, manners, learning and law, due to an absence of religious faith and unity. Professor Weidlé, who is the more colourful if less precise writer, expresses their common point of view in these words:

> 'In a world whose soul is growing dark and cold, art cannot remain the only source of heat and light. All its roots are deeply embedded in the religious life, but that does not mean that it could itself replace religion. On the contrary, it is perishing itself precisely because of the lack all round it of a world imbued with religion.'

Professor Weidlé assumes that Christianity had its ideal embodiment in the art of the Middle Ages. 'For a thousand years and more,' he writes, 'the arts of Christian Europe remained indissolubly tied to the religious life, and that meant to the whole of life. The artist worked not merely for the Church but in the Church. He did more than provide for the needs of worship: he took part in it, for the planting of his work was an act of adoration and its growth to maturity was one long prayer.'

This romantic conception of the Middle Ages, and of the place of the artist in the society of that time, has little correspondence with the historical facts. Professor Weidlé is presumably a member of the Eastern Orthodoxy and he may have more justification in the history of Byzantine art and religion; but of the West no such dogmatic statement could be made. Recent scholarship has entirely discredited the notion of a pious craftsman devoting his art to the service of God. Much of medieval art is neither pious nor anonymous; on the contrary, as Meyer Schapiro has shown in an essay on *The Aesthetic Attitude in Romanesque Art*, 'by the 11th and 12th centuries there had emerged in Western Europe within church art a new sphere of artistic creation without religious content, and imbued with values of spontaneity, individual fantasy, delight in colour and movement and the expression of feeling, that anticipate modern art.' The texts which Professor Schapiro has studied show that the medieval attitude to art was very much what it is today: 'contrary to the general belief that in the Middle Ages the work of art was considered mainly as a vehicle of religious teaching or as a piece of craftsmanship serving a useful end, and that beauty of form and colour was no object of contemplation in itself, these texts abound in aesthetic judgments and in statements about the qualities and structures of the work. They speak of the fascination of the image, its marvellous likeness to physical reality, and the artist's wonderful skill, often in complete abstraction from the content of the object of art.' We are driven to the conclusion that there was just as much sheer delight in the sensuous qualities of art then as now; that the artist had the same freedom of expression and was prized for the same kind of skill; and that he was only incidentally religious. It is of course true, and it is an immensely important fact, that the artist was living in a stable religious community; he had a steady job and patrons who knew what they wanted. But the fact remains, as Hegel said, that in an age of piety one does not have to be religious in order to create a truly religious work of art, whereas today the most deeply pious artist seems to be incapable of producing anything comparable to the art of Ancient Greece or the Middle Ages.

It is essential to get this point clear, because the whole of Professor Weidlé's case depends on it. I shall presently put forward a different theory of the relation of art to society, but first let us note some of the curious inconsistencies. The art which does not fit into Professor Weidlé's theory he calls romantic art, and in general he has no words too bad to describe it. It is the death of style, the paralysis of the creative will, the genuine *mal du siècle*, the disease of a century, a fever that has attacked great souls, the men of genius. No poet worthy of his name has escaped it, after Goethe, after Pushkin. Why Goethe and Pushkin are excluded from a company which includes Hölderlin and Kleist, Coleridge and Keats, Leopardi and Baudelaire, Flaubert and Chateaubriand, Carlyle and Browning, De Quincey and Wordsworth, is not made clear. Constable and Turner, Ingres and Delacroix, von Marées and Cézanne, Wagner and Verdi, Yeats and Mr Eliot himself are thrown onto the flames, with the assurance that nothing is to be gained by despising an evil which one cannot cure.

Professor Weidlé can point to many qualities in modern art which justify his poor opinion of it, but they all amount to the same lack of a unity of style. We must not be mesmerised by this word 'unity' – it is a word dear to tyrants and dictators no less than to religious fanatics and historians of art. Words like diversity, variety and individuality also have their charm. But there can be no doubt that the 'greatness' of a style, such as the Doric, or the Gothic, or the Baroque, is related to a certain coherence in the societies responsible for such styles. But in my opinion, and I think I have Meyer Schapiro's support on this point, such unity is not determined or even guaranteed by religious faith. It is due to something still more basic, a collective consciousness, or group unanimity, which is the substance of life itself – life in its economic, familial and associative groupings and activities. At the base is an active civil community, participating in joint enterprises, spontaneously creating an expression of expanding life and joy. What puzzles me in Professor Weidlé's book is that in more than one place he seems to recognise this fact. For example, he says that 'Style is a universal principle which does not in the least infringe upon the play of the particular and the unique. It is not the individual creation of a genius, not the final result of a great number of convergent efforts; it is only the external manifestation of a deep community, an abiding fraternity of souls; its roots are in the unconscious; it is impossible to replace it by reasoning, by desire, by an exact description of forms and methods, of the grammar and vocabulary of a given style. When community breaks up, style is extinguished and nothing can bring it to life again.'

I can accept that as the truth of the matter. But there is nothing here about 'higher' and 'lower' religions, nothing about the necessity of a Christian interpretation of the world. There are, instead, two or three phrases which imply both more and less – 'a deep community', 'an abiding fraternity of souls', and a reference to the unconscious. I wish Professor Weidlé had said a little more about the unconscious, because it should be very much in evidence in our discussions of art and religion.

But for the moment I would like to concentrate on the meaning of 'community' and 'fraternity', for therein lies the whole of our dilemma.

Mr Eliot defines culture as 'a way of life of a particular people living in a particular place', and, on another page, as 'a peculiar way of thinking, feeling and behaving'. It is the 'pattern of the society as a whole' and it is 'the creation of the society as a whole'. But he agrees that it is not a conscious creation – it is in some sense an unconscious phenomenon and cannot be deliberately produced by education or political action.

Culture must therefore be distinguished from the cultivated taste of an individual, as well as from the culture of a professional group or separate class within a society. Again, it is misleading to identify culture with any of its specific manifestations – it is just as much a question of good manners and good cooking as of great architecture and immortal poetry. Nevertheless there is one quality that, in Mr. Eliot's opinion, has characterised all cultures. 'No culture,' he asserts, 'has appeared or developed except together with a religion: according to the point of view of the observer, the culture will appear to be the product of the religion, or the religion the product of the culture.'

At this point Mr Eliot joins forces with Professor Weidlé, but he is more precise in his definitions. He takes great pains to define this 'togetherness' of religion and culture. He warns us several times not to make the mistake which Matthew Arnold made and assume that culture is something more comprehensive than religion. Equally we must avoid the error of regarding religion and culture as two separate things between which there is a *relation* – which is as bad as the alternative error of *identifying* religion and culture. Such descriptive statements miss the essential point, and though he is 'aware of the temerity of employing such an exalted term', Mr Eliot cannot think of any other which would so well convey his intention as the word *incarnation*; the culture of a society is the incarnation of its religion.

But there are still further qualifications to be made. Mr Eliot, like Professor Weidlé, assumes that there are religions of 'partial truth' and people with 'a truer light', 'higher' religions and 'lower' religions, and if we should be compelled by the objective evidence to admit that a religion of partial truth, such as Buddhism, is incarnated in a culture superior to our own, the explanation lies in the fact that our culture is not really Christian. But surely a Buddhist might retort that if in some respect the culture of India or China is in our view inferior to our own, that is only because it is not really Buddhist. If we are to have what might be called a science of comparative culture, then we must have too a science of comparative religion; and all that the scientists would be able to conclude is that while culture is generally found in association with religion, there is no evidence to show that one type of religion is more productive of culture than another. There is one way of life (comprising religion and art and every other kind of cultural manifestation) and there is another way of life (equally comprising all these things), and the only *objective* test of their worth would seem to be the degree of happiness generated by each way of life – Bentham's sensible test of the greatest happiness of the greatest number.

I agree with Mr Eliot on so many essential points that it is only a feeling of hopeless bafflement compels me to confess my scepticism on the issue which he obviously regards as the most important of all. If I do not misunderstand him, he assumes that our European destiny is to work out a pattern of culture ordained nearly two thousand years ago. I am genuinely anxious to understand the Christian sociologist on this point. I agree with Professor Weidlé in thinking that Christian culture reached its perfection in the Middle Ages – in the Christian society of Saint Louis, for example. It is surely not very realistic to suggest that we should try to re-establish the cultural pattern of the thirteenth century; but at the same time any incarnation of the Christian faith would seem to imply a society far more like the feudal societies of the Middle Ages than anything we have experienced in modern history. If that kind of medievalism is not in Mr Eliot's mind, then he must envisage a very different kind of society – a society different from that of the thirteenth century no less than from our present society. But a *different* society – a society different from the Christian society of the Middle Ages – would seem to imply the incarnation of a *different* religion. That, obviously, is not what Mr Eliot or any orthodox Christian would admit as a possibility.

That Mr Eliot does – at any rate in broad outlines – seek to restore a past order to correspond with a past stage in religious evolution is shown by his treatment of the question of *élites*. This fashionable word hides the social phenomenon more realistically known as a dominant or privileged class. Admittedly, a culture is never uniform in its manifestation: the fact that people are variously endowed at birth with genius or talent means that if a society is to benefit to the full from its membership, it must allow its best brains, its wisest minds, to rise to positions of influence in the public service. It would seem, from what might be called the biological point of view, that the best system would be one that allowed this talent to rise freely to the top, like cream on milk. That is the system known in politics as 'equality of opportunity'. Mr Eliot is opposed to it, with a somewhat surprising violence. He argues that it 'is an ideal which can only be fully realised when the institution of the family is no longer respected, and when parental control and responsibility passes to the State.' Any system which puts such a policy into effect, Mr Eliot thinks, 'must see that no advantages of family fortune, no advantages due to the foresight, the self-sacrifice or the ambition of parents are allowed to obtain for any child or young person an education superior to that which the system finds him to be entitled.' I should have thought that the family, in Mr Eliot's no less than in my own view, was bound together by something more spiritual than self-interest. I should also have thought that our recent experiences in war and in peace had shown not merely the danger, but even the impossibility, of relying on an élite produced by privileged education. When a nation is at the end of its tether, it is not education that counts, but something which would usually be called 'character', and which is just as likely to be found in Wigan or in Stepney as in Eton or Oxford.

Mr Eliot is contemptuous of the doctrine of egalitarianism; he thinks it leads to licentiousness and irresponsibility. I do not think he has given due consideration to what might be called the *mystique* of the doctrine. Some Christians argue that this mystique is implied in the Fatherhood of God, in the Brotherhood of Man; I am not in a position to substantiate their theology. I take my evidence from the natural sciences and history, and this evidence suggests to me that the highest achievements of man, moral and material, are due to the impulse of mutual aid. There is, of course, an individualistic, one-way expression of this impulse – we then call it sympathy or charity. But the higher form of its expression is mutual, an 'I-Thou' dialogue, a sinking of differences, an exercise of humility. To the extent that this relationship prevails in a society we have that social unity, that 'peculiar way of thinking, feeling and behaving', which generates and transmits a culture. It is this unconscious and instinctive sense of social communion which underlies the whole of the religious, artistic and social development of man from the dawn of civilisation.

At this point I can imagine Professor Weidlé and Mr Eliot, in the unlikely event that they were listening to me, getting a little impatient. But we have admitted all that, they might say; indeed it is the very substance of our thesis. But no. It is the substance of their thesis so long as they write in the abstract, and so long as they speak of the past. But when it comes to the present, by which I mean the past hundred years or so, they become illogical. To be logical they should say that during the past hundred years or so there has developed in Western Europe a particular way of life involving practices and experiences almost totally different from any that have hitherto been characteristic of human communities. Science has resulted, not only in a mechanised civilisation, but in materialistic beliefs about the origin of the world and the destiny of mankind. In conformity with this profound revolution in our ways of thinking, feeling and behaving (Mr Eliot's definition of a culture, you remember), a new type of art has sprung into existence, as expressive of our modern way of life as the art of the past was of the way of life in the Stone Age, or in Ancient Rome, or in the Christian communities of the Middle Ages.

It follows from this line of argument – which, I submit – is the only logical line, that we cannot hold the modern artist responsible for the art which we don't like. Professor Weidlé does not like the art of Picasso and Léger; he has a nostalgic reverence for the art of Titian, Correggio and Raphael. What he cannot see, or will not admit, is that Picasso and Léger are doing for our society, for our way of life, exactly what Titian, Correggio and Raphael did for theirs. And in my opinion they are doing their job just as effectively as the artists of the Renaissance. From the strictly artistic point of view there is no dilemma: the artist cannot escape the way of life into which he is born. He must accept it and make the best of it.

Professor Weidlé has an apocalyptic vision of the artist's loneliness in the modern world – of his agony in a faithless, irreligious society. This may be true of a few artists like Rouault and Claudel, particularly admired by Professor Weidlé, who are completely out of sympathy with the modern age. It is not true of artists like Picasso and Léger, or, to give an English example, Henry Moore. I am not suggesting for a moment that these artists are complacently satisfied with our way of life; Picasso has expressed his strong disapproval of that way of life by joining the Communist Party. I would say that most modern artists are fully aware of the disintegrated nature of the societies in which they live, and they yearn for an 'abiding fraternity of souls'. But most of them realise that such a fraternity is not brought into existence by wishful thinking, by nostalgic conversions, by any form of contracting out of our social responsibilities. A deep sense of community will be created in the fields and the workshops; it requires in the first place an economic revolution, and those who oppose such a revolution on the basis of traditional conceptions of religion and society, are merely hindering the rebirth of a culture whose death they so eloquently lament.

24
Americanism

The American Democracy by Harold Laski.

An Inquiry into the Principles and Policy of the Government of the United States by John Taylor. With an Introduction by Prof. R.F. Nichols.

Pioneers of American Freedom by Rudolf Rocker.

PROFESSOR LASKI'S book was published nearly a year ago, and my only excuse for the lateness of this review is that it reached me on the eve of one of my own visits to the United States, and that it is nearly half-a-million words in length – nearly eight hundred very solidly printed pages. Owing to my absence I did not hear what kind of reception it had in this country, but I doubt if it was adequate. For it is a very fine and important book. America has inspired several good books, generally written by Europeans, but I would put Laski's book with the best of these – that is to say, with de Tocqueville and Bryce. It has not got the amazing prophetic quality of *Democracy in America*, nor the same eye for significant detail, but de Tocqueville was a pioneer, and every observation was news. And he had less to cope with – less history, less civilisation, fewer contradictions and complexities. Laski's book is very long, but it is amazingly unified and comprehensive. It deals not only with the traditional and historical aspects of American civilisation, but also gives a clear account of the present political institutions, federal, state and local. There are chapters on American business enterprise, American labour, religion, education and culture. The minority problems are treated realistically (they 'require a new America for their solution... America will not go forward to the solution of these grave and growing issues until its citizens have displaced the businessman as the idol to be worshipped in its market-places'). There are further chapters on America as a world power, on the professions, on the press, cinema and radio, and a final chapter on 'Americanism as a Principle of Civilisation'.

If there is a central argument in this book, it is expressed in the following sentence: 'I have argued here that in the main realms of American thought the sense of openness and expansion diminishes, and that, with its diminution, there emerges the scepticism, even the pessimism, which men reveal when they measure the distance between the promise for which they had hoped and the reality which they had found to be possible.'

This idea is expanded in a concluding paragraph to the chapter on American culture, and as this is perhaps the most significant passage in the whole book I will quote it in full:

> The crisis of American culture is the outcome of the fact that those values [the values originally expressed in the American Constitution] are in such obvious decay. Whatever the avenues they opened in the past, their application now evokes in most forms of thought a sense of inadequacy and frustration. They prevent growth; thereby, they belittle man. They are prohibitions against the emergence of those productive relations in society which enable its members to feel that whatever is accessible of well-being they can both explore and use. By the very fact that expansion of well-being has become a threat to the supremacy of the businessman, he is compelled to frustrate that expansion; and when he so acts, he frustrates simultaneously the expansion of culture too. For it is no accident that the great ages in the history of culture are also the ages in which the consciousness of culture is most widely shared. Once more the right to share is rigidly limited by a profit-making system which must impose its discipline ever more stringently as its central objective becomes ever more difficult; the whole of civilised life is bound to be sacrificed to a part of it; and both the quest for happiness and the search for beauty will be sacrificed to its claims. The curse of Midas has been heaped upon the businessman in the United States, and he has sought, out of fear, in his turn, to impose its narrowing obligations upon the society he dominates. That is why a fundamental change is needed in the direction of American life; for nothing is more fatal to the greatness of a culture than impotence to translate the mind of man from the relation of past tradition to the relation of emerging creativeness.

The agent of such a change should, of course, be the labour movement, but at the end of his acute analysis of American labour, Laski is not in a very hopeful mood, and the only course he can recommend is the bankrupt one of indirect political action. Direct productive action does not enter into his picture of the future – in fact, the whole of the co-operative movement, which is not without its significance in the United States, is ignored. But if it is essential, as Laski argues, for the labour movement 'to take up the work of re-stating, in twentieth-century terms, that problem of freedom which Jefferson saw so clearly in the first American Revolution and Lincoln so supremely in the second,' then American labour must do something better than imitate the tactics of the British Labour Party, which has nothing better to offer than a timid version of the totalitarian state. The whole of this national political party game is totally inconsistent with the libertarian ideals of Jefferson and John Taylor.

* * *

The republication of Taylor's classical treatise comes very opportunely. First published one hundred and thirty-five years ago, it is one of the basic documents of American political theory. John Taylor was a lawyer by education but a plain Virginia farmer by preference. His treatise is in the eighteenth-century tradition of political thought, but directed to the practical problems of a new democracy. Taylor's main concern is to design checks on authority, and his views on the corrupting influence of power anticipate Acton's in vigorous expression:

> The Republican and federal parties of the United States are evidently clambering towards the system for consigning a nation to the constant spoliation of a successive authority, more aggravating to vicious passions, because more unsettled than monarchy itself. Far from correcting the abuses with which they charge each other, their leaders, trusting to the pernicious doctrine of confidence and authority, will convert their mutual abuses into mutual precedents. Neither parties nor individuals will voluntarily diminish power in their own hands, however pernicious they have declared it to be in the hands of others, because if they are vicious, they are willing to abuse it, if virtuous, they presumptuously confide in their own moderation; therefore abuses can never be corrected, where confidence and authority have subverted national principles.
>
> As authority generates the same effects upon all men, the men are not blameable, because it is obvious from the constancy of the effects, that the force of authority is irresistible by human nature.

Which is precisely the anarchist point of view!

* * *

Comrade Rocker's book is to be welcomed as a supplement and in many respects a corrective to Laski's. In the first part he covers much the same ground (Jefferson, Emerson, Thoreau, and Lincoln), but deals more fully with William Lloyd Garrison and Wendell Phillips (he does not mention Taylor). In the second part of his book he deals with American radicals none of whom is as much as mentioned by Laski – Josiah Warren, Stephen Pearl Andrews, Lysander Spooner, William B. Greene, and Benjamin Tucker. He emphasizes the strong individualistic trend in American anarchism.

> 'They all agree on the point that man be given the full reward of his labour and recognise in this right the economic basis of all personal liberty. They all regard the free competition of individual and social forces as something inherent in human nature, which if suppressed will inevitably lead to the destruction of the social equilibrium. They answered the socialists of other schools who saw in *free competition* one of the destructive elements of capitalistic society that the evil lies in the fact that today we have too little rather than too much competition, since the power of monopoly has made competition impossible. Starting from this viewpoint, they rejected fundamentally every communistic solution of the social problem and opposed just as intensely the ideas of state socialism as the tendencies of Kropotkin and communistic anarchism. This is particularly true of Tucker and his circle.'

This throws a new light on American anarchism and explains why it has never had much appeal to the corresponding European movement. The American anarchists were all 'one hundred per cent American' by descent, and 'influenced in their intellectual development much more by the principles expressed in the Declaration of Independence than by those of any of the representatives of libertarian socialism in Europe.' This is not altogether true of contemporary American anarchism, and with a figure like Randolph Bourne libertarian thought in the United States enters into the main current.

25
Marie Louise Berneri

Marie Louise Berneri, 1918-1949 – A Tribute.

IT is appropriate that the first publication of the Marie Louise Berneri Memorial Committee should be a tribute to Marie Louise herself. It is a beautifully produced brochure of 52 pages, cloth-bound. The fourteen illustrations show Marie Louise at various stages of her development, and in various moods – straight portraits which catch the beauty and gaiety of her spirit, snapshots of Marie Louise at work or on holiday, with a group of Spanish refugees and addressing a meeting of factory workers in Glasgow. To all who knew her, these are precious memorials, and we must be thankful that among her nearest friends were two such excellent photographers as VR and PD. The Introduction relates the main facts of her life – her childhood as the daughter of political refugees, her growth to maturity in an atmosphere of intense revolutionary activity, and the final twelve years in which she herself took up the leadership from her assassinated father. She was the great daughter of a great father. There is about everything that Camillo Berneri wrote the clear impression of genius – he himself would have preferred the word 'style'. In a letter to Marie Louise printed in this brochure he says: 'Whenever conscience is involved, reason leads me to no decision. The *ultima ratio*, what really decides the issue, is *style*: this is not my style – for me that is the last word.' It was the last word for his daughter, too. She had this instinct for living with style, and if this should seem a modish word, let us remember that her style took the form of love for humanity. Camillo Berneri wrote his letter a few hours before he was seized by the communist assassins in Barcelona, while he was keeping watch over his sleeping comrades, and in it he says – '...I am watching over all of them, working for those who will follow. This is the only thing which is wholly fine. More absolute than love, more true than reality itself. What would man be without this sense of duty, without being moved at the thought of his oneness with those who have been, with the unknown men of the past and with those who are to come?' This is the feeling that Marie Louise inherited from her father, and which she communicated to all who came into contact with her brave spirit.

There is a tribute from one of the comrades she worked with in France (S. Parane); an account of her work for Freedom Press by the Freedom Press Group; a tribute from a Spanish refugee (Manuel Salgado); and another from George Woodcock, who worked with her so closely on the Freedom Press publications. All these contributors emphasize her beauty, her sympathy, and her vitality; I am glad to see that Woodcock also brings out clearly that quality in her which superficially might seem to be inconsistent with her great charm – her penetrating intelligence and clarity of vision. These qualities will become more evident to the general public as the publications of the Memorial Committee take shape, and the full range of Marie Louise's influence is felt.

26

The Utopian Mentality

Journey through Utopia by Marie Louise Berneri.

IT is not necessary, in *Freedom*, to write a conventional review of this book. But even our readers, once so familiar with the journalism of Marie Louise, may allow themselves to be a little dazzled by the brilliance of this posthumous work – it is so calm and coherent, so well organised and well written, and so disinterestedly readable. Though not specifically libertarian in its subject-matter, it is a great contribution to the growing body of sociological literature written by libertarian authors – literature that is very necessary as a definition of the libertarian concept of reality. Anarchists in the past have been too inclined to confine their writings to anarchism. What we require, now that anarchist principles have been adequately defined, is a general orientation towards the sociology of knowledge. Kropotkin was very conscious of this need, and *Mutual Aid* and *Ethics* were his own contribution to it – books which belong to the general categories of science and philosophy, rather than specifically to anarchist propaganda.

Marie Louise's book is of this kind. She makes no attempt to disguise her sympathies, but she writes dispassionately and is as fair to Plato as to Winstanley, to Bellamy as to Morris. Her scope is universal – she begins with Plato and ends with Orwell (unfortunately she did not live to include *1984* in her survey, for that, for the present, is the last of the utopias). It is true that by extending the scope of her definitions she might have included many marginal works, from the Hebrew prophets to Giraudoux (whose *Suzanne and the Pacific* is a very agreeable utopia). But she has kept to a strictly political conception of the term, and that limitation gives her book its logical unity.

Utopia is the principle of all progress, said Anatole France; Oscar Wilde said the same thing ('progress is the realisation of Utopias'). With utopias, said Kautsky, modern socialism begins. And so on – all recent political philosophies have been aware of the significance of the utopianising faculty. The greatest of modern sociologists, Karl Mannheim, devoted a whole book to a discussion of this significance (*Ideology and Utopia*), and it is a book which can be usefully read in conjunction with Marie Louise's historical survey. Mannheim defined the utopian state of mind as one 'that is incongruous with the state of reality in which it occurs', and he pointed out that this state of mind becomes revolutionary and dangerous to the existing order of society as soon as the utopia ceases to be part of the cosmic ideology of a period. For example, so long as the utopian wish is satisfied by a belief in an other-worldly paradise, it is not likely to take the form of an idea that is politically realisable. The serious 'utopias' therefore belong either to the classical period (Plato) or to the humanistic period (More onwards, with increasing political significance). The really dangerous people were those Christians (Hussites and Anabaptists) who had the temerity to suggest that the kingdom of Heaven could be and should be realised here on earth. Such utopians have always been treated as criminals.

Utopianism is for this reason closely linked with the history of the freedom of thought. But, as Marie Louise makes clear, it by no means follows that all utopians are libertarians. On the contrary, left to itself to imagine an ideal state of existence, the human mind betrays a distressing tendency towards authoritarianism. One sees here the dangers of rationality. There exists in the human mind an itch for tidiness, for symmetry and formality. This leads to good results in purely mental categories, and to it we owe the achievements of logic and science. But life itself is not tidy and cannot be made tidy so long as it is life – 'we murder to dissect,' as Wordsworth said. Most utopians have forgotten this distinction, and as a result their ideal commonwealths can never be, or ought never to become, real. I have a suspicion that Plato realised this, for his *Republic* is based on an ideal human type (the Guardian) about as remote from actuality as Nietzsche's Superman. The *Republic* is a fairy-tale full of beautiful fancies, and intended to teach a moral (that morality and beauty are identical), but it is only in his later utopia, *The Laws*, that Plato begins to plan society with realism – and in that sense in his old age he was reconciled, as Marie Louise says, to the idea of 'a second-best state'. But the totalitarianism is still there, as it is in most of the utopias of the Renaissance and the Enlightenment. For totalitarianism is precisely the imposition of a rational framework on the organic freedom of life. It is only in those writers who retain a sense of organic freedom – Rabelais, Diderot and Morris – that the utopia is in any sense libertarian. It is no strange coincidence that these are the only inspiring utopias. As we approach the era of socialism utopias, indeed, become increasingly depressing.

> 'There are few utopias of the nineteenth century [writes Marie Louise] which can be read today without a feeling of utter boredom, unless they succeed in amusing us by the obvious conceit of their authors in thinking themselves the saviours of mankind. The utopias of the Renaissance contained many unattractive features yet they had a breadth of vision which commanded respect; those of the seventeenth century presented many extravagant ideas, yet they revealed searching, dissatisfied minds with which one sympathises; but though we are in many ways familiar with the thought of the utopias of the nineteenth century, they are nevertheless more foreign to us than those of a more distant past. In spite of the fact that these utopian writers were no doubt inspired by the highest motives, one cannot help "feeling bitter about the nineteenth century," like the old man in *News from Nowhere*, bitter even about the love these utopian writers lavished on humanity, for they seem like so many over-affectionate and over-anxious mothers who would kill their sons with attention and kindness rather than let them enjoy one moment of freedom.'

It is well said. The most terrible utopias are the scientific utopias of the marxist socialist and the monopoly capitalist. With the same rational instruments of thought that have perfected science and technology, they now advance on the spontaneous sources of life itself. They presume to plan what can only germinate, to legislate for the forms of growth and to mould into infrangible dogmas the sensitive graces of the mind. They are doomed to failure, for the threatened sources of life are always driven underground, to emerge in some new wilderness. But the process is long and painful, and mankind must suffer in terms of war and tyranny for the satisfaction of a spurious logic.

The realisation of a rational utopia leads to the death of society (that, I mention in passing, was the theme of *The Green Child*). This does not mean that the utopian mentality itself is necessarily evil. On the contrary, we must repeat with Anatole France, the utopia is the principle of all progress. Society exists to transcend itself, and the progressive force of its evolution is the poetic imagination that moves with the organic principle of all evolution, to take possession of new forms of life, new fields of consciousness.

27
A One-Man Manifesto

THE most terrifying object in the world today is not the atom bomb but the political cliché. The political cliché is not merely verbal: the words reflect a mental reaction which is as automatic as it is false. It projects its own guilt feelings onto a chosen object – it used to be a harmless animal object, the scapegoat, but now it has to be a human object, the enemy, to whom we give a dehumanised name: the boche, the nazi, the red. Human guilt is now so enormous, that millions of scapegoats are needed to carry it. The human race is accordingly divided into two moieties, each serving as the scapegoat of the other.

To listen to the purveyors of clichés, the so-called statesmen, the politicians, generals and journalists, has become an inescapable infliction. Not to know the news is now a crime: ignorance is connivance and innocence is guilt. In a spirit of scientific detachment it becomes almost fascinating to watch this automatic projection of clichés: Dulles, Truman, Taft, Attlee, Bevin, Eden, Schuman and Adenauer – they are all the same. If by chance a public figure gets up and makes an utterance that is not a cliché – as Pastor Niemoller has been doing lately – there is a shocked surprise, as if an indecency has been committed in public. But that is a very rare occurrence.

The present alarm is not difficult to understand. Since the end of the last war (indeed since the end of the First World War) the spread of a phenomenon to which we give the name 'communism' has been continuous. It suffers from apparent set-backs (Yugoslavia), but these are not of a nature to give any real satisfaction to the opponents of communism. Communism now embraces about half the world, and the more widely diffused it becomes, the less easy it is to define. The conversion of the four hundred millions of China to communism is not an ideological phenomenon: it is in the nature of a mental landslide. Millions wake up one morning and find that they are communists. Theirs not to reason why: life goes on as before, with perhaps a change of landlords to mark the event; and, of course, a different symbol on the flag and a call-up to a people's army. But in the army it is the same drill, just as in the fields it is the same relentless toil.

The people who get excited (Dr Comfort's delinquents) are the people who run the bulldozers that cause the political landslides. These bulldozers are very powerful machines, serviced by fanatical politicians and journalists, and they go about the world bulldozing over peasants and workers and in a general way creating chaos – shovelling millions into the armament factories, millions into the armed forces, and millions more into the 'lines of communication'. No one is allowed to get on with his natural function, which may be producing food, or building houses, or writing poetry.

The odd thing is that we all submit to this bulldozing. Hardly a squeak is to be heard. We are pushed here and we are pushed there, and at the end of the week we hand over up to half our pay in taxes to feed the bulldozers, to keep them going against us. Nothing is so significant of the present age, and perhaps a symptom of its incurable decadence, as the prevailing apathy in all countries – the refusal to fight the bulldozing politicians and generals, *the willingness to pay*. It was not always so. Our liberties were won by the simple expedient of refusing to furnish the means (ship-money, etc.) of bulldozing the people. Such a practical procedure is not even discussed these days. Technically it may be treason: but it was by 'treason' that we won the Magna Carta and every other advance in political liberty.

Most significant in this muted slaughterhouse we live in is the apathy and inefficiency of the Christian churches and of the secular pacifist movements. Though the churches profess, in accordance with the teachings of Christ, a belief in peace, they take no effective steps to instil that belief in their congregations (Pastor Niemoller and his following excepted). They merely bless the rival combatants.

As for the breakdown of secular pacifism, it seems to be pathological. A belief requiring the highest degree of moral courage and personal sacrifice, there are no more than a handful of men in any country who are ready to propagate this belief, and they are mostly of an older generation. The youth in all countries is indifferent to pacifist propaganda and accepts with fatalistic indifference the militaristic evils which they have inherited.

So much for the general diagnosis. Immediately, at the opening of the year 1951, there is the danger, indeed already the actuality, of a Third World War. The communist revolution in China, completely successful, has thrown the United States into a truculent panic. In defiance of all political decorum or absolute justice, this powerful nation clings desperately to a discredited régime lodged precariously in the Chinese island of Formosa. On the mainland, with the support of the democratic half-world, she has invaded Korea on a pretext of broken treaties. China has now retaliated and threatens to drive the invaders across the sea. The United States call for a wider war, a war that cannot be restricted to China, but must inevitably involve Western Europe and virtually the whole world.

It is at this point that the complete unreality of the situation becomes evident. The United States has a cover in the United Nations, an organisation dedicated to high ideals of a democratic character. Such ideals are supposedly an expression of the will of the people, and they do indeed represent the popular desire for peace. It is difficult to say *who wants war*. Certainly not the people – not the people in any country in the world. Certain politicians, perhaps; certain military commanders, perhaps; some calculating financiers and manufacturers. But it is difficult to believe, in the pre-war fashion, that a few scheming politicians, generals and capitalists are capable nowadays, for their private benefit, and against the will of the people, of precipitating a world war twice in a generation. Preparations for war keep certain industries at full stretch, but we have discovered that there is no certain profit, material or moral, for anybody in modern war. We can only conclude with a psychologist like Jung, that unconscious motives of a collectivist nature are responsible for such mass insanity.

If that is the case, there are only two possibilities – either to acquiesce in the drift to world destruction, on the assumption that individual action is futile; or to enter upon a course of action which would in effect be a mass self-analysis, leading to the exposure of unconscious motives. What form such analysis should take is more than I can say, though I have made suggestions in *Education for Peace*. But no analysis or cure can take place unless the patient has the will to be cured. There is no sign of such a will anywhere among the peoples of the world. How should we recognise such signs? The first would be an absence of fear. Fear inhibits the cure of sick minds. In our half-world we fear the unknown, perhaps in the shape of communism, perhaps in no shape at all.

Why are we afraid of communism (in its Russian shape)? Fundamentally because we are afraid of insecurity, of any change in our standards of living. But those standards of living are changing all the time, and insecurity already exists. It is war, and the immense economic burdens due to war, that have created insecurity in our minds and inflation and uncertainty in our economic affairs. It is doubtful if any of the political and economic rigours of a communistic state *without* the burdens of war, could be worse than our so-called democratic way of life *with* the burdens of war. This is to leave out of account the non-material aspects of communism ('freedom'), but to that problem I will come presently.

Our fear of communism is fundamentally a distrust of our own social and economic order – it is the sick man's fear of vitality in others. We do not believe passionately, mystically or even rationally, in whatever social and economic order prevails in our half-world today, for the truth is that no order of any positive kind does exist. There are only various degrees of disorder – of private capitalism in decay, of monopoly capitalism at war with labour monopolies, of state capitalism the prey of apathy and absenteeism. There is no healthy society anywhere in the world today, unless (which I doubt) in Russia.

The way to lose fear, and incidentally to oppose the communism of the Soviet half-world, is to create an integrated social order in our half-world – an order that would challenge the Soviet order, not in military terms, but in social amenities and cultural achievements.

This cannot be done without a revolutionary desire to create such an order throughout our half-world; and there can be no question of creating such an order in a war atmosphere and with an economy dedicated to the provision of armaments.

Immediate unilateral disarmament is the necessary preliminary to the creation of such an order. The decision to disarm would in itself be an act of moral strength sufficing for a further advance to a new world. But such a decision can only be made as an act of faith – an act of faith in humanity.

With such a faith we could resist communism in the only sense which it can be effectively resisted – by conversion. Even if we had to go through a stage of Soviet domination of the world, the passive fortitude of our humanism would in the end triumph over the active evil of inhumanism. That is the minimum faith on which a rational view of life can be based. All this can easily be dismissed as vague idealism, but there is no alternative belief – only as alternatives a nihilistic despair or a destructive spirit of aggression that must overwhelm the whole world.

28

The Death of Kropotkin

Emma said there had been snow
and a keen wind sighing in the withered branches.
And I imagined little details
sheepswool caught in the thorns
red berries
and a prophet's dead face on the pillow.

She said he had died in peace
and the eternal intelligence on his brow
had seemed like a light
in the dark unlit hut.
And I imagined
steel-rimmed glasses on a side-table
and eyes forever hidden.

She said there had been a great concourse of people
walking out from Moscow
or the nearest station
poor humble people – Lenin had let them come
to sidle lovingly past
his silent form.

Several hundred people, simple people
fur caps down to their ears
their padded trousers criss-crossed with string
standing there on the obliterated road
waiting for the cortège.

Dmitrov was the name of the place.
They took his body to Moscow

and there formed a procession
perhaps a mile long
old revolutionaries, young students
and children carrying wreaths
of holly and laurel.

They marched five miles
carrying the black and scarlet banners
and I imagined the feathery snow falling
gently on his bier
gently on the bowed heads
and the patient streets.

But when they reached the burial place
the snow had ceased
and the winter sun
sinking red
distained the level glittering plain.

A river of glowing light
poured into the open grave
all the light in the world
sank with his coffin
into the Russian earth.

It was seven versts outside Moscow.
On the steps of their museum
the Tolstoyans had gathered
to play mournful music
as the cortège passed.

Dark then it was, and silent.
I remembered, said Emma, the cairn on the mountain ridge
a heap of stones and broken branches
with tokens attached of horsehair or rag
and the cry: 'The waters before us
flow now to the Amúr.
No mountains more to cross'.

No mountains more to cross for you
dear comrade and pioneer.
You have crossed the Great Khinghán
travelling eastward into rich lands
where many will follow you.

29

Art and the Evolution of Man

Something drops from eyes long blind,
He completes his partial mind.
                                    Yeats

THE place hitherto assigned to art in the theory of evolution is secondary or even non-existent – the word 'art' does not find a place in, for example, Dr Julian Huxley's 'modern synthesis' of evolution.[1] I propose presently to give a short review of the various suggestions that have been made, but it may be said at once that all agree in regarding art as in some sense a late and perhaps unessential addition to human faculties, a means of dispersing surplus energy, of attracting sexual attention, or at best an adornment of existence – something that makes life pleasanter, or even nobler. In general it has seemed only too evident that the human species can get along quite nicely without art, and if a whole nation or a civilisation is devoid of aesthetic culture, we might piously regret the fact, but would not seriously regard such a condition as one of social or biological degeneracy.

The hypothesis which I shall put forward is very different. I shall argue that art – or, to use a more exact phrase, aesthetic experience – is an essential factor in human evolution, and, indeed, a factor on which *homo sapiens* has depended for the development of his highest cognitive faculties.

I must begin by making clear that I am not going to deal with the evolution of art. Indeed, I would say that the fundamental paradox underlying my approach to the subject is a realisation that art does not, in any strict sense of the word, *evolve*.[2] The history of art is the history of a constant factor which we may describe as *maximum aesthetic sensibility* – combined with other factors which may be social or ideological.

160 Art and the Evolution of Man

The constant factor is present in the earliest examples of human art that we know – the cave-paintings and cave-drawings of the Upper Palaeolithic culture, which were executed perhaps 40,000 years ago – and again in the paintings and drawings of a modern artist like Picasso. We may take the art of drawing as a convenient testing-ground of aesthetic sensibility, and then affirm that at no intervening stage has this original quality been surpassed by any phase of art or individual artist. Some of the painters of Greek vases, some of the medieval illuminators of manuscripts, the great painters of the Renaissance, certain painters of the 19th century – all these have perhaps reached the level of aesthetic quality present in the cave-paintings at Lascaux or Altamira, but they have not exceeded that original standard.

Now this, it will be said, is a subjective judgment: we are scientists and we demand objective measurements. How are we to measure and record this aesthetic quality, and on what statistical evidence may we assert that it is a *constant* factor? Well, here at the begining of my lecture I have to admit that no infallible test for aesthetic quality has yet been devised, though it is possible that we may one day find such a test. We can already demonstrate the presence of a 'general factor' in aesthetic judgment,[3] and I would not despair of relating this general factor to specific qualities in works of art. But for the present I can only rely, primarily on my own aesthetic sensibility, and secondarily on what I believe to be the consensus of appreciation. I am quite prepared to be told that this is not good enough, and I can only offer these remarks as speculations in a field which is notoriously resistant to scientific investigation. But I am obstinately naturalistic even in this field, and I would therefore say that the vital and formal features which account for aesthetic quality are conceivably measurable, and that our consensus of opinion about aesthetic quality will finally be based on scientific grounds. At present that ground is uncovered, or unexplored and what I have to say must therefore to some extent be taken on faith – faith, to be quite honest, in the infallibility of my own aesthetic sensibility.

Two things we must keep clearly distinct in this context: the aesthetic faculty or experience, and the use which the individual artist, or the particular culture, makes of this faculty. The great debate, for example, which goes on about the significance of the Palaeolithic cave-paintings, is of supreme interest for the history of culture, but from our present point of view it does not matter whether the paintings were produced in conjunction with fertility rites, or were merely the exercise of a representational ability. Naturally, we must assume that such drawings were produced as expressions of an intense desire to represent realistically the animals they do actually depict: obviously they are not casual scribblings. But we know nothing, absolutely nothing, about the ideological promptings or social practices of these men of ten to forty thousand years ago. We can only judge the paintings as paintings, and that is precisely all we need to do for our present purposes.

What is significant is that the drawings were made for the most part in the depths of caves, where no daylight was available. It is, of course, remarkable that drawings so precise as some of them are, could be drawn at all in a primitive artificial light – firelight or rushlight. But what should interest us more particularly is the fact that such vital and accurate representations of animals could be drawn without an accompanying model – that is to say, from memory. We have to assume, therefore, that Palaeolithic man carried into the depths of his cave a very clear, *eidetic*[4] image of the animal he wished to depict.

Here we come across the first significant factor: why did Palaeolithic man confine his artistic activities to the depiction of animals? It is, as a matter of fact, not quite true to say that only animals were represented: in addition to the so-called 'Sorcerer' at Les Trois Frères (Ariège), which is a human figure clothed in a stag's pelt and might therefore pass as an animal representation, there are at Lascaux some abstract geometrical designs to which the question-begging name of 'blazons' has been given by the Abbé Breuil, and also what is indubitably a human figure. Apart from the curious fact that this figure, complete with human arms, legs and penis, has a bird-like head, it is drawn in a rough schematic style totally at variance with the organic vitality of the representations of the neighbouring animals. In general it looks as though Palaeolithic man had no desire to represent anything but animals, and that when he did represent anything else, he used a purely conventional, non-eidetic schema.

This exclusive character of prehistoric art seems to me to destroy at one blow all those theories of the origin of art which are based on the play hypothesis, or the surplus energy hypothesis. It may be true, as Herbert Spencer[5] suggested, that the stimulus to representation is a simulation of normal activities which cannot at the moment be followed – on this assumption, the cave-paintings would have been executed at a time of the year when the hunting scenes they depict could not take place owing to snow and ice. But a stimulus does not explain the result. A more adequate extension of the play theory was therefore put forward by Karl Groos, who introduced what is really an application of the recapitulation theory of development. That is to say, he assumes that animals and man are endowed with a play instinct which enables them to practice in childhood the activities that will engage their full energies when they come to maturity. In other words, 'the creature does not play because it is young, but is young because it has to play': nature provides a period of development to fit its creatures for the serious business of life.[6]

I am not sure whether on the basis of this theory – which precedes the main discoveries of Palaeolithic art – we should be driven to assume that the cave paintings were the work of children: it would seem to follow logically. But I do not think that in any case the theory will hold: apart from the objection I am going to make in the particular case of Palaeolithic art, there is the general objection which has been well expressed by Professor Huizinga:[7]

> 'An almost instinctive, spontaneous need to decorate things cannot, indeed, be denied; and it may conveniently be called a play-function. It is known to everybody who, pencil in hand, has ever had to attend a tedious board meeting. Heedlessly, barely conscious of what we are doing, we play with lines and planes, curves and masses, and from this abstracted doodling emerge fantastic arabesques, strange animals or human forms. We may leave it to the psychologists to attribute what unconscious "drives" they will to this supreme art of boredom and inanition. But it cannot be doubted that it is a play-function of low order akin to the child's playing in the first years of its life, when the higher structure of organised play is as yet undeveloped. As an explanation of the origin of decorative motifs in art, let alone of plastic creation as a whole, a psychic function of this kind must strike us as somewhat inadequate. It is impossible to assume that the aimless meanderings of the hand could ever produce such a thing as style. Apart from this the plastic urge is by no means content with the mere ornament of a surface. It operates in three directions: towards decoration, towards construction, and towards imitation. To derive art wholly from some hypothetical "play-instinct" obliges us to do the same for architecture and painting. It seems preposterous to ascribe the cave-paintings of Altamira, for instance, to mere doodling – which is what it amounts to if they are ascribed to the "play-instinct".'

My own criticism of the play-instinct theory of the origin of art is more specific. I cannot conceive that such an instinct could be anything but diffuse, and though I can conceive a style arising almost accidentally out of such a diffuse activity, I cannot imagine a canalisation of such an instinct into imagery so precise as the Palaeolithic paintings. It is true that the art of children tends to repeat their dominant interests, and boys will draw engines while girls draw houses; but there is nothing exclusive in their play-instinct, and they do draw, along with their favourite subjects, hundreds of other objects. And what they draw is relatively consistent in style – at one stage of development they will draw entirely schematically, and engines, animals, houses and human beings will have the same general character. But at Lascaux we have, side by side, the eidetic image and the schema, and we must construct an hypothesis which accounts for this fact.

Incidentally, to answer an objection that may occur to the reader, there can be no doubt that the Lascaux man and the bison were painted at the same time – pigment and surface condition of the rock, not to mention the actual composition of the scene (a disembowelled bison attacking the hunter whose spear has wounded it[8]) are conclusive on this point.

What we require, *a priori*, is a theory which would account for art as a functional tendency of some kind, achieving efficiency when specifically challenged. Such a challenge should have biological urgency, and its function, seeing that perceptual imagery or symbolism is involved, would presumably be cognitive. That, at any rate, is my preliminary guess.

The function of imagery in the evolution of consciousness is not a subject that can be fully investigated on the basis of historical evidence.

The most primitive minds we know, those of the few surviving aboriginal tribes, already possess complete consciousness, and can by training acquire the educated outlook of more civilised peoples. The mind in its evolution has left no fossils, no concrete evidence of any kind beyond the Palaeolithic cave-paintings and the later phases of prehistoric art. Apart from this evidence, we are driven to a reliance on the recapitulation theory, which assumes that the evolution of the species can be traced in the early stages of the individual's growth.

If we ask the simple question: at what stage in the development of a human being is consciousness born? we are at once aware of the relativity of the term. In some sense, no doubt, and at some stage, the foetus is conscious: a Caesarian operation brings into the world a seven-months-old child whose consciousness does not perceptibly differ from the consciousness of a child born normally at the end of nine months' gestation. But in what sense is a new-born child 'conscious'? It will be said that the new-born child is 'conscious' of its environment, of pain and pleasure, of hunger and satiation. But 'it is questionable', writes Karl Bühler, 'whether the nervous impulses are at this stage conducted as far as those areas of the cortex in which the sensations of taste arise. Automatically those parts of the cortex are ready to function at birth. But observations of children who are born without a cortex, who are no different from normal children during the first few days, at any rate as far as the broader manifestations of life are concerned, would seem to indicate that the cortex does not function at once. It is quite impossible that the new-born child is a pure "spinal being", of whose central nervous system only the spinal cord and those parts of the brain belonging functionally to the spinal cord are active.'[9]

Even when the various sensory and motor centres of the brain begin to function, it is not possible to draw any conclusions as to the states of consciousness of the infant. Indeed, the scientist is driven to conclude that *he does not know what the biological functions of consciousness are*, and for that reason, no doubt, there is little or no reference to them in works on biological evolution.[10]

Nevertheless, in *homo sapiens* a specific form of perception, which we call consciousness, does evolve, and we want to know how and why.

I cannot, in the course of a lecture, attempt even to summarize the investigations that have been made in recent years into the development of perception in the child – the experiments of Stern, Bühler, and above all, those of Piaget and his colleagues. But it is evident that what we call consciousness, the faculty peculiar to *homo sapiens*, arises not from the perception of space, time, size, shape and number as discrete phenomena, but from certain significant arrangements of those phenomena which permit comparison and judgment. Those arrangements in their turn depend on the development of memory and imagination – that is to say, on the ability to store images and recall them at will. Language and conceptual thinking can only develop later, on the basis of imagination. For the moment let us halt at the evident fact that consciousness can only have come into existence on the basis of memory-images – of those images which the scientists call *eidetic* because they are virtually clear and intense, uncontaminated, as it were by any conceptual association.

I do not know whether it has ever been put forward as a hypothesis by scientists, but it seems to me very likely that the human race, like the child of historical times, could draw before it could speak. We have no evidence that Palaeolithic man possessed a language, or that he was capable of conceptual thought. But we do know that he could depict, that is to say, project and record plastic representations of his memory-images. It is undoubtedly possible, and I would say even likely, that a language of pictures preceded a language of words – that man thought in images before he thought in signs. But we must first ask – what kind of images?

I have already mentioned the fact that at Lascaux and elsewhere two kinds of images are found – the eidetic or naturalistic image, and the arbitrary or schematic image. In its development of expression the normal child begins with a schematic image, and only very slowly, and sometimes with great difficulty, learns how to project eidetic images. It seems likely that prehistoric man followed the same development, but again we must remind ourselves that we are in the field of hypothesis, and at least one scientist, Max Verworn, has put forward the contrary hypothesis[11]. He suggests that before conceptual thinking developed, more particularly before animistic cults developed, man had a natural talent for the projection of eidetic images into plastic form. All schematic and geometrical art is a degeneration from this original endowment. Bühler has effectively criticized this theory,[12] but we can now point out that the long evolutionary decline required by Verworn's theory is contradicted by the co-existence of naturalistic and schematic drawings, as at Lascaux.

I think we must assume, on the basis of general genetic principles, that the ability to give plastic expression to memory-images arose like any other human skill. The faculty may well have arisen in the course of normal perceptual experience, as a result of the 'recognition' of a familiar or memorised image. A rock formation, a scratch on some even surface of clay, 'reminds' primitive man of some animal or object of which an image is stored in his memory. A natural or casual reminder suggests an artificial and purposive reminder, and man begins to draw a schematic representation of his memory-image. There are other possible explanations, but this one seems to me to be adequate.[13]

But once possessing this gift, and having developed it as a conscious skill, what use did man make of it? There seems to be an almost unanimous answer to this question – he used it, say the anthropologists and archaeologists, the historians of civilisation and culture – he used it for ritualistic purposes. 'At the bottom of art,' we are told, 'as its motive power and its mainspring, lies, not the wish to copy Nature or even improve on her... but rather an impulse shared by art with ritual, the desire, that is, to utter, to give out a strongly felt emotion or desire by representing, by making or doing or enriching the object or act desired.

The common source of the art and ritual of Osiris is the intense, worldwide desire that the life of Nature which seemed dead should live again. This common emotional factor it is that makes art and ritual in their beginnings well-nigh indistinguishable.'[14]

This is Jane Harrison's formulation of the answer to my question; it is representative, and my only objection to it is that it lacks evolutionary perspective. There is simply no evidence to show that in its origins art was in any sense the expression of an emotional need. It gradually became that, but to say that 'all art springs by way of ritual out of keen emotion towards life' is to place the origins of art far too late in human evolution, and to restrict its function far too drastically.

Let us return to the Palaeolithic artist. I have said that there are two co-existing types of art – the naturalistic and the schematic. Actually there are three types, for there are certain figures of women – the ivory fragments from Brassempouy (Landes), the statuette from Grimaldi, the woman with the horn from Laussel (Dordogne), the famous 'Dame de Lespugue' (Haute-Garonne), the Gagarino statuette (Don) and the Willendorf statuette (Austria), which are neither naturalistic nor schematic, but rather symbolic or stylised. That is to say, unless the female form has undergone some extraordinary variation, certain features are exaggerated, notably the breasts, hips and stomach. Though we are still in the region of speculation, there can be little doubt that these figurines were portable fertility charms.

The frequent portrayal of animals in a state of pregnancy also suggests some connection with fertility, and I have no wish to deny a connection between the art and the religious conceptions of the Stone Age. On the contrary, we must not make any distinction between art and religion at this stage of human evolution. It is not a question of ritual being the motive power of art, or of art providing the instruments of religion. It is certainly not a question of art for art's sake, or of art for play's sake. Art and religion are rather to be regarded as an 'integral organism', as inseparable aspects of the same evolving consciousness. I do not know exactly what the archaeologists envisage as cave ritual – perhaps dancing and chanting; but these activities are arts, too, and no important distinction is to be drawn between such arts and the arts of painting and sculpture. The art was the ritual; the ritual was art.

Why, then, is the art not in itself integral – why these three types of representation: naturalistic, abstract and symbolic?

It has been suggested that taboos would explain the absence of certain subjects – for example, the male figure. But must we invent a taboo to explain the absence, or extreme rarity, of birds and fishes, of trees and flowers, of innumerable other species of fauna and flora? No: the reason for a selective emphasis must be a positive one. Palaeolithic man had a special and exclusive interest in the animals he depicted, and the presence and force of this interest explains, in some way, the vitality of his plastic representations of the animals.

His dependence for his survival on the hunting of these animals is the obvious explanation. But granted this explanation, why should it lead to a desire to paint vivid images of these animals in the depths of his caves – of these animals and nothing else?

Again, there is the simple explanation: animals were his mental preoccupation. Their images danced before his eyes even in the depths of the caves. We must all of us have experienced the persistence of images connected with some occupation we have been intensely engaged in for many hours. The sensation has been well described by Robert Frost in his poem 'After Apple-picking':

> Magnified apples appear and disappear,
> Stem end and blossom end,
> And every fleck of russet showing clear.
> My instep arch not only keeps the ache,
> It keeps the pressure of a ladder-round.
> I feel the ladder sway as the boughs bend.
> And I keep hearing from the cellar bin
> The rumbling sound
> Of load on load of apples coming in
> For I have had too much
> Of apple-picking: I am overtired
> Of the great harvest I myself desired.

In the same way, Palaeolithic man, retiring to his cave after a day or days of hunting the buffalo and the wild horse on the icy steppes, would see magnified animals appear and disappear, with every detail of hoof and horn, of plunging charge and bleeding death, cast like a modern lantern projection on the bare cave-walls. But he still has to make the step between visual hallucination and painterly craft, and for any light in that evolutionary leap we must return to the child and the savage among us.

There is no doubt, as the researches of Piaget, Bühler and Koffka have shown, that the earliest stages in the development of memory in the child take the form of revived experience. The child (and the primitive) has no capacity to remove images to a conceptual distance, and manipulate them as significant counters. Memory involves a sensational reaction for the child, becoming feebler as the mind matures. We must also remember that for the child, as for primitive man, there is no consciousness of self standing apart from the object or the event: there is complete 'participation'. I think we must assume, therefore, on the basis of the very considerable research that has been given to this problem, that the plastic realisation of his eidetic imagery was no playful experience for prehistoric man: it was an awful achievement, not to be lightly undertaken. But once the objective image had been made then it served as an enlargement of experience – not only in the sense that the experience could be repeated again and again, until a distance was bred by familiarity, but also in the sense that two or more experiences could be combined simultaneously, and unconsciously – but with increasing consciousness – compared. The function of memory then becomes clearly visible – it is the means by which the child, and primitive man, and, we can assume, prehistoric man, builds up a rational conception of its environment, and by recognition of this memorised and realised conception, is able to establish the rudiments of cognition. No doubt Palaeolithic man had through millions of years elaborated a technique of hunting – just as the wolf or the spider has its technique. But animal techniques are, as we say, instinctive – chained reflexes – and though man has an instinctual component in his make-up, his distinction is that he has evolved another and a superior faculty which we call intelligence, and by virtue of this intelligence has been able to survive. *Homo neanderthalensis* learned to think and thereby became *homo sapiens*. It is impossible to conceive this evolutionary transition in any manner that does not involve the aesthetic faculty – that is to say, the ability to project and compare (i.e., compose) eidetic images, which then became memory-images, and much later in human evolution, intellectual concepts.

The concentration on animal imagery is, with such a hypothesis, not difficult to understand. The most vivid images are those which accompany the intensest experiences, and there can be no doubt that the intensest experiences of Palaeolithic man were for the most part connected with the hunting of animals. The begetting of children would be another such experience, but as the man's part in that experience was probably a mystery, as it still is to primitive men and savages, it is easy to see how a stylistic differentiation arose: the carver (unless, as is perhaps possible but not likely, a woman) would have no experience to relive, but only a desired event to encourage by sympathetic magic, by prophetic realisation. As for the man himself, not being conscious of his separateness, of his uniqueness, he would tend to represent himself, if at all, by the most summary means, the schema.

As a matter of fact, a similar differentiation does take place in children today. When a child has an obsession for some animal – as many young girls have for ponies – they tend to draw such animals with a degree of realism altogether absent from their normal drawings. There are, of course, many influences, that counteract this tendency – the uniformatory tendency of education, for example – but the evidence exists.

We must now leave the Stone Age and the age of innocence and take into view the wider sweep of human evolution. Can we show that the aesthetic faculty, the ability to give the mind's imagery the concrete forms of art, has played a decisive part in the further evolution of human consciousness ? Does the same intimate and indivisible connection which evidently existed between art and the origin of consciousness, between art and primitive skill and ritual, persist through the later phases of mankind's history? Does art, that is to say, persist as an offspring of magic, religion, science, philosophy, of all we mean by civilisation and culture; or is it rather the mainspring, the mental faculty without which none of these other graces of mankind would have had a chance of coming into existence?

I shall, of course, take this latter view, but in the time left to me I can do no more than give a brief indication of the direction in which an answer to this question is to be found.

I have to confess, at this point, that I am an unregenerate Bergsonian. From the scientist's point of view Bergson has been dismissed as a 'good poet but a bad scientist',[15] and no doubt he was unscientific in method. But he had what the scientist so often lacks – a synoptic vision. He gave us a coherent picture of life, and though some of its terminology may be old-fashioned, or even downright misleading, nevertheless it is one of the last of such intuitive efforts that makes sense. In particular, it makes sense because it includes within its scope, not only the evolution of species in the broad sense, but the intensive evolution, within the species man, of such faculties as instinct, intuition and intelligence. Bergson found a logical place in evolution for that phenomenon which is our main concern now – consciousness. More particularly still, he gave a convincing explanation of the fact that this phenomenon, consciousness, has evolved in *relative* independence of the brain – 'there is indeed solidarity and interdependence between the brain and consciousness, but not parallelism: the more complicated the brain becomes, thus giving the organism greater choice of possible actions, the more does consciousness outrun its physical concomitant'.[16] I cannot repeat the argument on which Bergson bases his statement, but I must give his resulting hypothesis in his own words:

'The evolution of life, looked at from this point, receives a clearer meaning, although it cannot be subsumed under any actual idea. It is as if a broad current of consciousness had penetrated matter, loaded, as all consciousness is, with an enormous multiplicity of interwoven potentialities. It has carried matter along to organisation, but its movement has been at once infinitely retarded and infinitely divided. On the one hand, indeed, consciousness has had to fall asleep, like the chrysalis in the envelope in which it is preparing for itself wings; and, on the other hand, the manifold tendencies it contained have been distributed among divergent series of organisms which, moreover, express these tendencies outwardly in movements rather than internally in representations. In the course of this evolution, while some beings have fallen more and more asleep, others have more completely awakened, and the torpor of some has served the activity of others. But the waking could be effected in two different ways. Life, that is to say consciousness, launched into matter, fixed its attention either on its own movement or on the matter it was passing through; and it has thus been turned either in the direction of intuition or in that of intellect. Intuition, at first sight, seems far preferable to intellect, since in it life and consciousness remain within themselves. But a glance at the evolution of living beings shows us that intuition could not go very far. On the side of intuition consciousness found itself so restricted by its envelope that intuition had to shrink into instinct, that is, to embrace only the very small portion of life that interested it; and this it embraces only in the dark, touching it while hardly seeing it. On this side, the horizon was soon shut out. On the contrary, consciousness, in shaping itself into intelligence, that is to say in concentrating itself at first on matter, seems to externalise itself in relation to itself; but, just because it adapts itself thereby to objects from without, it succeeds in moving among them and in evading the barriers they oppose to it, thus opening to itself an unlimited field. Once freed, moreover, it can turn inwards on itself, and awaken the potentialities of intuition which still slumber within it.

'From this point of view, not only does consciousness appear as the motive principle of evolution, but also, among conscious beings themselves, man comes to occupy a privileged place. Between him and the animals the difference is no longer one of degree, but of kind.'[17]

Having disengaged intellect in this way, Bergson defines its function as that of 'embracing nature in its entirety'. I would prefer a more philosophical phrase, such as 'apprehending the nature of being, or the process of reality', but let that pass for the moment. The intellect, for Bergson, is regarded as 'a special function of the mind, essentially turned toward inert matter'. Matter does not determine the form of intellect, nor does the intellect impose its form on matter, nor have matter and intellect been regulated in regard to one another by we know not what pre-established harmony – intellect and matter have progressively adapted themselves one to the other in order to attain at last a common form. 'This adaptation has, morever, been brought about quite naturally, because it is the same inversion of the same movement which creates at once the intellectuality of mind and the materiality of things'.

But intellectuality is essentially order. 'All the operations of our intellect tend to geometry, as to the goal where they find their perfect fulfilment', and it is evident, says Bergson, that 'a latent geometry, immanent in our idea of space... is the mainspring of our intellect and the cause of its working'. This tendency to geometry described by Bergson is given a more universal interpretation in the hypothesis of a unitary principle in biology and physics recently formulated by Lancelot Law Whyte[18] in these terms: 'Asymmetry tends to disappear, and this tendency is realised in isolable processes' – a principle, which although as old as Aristotle, has been emerging, as Mr Whyte has shown, with increasing clarity in modern scientific speculations. That matter, in Bergson's vivid phrase, is 'weighted with geometry' has perhaps been obvious since the time of the early Greek physicists; it is now suggested that mind is in a similar condition. The faculties of induction and deduction, on which our reason depends, are patterns of relationship determined by geometrical laws. Indeed, we finally come to the conclusion, which Mr Whyte expresses in this way: that 'the invariant characterising mental processes is not a physical quantity, *but some unknown law of the development and transformation of patterns'*.

It is obvious why the patterns must be transformed – there would otherwise be no physical or mental evolution. But what is the nature of the transforming act? Bergson calls it 'creative', and uses the analogy of the spontaneously created work of art – a symphony of Beethoven, to be exact. The point I am trying to make, the whole point of my hypothesis, is that the work of art is not an analogy – it is the essential act of transformation; not merely the *pattern* of mental evolution, but the vital process itself.

Actually, as Bergson pointed out, there are two kinds of order which we generally confuse:

> 'In a general way, reality is *ordered* exactly to the degree in which it satisfies our thought. Order is therefore a certain agreement between subject and object. It is the mind finding itself again in things. But the mind... can go in two opposite ways. Sometimes it follows its natural direction: there is then progress in the form of tension, continuous creation, free activity. Sometimes it inverts it, and this inversion, pushed to the end, leads to extension... to geometrical mechanism... In both cases we say there is order.... As for the first kind of order, it oscillates no doubt around finality; and yet we cannot define it as finality, for of a free action or a work of art we may say that they show a perfect order, and yet they can only be expressed in terms of ideas approximately, and after the event.'

But Bergson is still using the work of art as analogy. 'Life in its entirety,' he says, 'regarded as a creative evolution, is something analogous [to a free action or a work of art]; it transcends finality... the vital is in the direction of the voluntary... We say of astronomical phenomena that they manifest an admirable order, meaning by this that they can be foreseen mathematically. And we find an order no less admirable in a symphony of Beethoven, which is genius, originality, and therefore unforeseeability itself'.[19]

That is perhaps to betray a romantic conception of the work of art, for really there is no essential distinction between the creative process as operative in a world of art and the creative process operative in a scientific generalisation – both processes involve the subsuming of discrete phenomena within a meaningful pattern, a significant form. What is important, and confined to a few individuals, is the capacity to stretch the pattern, to transform the form, the process which we can best call symbolisation.

I ought at this point to bring in the evidence of Gestalt psychology, which, approaching the problem from the analysis of perception, has come to the conclusion that 'art psychologically considered, is not an idle play on our emotions, but a means of helping us to find our place in the world.'[20] What the Gestalt psychologists have tried to establish, in my opinion succesfully, is that perception, too, tends towards balance and symmetry – 'balance and symmetry are perceptual characteristics of the visual world which will be realised whenever the external conditions allow it; when they do not, unbalance, lack of symmetry, will be experienced as a characteristic of objects or the whole field, together with the felt urge towards a better balance'[21]. Now this process, under normal circumstances, is haphazard – 'the organism... does the best it can under prevailing conditions, and these conditions will not, as a rule, allow it to do a very good job... A work of art, on the other hand, is made with that very idea; once completed it serves as a source of stimulation specifically selected for its aesthetic effect'. This is Professor Koffka's formulation, and it is one that betrays a certain limitation, for it does not give us any clue to the purpose of art. The work of art makes its effect by virtue of a certain structure, a 'good', and even – we may suppose – an increasingly 'better' gestalt. But surely the conclusion to be derived from these considerations is that the search for the good gestalt is due to the need for 'finding our place in the world'. That constitutes the 'requiredness' of the work of art, and it is a requiredness that is fundamental to the onotological situation of man. In other words, aesthetic requiredness is the basic requiredness in biological and intellectual development.

If we now return to the historical development of mankind, as if to test our hypothesis, it seems to me that there should be, and indeed are, certain definite stages which mark an increase of mental awareness, of inward intensification, of increased consciousness or apprehension of reality, directly attributable to the aesthetic faculty. The first of these is the birth of language – an event lost in prehistory, about the nature of which we can but dimly speculate. Somewhere in the long interval between the birth of consciousness and the historical records of language, we have such decisive events as the rise of ritual, the birth of magic and science, the birth of the ethical conscience, the birth of religion and philosophy, and many more specific events, or isolable processes, such as the realisation of an ideal type of humanity in Greek art. All these stages in the evolution of mankind are due to refinements of perception involving a progressive transformation of perceptual patterns, a structure satisfying a 'requiredness' inherent in, or spontaneously generated by, the immediately preceding evolutionary situation.[22] The alternating phases of the history of art generally known as classicism and romanticism, for example, are to be interpreted as alternating phases of evolutionary stability and revolutionary transformation.

Susanne Langer, who is, as far as I know, the only philosopher with a comprehensive vision of these evolutionary processes, has described their serial nature in the following way:

'It is a peculiar fact that every major advance in thinking, every epoch-making new insight, springs from a new type of symbolic transformation. A higher level of thought is primarily a new activity; its course is opened up by a new departure in semantic. The step from mere sign-using to symbol-using marked the crossing of the line between animal and man; this initiated the growth of language. The birth of symbolic gesture from emotional and practical movement probably begot the whole order of ritual, as well as the discursive mode of pantomime. The recognition of vague, vital meanings in physical forms – perhaps the first dawn of symbolism – gave us our idols, emblems, and totems; the primitive function of dream permits our first envisagement of events. The momentous discovery of nature-symbolism, of the pattern of life reflected in natural phenomena, produced the first universal insights. Every mode of thought is bestowed on us, like a gift, with some new principle of symbolic expression. It has a logical development, which is simply the exploitation of all the uses to which that symbolism lends itself, and when these uses are exhausted, the mental activity in question has found its limit. Either it serves its purpose and becomes truistic, like our orientation in "Euclidian space" or our appreciation of objects and their accidents (on the pattern of language structure, significantly called "logic"); or it is superseded by some more powerful symbolic mode which opens new avenues of thought.'[23]

It is true that in this passage Susanne Langer does not use the word art, but in the very next paragraph she characterises the highest development of which myth is capable as 'the exhibition of human life and cosmic order poetry reveals'; and elsewhere in her writings she makes it abundantly clear that symbolic transformation only takes place by virtue of aesthetic effort. Language, for example, she sees as a development of ritual[24] – 'ritual, solemn and significant, antedates the evolution of language... song, the formalisation of voice-play, probably preceeding speech'. But in this sphere what is beyond dispute, and demonstrable in our own creative thought processes, is the significance of metaphor – metaphor is the law of the life of language. As a modern logician, Morris Cohen, freely admits: 'metaphors are not merely artificial devices for making discourse more vivid and poetical, but are also necessary for the apprehension and communication of new ideas... they are often the way in which creative minds perceive things, so that the explicit recognition that we are dealing with an analogy rather than a real identity comes later as a result of further reflection or analysis.'[25] The first perceptions of what is novel in any science tend to assume the form of metaphors – the first stages of science are poetic.

It is, of course, true that as science progresses it dispenses with metaphor and relies on conceptual or discursive forms of thought. That may be another aspect of the unitary principle – the tendency of mental processes to seek a state of equilibrium. Hegel came to the conclusion that such a state of equilibrium had been reached by modern philosophy, and that it must not be disturbed. Art he therefore regarded as 'a thing of the past'. But he is not complacent about the situation. 'As a matter of fact,' he says, 'the beauty of art does not appear in a form which is expressly to be contrasted with abstract thought, a form which it is compelled to disturb in order to exercise its own activity in its own way. Such a result is simply a corollary of the thesis that reality anywhere and everywhere, whether the life of Nature or mind, is defaced and slain by its comprehension; that so far from being brought more close to us by the comprehension of thinking, it is only by this means that it is in the complete sense removed apart from us, so that in his attempt to grasp through thought as a *means* the nature of life, man rather renders nugatory this very aim'[26]. Hegel regarded art as a permeation of the sensuous substances of the phenomenal world with intelligence, and for that reason he could assimilate art to the process of thinking which in his view 'constitutes the most intimate and essential nature of mind'. He could even admit that the true function of art is to bring to consciousness the highest interests of mind. What he did not perceive, or admit, was the priority, in the evolutionary sense, of the metaphorical or symbolic activity. He took the 'idea' of the beautiful as his starting-point, not realising that 'idea' itself, as logical form, has its starting point in beauty. Or, to express the same distinction in Susanne Langer's words: he did not realise that intelligence is not to be restricted to discursive forms – that there is such a process as non-discursive thought, and that the mind develops, and apprehends reality, as much by imagination and dream, by myth and ritual, by art, in short, as by practical intelligence. It is mere presumption to claim the essence and intimacy of the mind for abstract thought: that arcane region is reserved, if for anything, for acts of symbolic transformation, for the formative intuitions of the great artist. The essential truth was expressed by Goethe, whose excursions into the theory of art Hegel treated a little contemptuously; the formative process (*die Gestaltung*), Goethe said, is the supreme process, indeed the only one, alike in nature and art.[27] Or as he said to Eckermann (April 15, 1827): 'I have to laugh at the aestheticians who agonize over trying to formulate in a few abstract words that indefinable thing we call beauty. Beauty is an *Urphänomen* (archetypal phenomenon). While it never materialises as such, it sheds its glow over a thousand different manifestations of the creative spirit and is as multiform as nature itself.'

The aesthetic apprehension of reality has gone on, in historical times, side by side with the intellectual apprehension of reality, and though we must finally insist on the vital relationship between these two processes, thought becoming academic and sterile unless continuously inspired by art, we can allow discursive thought its unique achievements[28]. But these achievements do not, and never can, make art a thing of the past, for the process of original symbolisation must go on if human consciousness is to retain an ontological purpose. And art, in this sense, is continuously at its evolutionary task. Even since Hegel's day we can claim that in at least two directions art has refined the apprehending faculties of consciousness. Those movements in painting, music and literature to which we may give the general name of Impressionism have a direct relationship – the relationship of originators of the appropriate imagery – with the philosophy of Bergson and even with the physics of Einstein. The painting of Monet, the music of Debussy, the philosophy of Bergson, the psychology of Proust – can we separate them? Or take the Janus-spectacle of Sartre – from one aspect a discursive philosopher, from another a non-discursive artist. Does he keep his philosophy and his fiction in separate areas of his mind, or is there at the basis of both the same process of symbolic transformation ? The same stretched tension of an expanding consciousness? 'That which remains, that which endures,' wrote the poet Hölderlin, 'is established by the poets'; and commenting on this statement the philosopher Heidegger admits that 'the speech of the poet is establishment [of being] not only in the sense of the free act of giving, but at the same time in the sense of the firm basing of human existence on its foundation'.[29] I have mentioned the name of Marcel Proust, and I might perhaps close this lecture appropriately with a quotation from his great novel:

'The greatness of true art . . . was to rediscover, to recapture, to make known to us that reality so distant from our everyday existence, and from which we stray ever farther according to the increasing solidity and impermeability of the conventional knowledge which we substitute for it, that reality which we run a serious risk of never knowing before we die, and which is nothing more or less than our life, our real life, life finally discovered and illuminated, that life which, in a sense, is present at every moment in all men as well as in the artist. But they do not see it because they make no effort to illuminate it. And so their past is cluttered up with innumerable negatives which remain useless because the intelligence has not "developed" them. To recapture our life, and also the life of others; because style, for the writer as well as for the painter, is a matter not of technique but of vision. It is the revelation, which would be impossible by direct or conscious means, of the qualitative difference there is in the way the world presents itself to us, a difference which, but for the existence of art, would remain the eternal secret of each individual.'[30]

The revelation of the qualitative difference in the way the world presents itself to us – that is at once a description of the function of art and of the stages of the evolving consciousness of mankind.

Notes

1. *Evolution: The Modern Synthesis* (London : Allen & Unwin, 1942).

2. 'Non jamais nul artiste ne surpassera Phidias. Car le progrès existe dans le monde, mais non dans l'art.' Auguste Rodin, *L'Art*. (Entretiens réunis par Paul Gsell. Lausanne: H. L. Mermod, n.d.), p. 316.

3. H. J. Eysenck: 'The General Factor in Aesthetic Judgments', *Brit. J. Psych.*, XXXI (1940-1), 94-102; 'The Experimental Study of the "Good Gestalt" – A New Approach', *Psych. Rev.*, XLIX (1942), 344-64; *Dimensions of Personality* (London: Kegan Paul, 1947), ch. 6.

4. Cf. E. R. Jaensch, *Eidetic Imagery and Typological Methods of Investigation*, Eng. trans. (London, 1930), pp. 2-3: 'Optical perceptual (or eidetic) images are phenomena that take up an intermediate position between sensations and images. Like ordinary physiological after-images, they are always *seen* in the literal sense. They have this property of necessity... under all conditions, and share it with sensations.'

5. *Principles of Psychology*, part 9, ch. 9.

6. *Die Spiele der Menschen* (Jena, 1899). American translation: *The Play of Man* (New York, 1901).

7. *Homo Ludens: A Study of the Play Element in Culture*, trans. by R.F.C. Hull (London: Routledge & Kegan Paul, 1949), p. 168.

8. A departing rhinoceros seems to be included in the composition and may have been responsible for the disembowelling.

9. *The Mental Development of the Child*, trans. Oscar Oeser (London: Kegan Paul, 1930), p. 60.

10. Bergson, who dealt specifically with the problem in his Huxley Memorial Lecture on 'Life and Consciousness', 1911, is an exception, but perhaps he ranks as metaphysician rather than a biologist.

11. *Zur Psychologie der primitiven Kunst* (1907; 2nd edn., 1917); *Die Anfange der Kunst* (1909).

12. *Op. cit.*, pp. 123-4.

13 Cf. G. H Luquet, *L'Art et la religion des hommes fossiles* (Paris, 1926), ch. 5.

14 Jane Ellen Harrison, *Ancient Art and Ritual* (London, 1913), p. 26.

15 Huxley, *Evolution*, p. 458.

16 *Creative Evolution* (Eng. trans.) p. 190.

17 *Ibid.*, pp. 191-2.

18 *The Unitary Principle in Physics and Biology* (London: Cresset Press, 1949).

19 *Op. cit.*, 235-7.

20 K. Koffka, 'Problems in the Psychology of Art', *Art: A Bryn Mawr Symposium* (1940).

21 *Ibid.*, p. 261. Cf. also, by the same author, *The Unfolding of the Artistic Activity* (Berkeley, 1948).

22 L. L. Whyte calls such a situation a 'threshold' – 'the point of unstable equilibrium between two alternative tendencies' – and contrasts it with the 'terminus', which is the stable equilibrium where a tendency culminates in symmetry.

23 *Philosophy in a New Key* (Harvard, 1942), pp. 200.

24 At this point taking up an earlier and forgotten hypothesis put forward by J. Donovan in two articles on 'The Festal Origin of Human Speech', contributed to *Mind*, 1891-2 (XVI (o.s.), pp. 498-506, and XVII, pp. 325-39).

25 Morris R. Cohen, *A Preface to Logic* (London: Routledge, 1946), pp. 83-6.

26 *The Philosophy of Fine Art*, trans. by F. P. B. Osmaston (London, 4 vols., 1920), I, p.15.

27 'Kein Mensch will begreifen, dass die höchste und einzige Operation der Natur und Kunst die Gestaltung sey' (letter to Zelter, Oct. 30, 1808).

28 And its influence on non-discursive thought. Certain inventions, e.g., the telescope, the microscope, the pianoforte, have been the instruments that have made possible an expansion of aesthetic consciousness. See, for this aspect of the subject, the various works of Marjorie Hope Nicolson: *The Microscope and English Imagination* (1935), *A World in the Moon (1936),* and *Newton Demands the Muse: Newton's* Opticks *and the Eighteenth Century Poets* (Princeton University Press, 1946).

29 Cf. Martin Heidegger, *Existence and Being* (London: Vision Press, 1949), pp. 304-5.

30 *Le Temps retrouvé*, II, 48. Trans. by F. C. Green in *The Mind of Proust* (Cambridge University Press, 1949), p. 521.

30
Kicks and Ha'pence

The Bland Renegade

Very curious are the justifications which men now put forward for a change of heart, or for a loss of faith. It used to be a bold assertion of enlightenment, a confident step forward on to new ground. The socialist, the atheist, the religious convert – all were positive and militant. But now our philosophers and politicians rejoice in mere negation. They renounce their former beliefs as Buchmanites renounce their sins – they shed a burden and step up into the limelight, to celebrate their empty minds. Mr Joad writes an article (*New Statesman*, May 19th) on what he *still* believes. He has lost his pacificism ('naive optimism') and his socialism ('no longer a creed to conjure with. It is like a hat which has lost its shape because so many wear it; rightly or wrongly, few of us now look to it to revivify our early hopes.'). He has found a belief in 'the Christian doctrine of original sin,' which 'expresses a deep and essential insight into human nature' – in other words, forbids a belief that 'the equality of women, pacifism, socialism or science will bring about the millennium *or even markedly improve the human lot*'. In short, Mr Joad has substituted a sophisticated pessimism for his naive optimism. But he 'still believes' in two things – reason and democracy. By reason he seems to mean little more than expediency – you can convert people to 'reason' if you can show them that a particular policy is to their advantage. As for democracy, that is merely 'the necessary framework' for such a pragmatic process.

Well, it was expedient to cease being a pacifist in 1940, as it was expedient to cease being a communist a year or two later. But what has such expediency to do with reason; and by what process of reasoning does Mr Joad arrive at a belief in the doctrine of original sin? Twenty years ago, did Mr Joad base his pacifism and his socialism on expediency – or on reason? If his reasoning was at fault twenty years ago, on what grounds must we conclude that it is now in working order?

Expediency is a betrayal of reason, and Mr Joad must know it. If socialism is now a shapeless hat that no longer looks well on Mr Joad's head, the explanation may be under the hat. If socialism has failed, it is because socialists like Mr Joad did not reason clearly enough thirty years ago. To be specific, they surrendered their reason to the most irrational concept that has ever entered the brain of man – the State. Mr Joad should not be blandly celebrating his lost innocence, he should be trying to recover his common sense.

Picasso Paints a Bad Picture

This is surprising news, but there seems to be no doubt about it. It is inspired by the atrocities in Korea, and has been reproduced in some French periodicals. A friend who had seen the original told me that it lost nothing in reproduction, being painted in dirty greys. It represents a shooting squad on one side, a group of civilian victims on the other side. The composition is crude, the distortion ineffective even as a caricature. If the subject were not so tragic, we might say that it was a piece on the level of the comic strip.

One feels as if an innocent man had been compelled by mental torture to tell a lie. Picasso has always been an infallible artist – his merest scribble betrayed his subtle sensibility, his unerring grace. *Guernica*, a great painting with a political purpose, is still first and foremost a painting – a composition of great complexity but of overwhelming unity of effect. Picasso painted it spontaneously, with strong but controlled feeling. I do not doubt the genuiness of his sympathy for the massacred Koreans. But I do doubt the spontaneity of this gesture. It almost looks as though the Party had commissioned it – it almost looks as though the Arts Committee of the Council of Ministers in Moscow had dictated how it should be done. Some power not Picasso has inspired its hatefulness; and the pity it induces is not for the victims of war, but for an artist who has lost his integrity.

Picasso's Gift

'The British Peace Committee announces that Pablo Picasso has given a painting to help the work for peace in Britain. It shows a faun's head.' A faun, we hope, dishorned.

31
Kicks and Ha'pence: Machinism

Machinism

This is not a subject to be dismissed in a paragraph: it is perhaps the basic problem of our civilisation, embracing war, famine, social disintegration, moral degeneration, and metaphysical despair. It is not a subject on which anarchists have a clear and coherent point of view. Most of us, I think, tend to distrust the machine: the modern State could not exist without it and is in some undefined sense a creation of the machine. We tend to speak of the State in terms of the machine – 'the machinery of government', 'the bureaucratic machine', etc. Metaphors, no doubt, but the day is not so distant when Whitehall will become one vast calculating machine, with forms fed in at one end and infallible statistics controlling our lives coming out at the other end. A new word has been invented – cybernetics – and it comes from our most-mechanised society, the United States. It means 'the theory of communication *and control* in the man and the machine', and it is very necessary for all of us to understand its implications. We cannot do better than read Dr Norbert Wiener's *The Human Use of Human Beings*, a book on *Cybernetics and Society* as its subtitle more clearly indicates. Wiener is professor of Mathematics at the Massachusetts Institute of Technology, and one of the men responsible for the development of the 'mechanical brain' – 'which,' says the blurb, 'can do routine mental jobs better than any man, and which therefore make the untrained mind a drug on the market'.

The untrained mind means, apparently, the mind incapable of understanding and controlling these robots. 'Any machine constructed for the purpose of making decisions, if it does not possess the power of learning, will be completely literal-minded. Woe to us if we let it decide our conduct, unless we have previously examined the laws of its action, and know fully that its conduct will be carried out on principles acceptable to us! Woe, woe, woe! The hour is very late, and the choice of good and evil knocks at the door.' Dr Wiener is a very frightened man, and when he looks round for a principle or a faith that might conceivably control the machine for the benefit of humanity, he finds only Voices and Rigidity. His final remarks are addressed specifically to Americans, but in this sense we are all Americans. He slashes into Communists and Capitalists alike, and into the Catholic Church, and concludes:

> 'It is again the American worship of know-how as opposed to know-what that hampers us. We rightly see great dangers in the totalitarian system of Communism. On the one hand, we have called in to combat these the assistance of a totalitarian Church which is in no respect ready to accept, in support of its standards, milder means than those to which Communism appeals. On the other hand, we have attempted to synthesise a rigid system to fight fire by fire, and to oppose Communism by institutions which bear more than a fortuitous resemblance to Communistic institutions. In this we have failed to realise that the element in Communism which essentially deserves our respect consists in its loyalties and in its insistence on the dignity and the rights of the worker. What is bad consists chiefly in the ruthless techniques to which the present phase of the Communist revolution has resorted. Our leaders show a disquieting complacency in their acceptance of the ruthlessness and a disquieting unwillingness to refer their acts to any guiding principles. Fundamentally, behind our counter-ruthlessness there is no adequate basis of real heartfelt assent.'

A vague expression – 'heartfelt assent'. I suspect that Professor Wiener means 'mutual aid', and that he is one of our crypto-anarchists.

Jünger and Mounier

There are two other books which might be read with profit now that we are debating the problem of machinism. One, a furious onslaught on the machine and all its works, has not been published in this country. It is a translation of a book written in 1939 (but not published till 1946) by Friedrich Georg Jünger, the brother of the more famous Ernst Jünger, and is called *The Failure of Technology*. It is a powerful and persuasive book, and its thirty-eight short chapters attack every aspect of 'technological progress'. I will quote its conclusion:

'The state itself is now conceived by technology as an organisation which must be brought to perfection, which must be controlled by a perfect automatism. The technician asserts that the state can properly fulfil its tasks only when it becomes organised on a completely technical basis, when the idea of the state and its purpose are organized into a centralized functionalism, an all-embracing machine which nothing escapes. But precisely this definition annihilates the very essence of the state. For, indispensable to the state is that which is not state, and can never become state. This something by which alone the state can be a state is the people. The people may well be conceived as the carriers of the state; there are all kinds of relationships between the governed and the government, but never can the people be the state itself. The very idea of the state is null and void once this basis collapses whereon the state is built. The technical organisation of the whole people to the point where no sector of life remains unorganised, in the end brings the downfall of that state.'

Another crypto-anarchist?

The other book that deals to a considerable extent with the problem of machinism is *Be Not Afraid: Studies in Personalist Sociology* by Emmanuel Mounier. Mounier, whose early death about a year ago is to be greatly regretted, was a Catholic, a disciple of Péguy. But his attitude to the machine is very different from Gill's and other Catholic distributivists. He is almost lyric in his praises of the civilising influence of the machine, and takes the view that as a direct extension of man's faculties and intelligence, it is divinely sanctioned and should be developed for the benefit of mankind. But only, of course, within the controlling ethos of a Christian community. Mounier's personalist sociology has many points of contact with anarchism, and his general principle, that a morally healthy society could be trusted to make a right use of technology, is one with which we can agree. But how distinguish the good machines from the bad ones? It is simple, says Mounier. Good machines are an extension of the human hand; bad machines are automatic. A bicycle is a good machine – 'it is well adapted to the human body: the handlebars correspond to the arms and hands, the pedals to the feet, and it is entirely controlled by the human body'. The motor-cycle, however, is a bad machine – it is merely a mechanism that performs controlled automatic work. And now I am lost in contemplation of my typewriter! It is a good machine, I decide, for though it has its full share of 'that measure of disorder known to the statistical mechanist as *entropy*', it is the moving finger (or rather, two of them) that writes.

32
Kicks and Ha'pence

The Village Hall

The number of village halls established during the past twenty years is not known to me, though possibly the statistics are available. In any case, they are a new feature of country life, and a significant one. Their rise corresponds to the decline of the social influence of the Church; also, perhaps, to a shift in economic wealth – the rich are no longer so rich and the poor are no longer so poor. I know that there have been agencies (Carnegie Foundations, etc.) which have artificially stimulated this development, but fundamentally it has been a spontaneous growth, made possible by mutual aid. Take the case of my own village. It consists of about twenty-five households, with a few outlying farms. There is a church, but the nearest pub is two miles away. The possibility of erecting a village hall was mooted two or three years ago. A meeting was summoned in the only place available – an upper barn or granary which had formerly been used as a Protestant Sunday School, a Catholic Chapel, and an apple store. The stables beneath provided the characteristic odour. The meeting decided to launch the scheme with a whist drive. Excitement began to mount and the next move was a jumble sale, which realised the unexpected sum of £64. Throughout the following winter activities never ceased – more whist drives and socials, and on the Fifth of November even the children took their spontaneous part, parading a Guy on a pony and raising ten shillings. It was time to take the plunge. The local landowner was approached and a site in the village was given free. The committee began to look for a suitable building – an army hut in good conditions which could be re-erected on the site. Eventually it was found, approved by the local authorities, and bought. Next the site had to be cleared and levelled: it was done voluntarily by the men of the village in the summer evenings, after a hard day's work in the fields.

Stones for the foundations were collected by one of the farmers from a quarry on his land. The landowner lent a mason to supervise the mixing of the cement and the laying of a course of brickwork. Then the hall, in sections, was delivered and the men of the village erected it (small as it is, the village luckily includes a skilled joiner). But what we then had was merely a bleak shell: it had to be painted, and, worst snag of all, it had to be provided with a floor. Anxious meetings followed, for timber is controlled, and extremely expensive. But the timber was found and the floor was laid by the joiner. The last touches were given to the building and its surroundings, the roadman trimmed the road, the village green was mown by the blind quarryman (who also mows the churchyard, rings the bells and looks after his own cow and garden), and everything was now ready for the Opening Fête (this foreign word, along with bazaar and gymkhana, persists in the country). It was a 'splendid occasion'. There were speeches, of course; there was also a sale of work, and sports, and a concert given by the children, and a final whist drive – altogether another £100 was raised. There is still a debt – quite a substantial one – but with a Hall in their possession, the village feels secure. Now there will be, not only whist drives and socials, but dances and the mobile cinema. There is even talk of an opera.

Is this small beer to you? The Village Pump used to be a symbol of all that was parochial and self-centred. Is the Village Hall its present equivalent? Or is it, as I would suggest, a point of light in a dark world? A community of a hundred souls, unaided by national, state or local government, has brought into being, by its own spontaneous efforts, a centre for its communal life. It stands on the hill-side, a grey hut without any architectural graces, but it will weather into the landscape, and the villagers will use it and enjoy it because it was their own creation. It 'has brought the village together', they say. They mean that their lives will be happier, their activities will have a focus, their minds socially creative. Multiply this little event a thousandfold, and something like a social revolution will have taken place. But, of course, it can only take place in small communities. The problem is very different in a city. But even in a city it can be solved, as the Peckham Health Centre demonstrated. *Can* be solved, and yet the Peckham Health Centre has closed its doors. Its failure was a social tragedy, and what we want to know is whether such a tragic failure is inherent in city life, or merely the result of economic pressures which could have been avoided. A city can build a useless feature like the Dome of Discovery, but it cannot maintain a Home of Social Health. That is the paradox of an urban civilisation.

World Government

A conference on a very impressive scale is being prepared by the all-party Parliamentary Group for World Government. It will open in London on September 24th, and be continued in Cardiff, Edinburgh, Birmingham and Glasgow. Many fine speeches will be made and glowing sentiments will warm hearts chilled by the fear of atomic war. It is desirable that 'men of vision and goodwill with a sense of the realities of the age we live in' should be enabled 'to have a free discussion of the measures which might be taken to realise the just hopes or aspirations of the common peoples of all nations for a world of peace and plenty'. To people imbued with a governmental conception of society, it would seem that a World Government with absolute power over all people on the face of the earth is the only effective way of achieving the just hopes and aspirations, etc. One cannot doubt the sincerity and independence of men like Lord Boyd Orr and Mr Clement Davies, who are the leaders of this movement. But there are two questions that must be asked: Are their ideals realisable, and if realisable, are they desirable? I am not very concerned about the first question: if means can be found to persuade the USSR, China, Spain, the Argentine, Mexico, the United States and Mr Winston Churchill to surrender their sovereignties to an international government, then one miracle might give birth to another – an international government might succeed in establishing a world of peace and plenty (I assume, of course, that the process of persuasion would in itself be 'peaceful'). But what I find a little disturbing is the thought of such a concentration of power in relatively few hands. Would even our supermen have the nerves to stand the strain? Or would power absolute beyond any tyrant's dream be accompanied by corruption beyond the devil's own conception? But suppose we say, instead of World Government, NO GOVERNMENT AT ALL? We shall be told that that ideal is also unpractical, unrealisable. So in the end we are left with two projects of immense scope and significance each under the suspicion of being utterly idealistic, and we must make our choice. The difference is, that whilst people are accustomed to think along lines of the concentration and centralisation of power, towards an ideal of authoritarian control, they are not used to thinking along lines of the dissipation and decentralisation of power, towards an ideal of mutual aid. The choice is really between a few million village halls and one world government.

33

The Problem of Survival

The Estate of Man by Michael Roberts.

IT is a sombre book, piling up statistics to show that but for some miraculous turn of events, our civilisation is doomed. The cardinal fact which emerges from his survey of the economic and ecological condition of the world is that we cannot escape a gradual but finally swiftly accelerating reduction in the standard of living, accompanied by a bloody and lustful scramble for the last crumbs. 'There is no new land to plough,' he points out, 'and the land already ploughed can scarcely feed the present population of the world.' That population increases at the rate of 20,000,000 a year. In Asia alone the increase in the next ten years will be as great as the whole present population of the United States.

Roberts realised and said that 'If new measures are not taken to check the growth of population, the old ones will reinstate themselves, and the primitive forces that reinstate themselves will work through hunger, frenzy, bitterness, and hatred of one's fellow men... ' The obvious new measure – though in certain countries and among certain classes it is an old measure – is birth control, but birth control is most easily or most willingly practised by the most intelligent social groups. But what moral right have we to impose birth control on selected individuals or selected classes; and how, short of forcible sterilisation, are we to impose it? There are no 'reasons for optimism' listed in this new book – on the contrary, there is a new reason for pessimism in the two brilliant chapters in which Roberts investigates what he calls 'the reservoir of talent' showing how the increasing industrialisation and bureaucratisation of the world is leading to a relative decrease in intelligence, to a depletion in the ranks of those occupations where intelligence is most needed if we are to survive – the teaching and other professional services.

Michael Roberts did not finish this book, and apart from a stray note or two, we are left guessing as to *how* he would have finished it. One of the final notes reads: 'Man has been at war with nature and therefore at war with one another. Harmony with nature, then harmony with our neighbours. War springs from disequilibrium. We are being forced back to a harmonious relation with the soil, and that relation will solve our spiritual as well as our material problems. What ought *we* to do?'

Each of us must answer that question, and answer it practically. It is very difficult, perhaps impossible, voluntarily to reverse the processes of industrialisation and power economics. But one day, not very distant, the oil wells will be dry, our forests will have been consumed and our mines will be exhausted. To trust in the inventive resources of mankind is a dangerous illusion; they are more likely to lead to further weapons of universal destruction than to a harmony with nature. In the end we must return to the land, to the estate of man. We must love it and cultivate it as the only source of life. Ten million square miles is all it amounts to, or can amount to. How many millions of people that land can support is calculable. Michael Roberts believed that a gradual return to harmony with the earth, as farmers, not miners, will gradually re-establish an equilibrium between population and resources. There will be sacrifices, but they will be to Demeter and not to Moloch.

The final factors are not economic, but vital. They are controlled by impulses whose movements we cannot measure, or even detect. We close-shave our cornfields with combine-harvester and the corncrakes mysteriously disappear. They would mysteriously return with the scythes, or the horse-drawn reaper. This is a picturesque illustration of a process that has been going on now for many years; the machine has upset the equilibrium of nature, and our first action should be to put the machine into reverse.

We now accept the machine without question, and cannot easily imagine a future that does not depend on an increasing use of the machine. Nevertheless, in the long run the machine is anti-vital, and will, if unchecked, destroy the life of the world. Living things depend on the cultivation of organic growths, and on a limited store of natural resources. They consume certain products of the earth, but what they consume they return to the earth in the form of essential manures. Machines also consume natural resources, but render back only smoke, gases, cinders – dead and even harmful by-products of their power. It is logically and statistically certain that such a process must, sooner or later, end in the exhaustion of the earth's resources, and part of Roberts' purpose is to show that it will be sooner rather than later.

If we are to avoid ultimate doom, we must, as Michael Roberts says, learn a new husbandry. We must acquire the mentality of farmers and gardeners and discard the mentality of miners and excavators. We must stop burning and blasting, and resolve to conserve and cultivate. Vast schemes of reafforestation and reclamation must be undertaken, and the energy and cunning, the brain-power and man-power, now devoted to the sciences of exploitation, must be diverted to the sciences of growth and creation. A distinction must be made between the sciences that promote and preserve life, and the sciences that merely generate power – the general distinction between the biological and mechanical sciences. Degrees of interdependence will be discovered, and a point of equilibrium may be reached where the life-promoting sciences require a measure of support from the power-generating sciences.

To secure such a development, a mental and social revolution is required that will eventually exalt the biologist above the atomic physicist, the forester above the engineer, the schoolmaster above the air-pilot, the farm-labourer above the coal-miner. But it is not merely a question of revising emoluments and restoring prestige: we must renounce our deep-seated worship of power – the worship of power for power's sake. We must recognise, before it is too late, our unconscious surrender to the forces of death, our equally unconscious rejection of the forces of life.

34
Postscript to Posterity

DEAR POSTERITY:
By now you will be getting a little bored with the letters you have been receiving from my contemporaries in this year of grace 1952, but before you return to the more serious business of rebuilding the world we left in ruins, may I beg you to read this postscript? It will not take long, and it may hearten you to find that we were not all humbugs. Of course, I feel a bit of a humbug in making that claim, for how can I, and a few friends who share my indignation, be sure that we have not caught the prevalent infection? But you will have no patience with false modesty, so I hasten to explain that a minority does exist in our time which is not and never will be deceived by the stupidity around us. You will say, your side of all the disasters of a century, why did we not do something about it? If any records have survived you will find that we were not inactive; what you will not realise, perhaps, is the impotent insignificance of reason in a world gone mad. But let me try to explain.

At the moment of writing – it is the month of February, 1952 – we have just experienced a vast conspiracy of humbug which makes those letters you have been receiving hardly worth their postage. A king died – a decent, harmless fellow by all accounts, a perfect prototype of our bourgeois virtues. Though long deprived of any power, a mere symbol of pomp and circumstance, this king's natural decease is swollen, by press and radio, by film and television, into an event of universal, of supernatural significance. The whole life of the nation is disrupted, and uncounted wads of its shrinking pounds are expended in a delirious abandon to wholly fictitious grief. The parades and processions might perhaps be excused – the life we are accustomed to is drab and depressing, and the sight of a scarlet uniform, or the sound of a fanfare, rouses the indifferent heart. But the little man in his millions creeps out of his suburban home, carefully adjusting the black tie he last wore at his grandmother's funeral; looks round fearfully to see that his neighbour is giving his little gesture of support, buys his newspaper on which the printer's ink has taken on a blacker hue, presses through the milling crowds of ghouls that always emerge from God knows where on such occasions – myopic spinsters, wispy toothless hags, gawping adolescents – and finally arrives, ten minutes late, at his office, where he proceeds to carry on his little game of deceit.

His little game of deceit – he calls it earning a living, and we all play it in some way or another: punching the machines that now calculate the astronomical figures of finance, pulling the levers that control the machines that make the goods we exchange for food, collecting the taxes that pay for the bombs we shall explode in the Third World War. At the end of the week the little man gets his pay-packet – the solution of an equation whose factors are taxes and contributions, leaving a sum with which to pay more taxes and a final surplus for food. He will look at it ruefully, and when he gets home he will face as best he can the anguish of his wife, beset with petty cares, sinking into the zestless, sexless indifference of a middle age without fulfilment, of an old age without hope.

But you will know all this, or you can read it up in the social surveys and the fiction of our time. What you want to know, I imagine, is why we so complacently endured it all. Why, in this year of grace (you must excuse this cliché which I go on repeating: I use it wryly enough) why do we go on with the mad and monstrous comedy? Who knows? We have mass-psychologists, but they cannot give a convincing answer to this question. You must have foreseen (I imagine you saying) the coming of the Third World War; you must have seen the coming of the Great Famine – why did you do nothing about it?

I will try and answer that awkward question presently. Some things, you know, are too big to be seen – and some are too small. But some of us did see, for example, the fantastic folly of our money system – a system which only a college of lunatics could have evolved, and only a gang of criminals could have deliberately operated. Criminals? That is too crude and easy as an explanation. I have a friend who is a trained scientist, a physiologist who seems to have operated on his own eyes, for they see where others are blind, and he has shown that these people who sit in power are simply delinquents – people who in any lowlier sphere of operations would be recognised as such, and put under control. But the banking world, the stock exchanges, and those mysterious international committees that control the 'value of money' are exempt from any kind of control, moral or medical. They sit in some Delphic boardroom, furnished no doubt with statues of bronze (or portraits of past chairmen) and utter their oracles which immediately spread desolation throughout the world. A few of us saw the deception of it all, but for one voice that was raised against these Pythian priests, there were a thousand professors of economics to stifle it with pamphlets and broadcasts. (When one of us, in the Second World War, did eventually get behind a microphone, he was promptly denounced as a traitor and a lunatic, and put into a mental hospital.)

I shared the view (it is the view of a tiny minority among us) that the root of all our misery is in this irrational monetary system, and that therefore any direct action against secondary follies, such as war and famine was largely a waste of effort. At the moment of writing, we, who live in an island off the coast of Europe, dependent for half our food on the rest of the world, are engaged in spending £4,700 millions on rearmament. For a quarter of that sum, perhaps for less, we could transform our agricultural system and make ourselves self-supporting (a statement which the professors of economics will controvert after their fashion). The rest of the sum might go to a world fund for the aversion of famine... but you see how easy it is even for me to slip into the Pythian jargon. For what are funds, and what are pounds and dollars? The mumbo-jumbo of an obsolete magic. There is no wealth but life, as Ruskin said. We could see – the tiny minority whose voice was unheeded – that the human race was being crushed by machines of its own invention: verbal or ideological machinery rather than machinery of steel. We could see that the way to freedom was wonderfully simple: simply to abandon all that machinery and live as direct producers and distributors of the produce of the earth. Yes: to repudiate all debts, to make usury a mortal crime, to unite all men in a common effort to survive – to survive and celebrate a new-found leisure.

We saw the truth – we proclaimed the truth, and yet we were ineffectual. We left you a legacy of war and famine, and as I write this letter in the year of disgrace 1952 (at last I have found the right phrase) I feel very uncertain that it will ever reach you. I feel very uncertain that any of our efforts, in art, literature, philosophy, will survive the coming catastrophes. But I have to pretend that they will. One lives on an overdraft of hope, and it is a pitiful illusion. Either our ideas must penetrate into the caves where the oracles sit and spin their devastating myths (and can you ever convert people to a surrender of their power?) or we must persuade the deluded millions who listen and obey to turn away and seek the truth. The difficulty is to make our voices carry: the voice from Delphi roars across the cities and fields, and we have no amplifiers – no microphones to command, no forests to convert into newsprint, no delinquents to co-opt on our committees. On our overdraft we might live another century, and on your side of universal catastrophe you might take up the message, and in a world still as death your living voice might be heard.

I had no power, therefore had patience.

35
Ancient War and Modern Peace

Ancient History by Michael Grant.

HERE, at last is a history book that gets down to relevant facts and, what is still more rare, judges those facts in the light of reason and justice. The scope is immense – from the dawn of human civilisation to the end of the *pax Romana*. What emerges, as the central theme, is war, and the second part of the book is an analysis of the causes of ancient wars. Criticising previous historians for their callousness, their blind and immoral acquiescence in a criterion of success, Professor Grant proceeds to revalue the events and personalities of the past from the firm ground of the present, finding 'the real anomaly – a serious danger in education – in the current habit of condoning in the ancient world (unlike many ancient thinkers themselves) pernicious conduct, such as aggression, which must not be condoned today.'

He finds the causes of ancient war to be (i) sovereignty and self-sufficiency; (ii) irrational emotions such as racialism; and (iii) inequalities in the social structure. He recognises that 'the chief function of governments throughout the ages has been war-mongering,' and he makes clear that the economic consequences of war have always been the destruction of real wealth. He does not, perhaps, give sufficient attention to the role of money in the origins and development of aggression, though he does admit in one place that the trouble begins when the integrity of a food-producing society is disrupted by the need to procure metals for the manufacture of weapons of aggression. He does not mention the irrational basis of money-value, or estimate the pressures created by usury and the accumulation of public debts.

Professor Grant shows that war is always associated with the particularism of States, and he comes to 'the only possible conclusion that is not of a highly anti-social character... that there must be no division between the ethics of the State and of the individual.' He comes near to admitting that public immorality is due to the existence of the State, but he feels that the evils of the State can be mitigated by federation and eliminated by a World State. He does not explain how the evil impulses that seem inseparable from the possession and exercise of power are to be prevented. It is true, of course, that 'the alternation of war and peace rests with human decisions and efforts,' but there is nothing in his survey of ancient history to encourage the belief that such decisions and efforts will ever be the outcome of political organisation.

The author mentions the stoic philosophy of the Brotherhood of Man (later absorbed by Christianity but always relinquished by the Christian Church under pressure from the State). He assumes that such a brotherhood can co-exist with the administration of a World State. It has not yet been proved that brotherhood can co-exist with the administration of a trade union. He can show that many of the wars of the past 'were directly caused by extreme hereditary differentiation of political and economic classes,' but he does not tell us how a World State can be organised without an extreme differentiation of political and economic classes.

In short, though the book gives the most realistic view of history known to me, it ends on a note of 'somehow' which is very unrealistic. 'The elimination of particularism must *somehow* be achieved by peaceful and not by forcible means.' Naturally; but the the cure for particularism is not universalism so long as universalism is conceived as a concentration of power. The difficulty of governing people, as Lao Tzu said, is through overmuch policy.

> 'He who tries to govern the kingdom by policy is only a scourge to it; while he who governs without it is a blessing.
> 'To know these two things is the perfect knowledge of government, and to keep them continually in view is called the virtue of simplicity.
> 'Deep and wide is this simple virtue; and though opposed to other methods it can bring about a perfect order.'

It is possible that the cure for particularism is not universalism but egoism, which is the art of cultivating one's own garden, as recommended by Candide.

36

The Ape of Hitler

THE mass trials of political prisoners in Spain are a symptom of much wider suffering and resentment in that country. The conditions of the workers and peasants are now such that 'direct action' of some kind must be attempted by desperate men. Direct action may take many forms, and not the least effective are the non-violent forms – the sit-down strike, etc. But a fascist dictator does not distinguish between fine points of ethics: where there is no right to strike, no liberty to express an opinion, no freedom of association, a striker is treated as a criminal and handled with the same ruthless violence as any other enemy of the State. Violence should be met with Christian fortitude, no doubt, but not in Christian Spain where blood is thicker than Communion wine. Franco has made of Spain a vat fermenting with hatred, and if violence now answers violence, it is that gross tyrant who is responsible.

It is now thirteen years since that fascist dictatorship was established with foreign aid, over the dead bodies of hundreds of thousands of Spanish democrats. Never for a moment has that dictatorship been accepted by the Spanish people. Imposed by brutal force, it has been resisted and resented by all freedom-loving Spaniards. Inside Spain, those who survived the fascist guns and bombs were driven underground, where secretly but surely they have been gathering force. Outside Spain, thousands of refugees have been organising themselves and planning for the eventual overthrow of the tyranny. Never for a moment, inside or outside Spain, will the struggle be given up, for the spirit of freedom has this quality – that even if it sinks to a flicker, invisible springs will replenish its light, till it blazes out stronger than ever.

Spain is a land which offers only two possibilities of development: either an economy based on extreme contrasts of wealth, a few capitalists exploiting the masses; or a co-operative economy based on small units (the village or the factory) which would ensure a modest but decent living for all. The natural resources of the country, for internal expansion or for export trade, are not sufficient for a bourgeois economy on the American or British model. That is the economic justification of the anarcho-syndicalist character of the Spanish workers' organisations. A fatted trade unionism on the British model, muscling in on a degenerate aristocracy (scions of the house of Citrine!), sitting pretty on central boards of control, dominating hives of busy executives – all this is inconceivable in Spain, where the sun is hot, and men and women live in the intimate gusto of a hard and penurious struggle with the parched earth. This earthy intimacy dominates even a big industrial centre like Barcelona, where there is no sense of a proletariat, or even of a white-collared rootless middle class; but always the feeling of a people living in families, inside patios, cafés, workshops, but always as communities, cellular, independent. Fascism has tried to destroy this intimacy, to impose a corporate pattern on it; to merge the cells into a unique State; to destroy independence and individuality. It has not succeeded.

It will never succeed. The fascist fury has a rising tempo. Almost every day there is news of further mass arrests, all over Spain, in Barcelona and La Coruña, in Seville and in Vitoria, without discrimination of rank or religion. Catholics are among them, leaders of the Catholic Youth Organisation – yet Rome shows no public indignation. It is not a question of religion or of social status: the conscience of a people is outraged, and men are arrested, imprisoned and shot, because their consciences can no longer be stilled.

And what of the conscience of Europe; what of the conscience of America? Obsessed with the fear of the more powerful devil in the East, our politicians and militarists prepare to bargain with the fat little devil in the West for a few acres of his blood-stained land, on which to build their air-bases. They offer him dollars lest his fascist régime should crumble and Spain be held, if not by communists, then by some régime not dollar-minded. Better, apparently, a devil in the hand than two devils in the heretical bush; as though all devils did not come out of the same hell!

We have been complacent too long. At the end of the war, Hitler's fiery little friend could have been brought before the same court of justice that hanged Ribbentrop and tried to hang Göring. Franco does not differ and never has differed, in character, policy or conduct, from these scourges of Europe. One day his vile tyranny will end, as

Hitler's ended, as Mussolini's ended, and the friends of liberty throughout the world will rejoice.

Meanwhile, it is our duty to rouse the conscience of the world, to support the oppressed with our sympathy, and to see that our governments break off all relations with this ape of Hitler.

37
We Protest against This Spanish Tyranny...

THIS meeting has been convened on a non-political basis, but it is difficult to decide where politics begin and end when the lives and liberties of politically-minded men are in danger. Franco's prisoners, whether they are trade unionists, intellectuals, or members of the Catholic Youth Movement, are enemies of Franco's régime. In other words, they are anti-fascists. We, too, are anti-fascists, and we are anti-fascists not only because we disagree with fascism as a political doctrine, but more fundamentally because we believe in the freedom and dignity of man.

When we see those elementary rights of man denied in any part of the world, our indignation is aroused, and because we believe that the human republic extends over all national and political boundaries, we feel we have a right to protest, simply in the name of Man. Some of us may think of the spiritual brotherhood of man, and feel that we should protest in the name of God. In other days we might have left that privilege to the Church, but the Church, particularly the Church that prevails in Spain, is silent, although members of its own congregation are among the victims of fascism. Among Franco's prisoners at the present moment is Antonio Pérez Cuadrado, vice-president of the Catholic Youth Organisation of Vitoria.

A famous Catholic writer whom I invited to attend this meeting, excused himself on the ground that it was unseemly for intellectuals to clear their consciences in such an easy way. I replied that there was a difference between the uneasy conscience that is due to guilt, and the spontaneous expression of human sympathy, and that the example of a Voltaire or a Zola was not to be despised by an intellectual of our own time.

Other people with whom I have discussed the subject were planning a holiday in Spain. Naturally, for it is the cheapest country in Europe. It is the cheapest country in Europe because it is the poorest; because the worker is oppressed. I do not say that on that account the traveller should take a guilty conscience to Spain; a few of our pounds, and a lot of American dollars, might trickle down to the poorer classes and alleviate their lot. But we should not be such cowards as to refuse to protest against injustice because our cheap holiday might be put in jeopardy.

Personally I sympathise with the politics, though not always with the political methods, of the men opposed to Franco. I would like to say a word or two about those methods, for there is a disposition to excuse Franco's violence on the grounds that some of the men arrested had been guilty of 'direct action'. There is a grand phrase to frighten the bourgeoisie! What, in the actual situation in Spain, can any action be but 'direct'. It is forbidden to strike; it is forbidden to hold a meeting; it is forbidden to criticise the régime in any effective manner. To lift a finger against such an absolute tyranny is direct action! The least squeak of protest invites brutal retaliation. The Spanish temper is hot, and little wonder, then, that violence is answered by violence. I for one will not condone violence on either side; but I will protest eternally against the tyranny that invokes violence. Franco's régime was established by violence; has survived by violence; we should not be surprised to see it perishing in violence.

At the end of the war I believe that the Allied politicians could have secured the abdication of Franco; by rights he should have stood in the dock at Nuremberg, alongside Göring and Ribbentrop. But, looking fearfully to the East, our politicians allowed Franco to stay, and subsequently his tottering regime was stabilised by American dollars. The fear of communism goes to that length – that we are prepared to compromise with fascism in order to fight fascism, to the utter confusion of all moral values.

We stand here on that question of moral values. In the name of justice and humanity we protest against this Spanish tyranny, which at this moment is arresting, condemning, imprisoning and shooting men whose only crime is the love of freedom.

38
Beyond Nihilism

L'homme revolté by Albert Camus.

THE subject of the latest book by Albert Camus might be described as the philosophy of politics. It is the kind of book that appears only in France, devoted, in a passionate intellectual sense, to the examination of such concepts as liberty and terror. Not that it is a theoretical work – on the contrary, it is an examination of the actual situation of Europe today, informed by the precise historical knowledge of the past two centuries of its social development.

Camus believes that revolt is one of the 'essential dimensions' of mankind. It is useless to deny its historical reality – rather we must seek in it a principle of existence. But the nature of revolt has changed radically in our times. It is no longer the revolt of the slave against the master, nor even the revolt of the poor against the rich; it is a metaphysical revolt, the revolt of man against the conditions of life, against creation itself. At the same time it is an aspiration towards clarity and unity of thought, even, paradoxically, towards order. That, at least, is what it becomes under the intellectual guidance of Camus.

He reviews the history of this metaphysical revolt, beginning with the absolute negation of Sade, glancing at Baudelaire and the 'dandies', passing on to Stirner, Nietzsche, Lautréamont and our contemporary surrealists. His attitude to all these figures is not unsympathetic, and this section of the book is particularly notable for a warm appreciation of the significance of André Breton's ideas. Camus then turns to the history of revolt in the political sense, his main object being to draw a clear distinction between revolt and revolution. Here, and not for the first time, Camus's ideas come close to anarchism, for he recognises that revolution always implies the establishment of a new government, whereas revolt is action without planned issue – it is spontaneous protestation. Camus reviews the history of the French Revolution, of the regicides and the deicides, and shows how inevitably, from Rousseau to Stalin, the course of revolution leads to authoritarian dictatorship. Saint-Just is the precursor of Lenin. Even Bakunin, to whom Camus devotes some extremely interesting pages (pointing out, for example, that he alone of his time, with exceptional profundity, declared war against the idolatry of science) – even Bakunin, if we examine the statutes of the Fraternité Internationale (1864-7) which he drew up, is found insisting on the absolute subordination of the individual to a central committee of action.

All revolutions in modern times, Camus points out, have led to a reinforcement of the power of the State. 'The strange and terrifying growth of the modern State may be considered as the logical conclusion of unrestrained technical and philosophical ambitions, foreign to the true spirit of revolt but nevertheless giving birth to the revolutionary spirit of our times. The prophetic dream of Marx and the powerful anticipations of Hegel and Nietzsche have ended by building up, in the place of the city of God which they have destroyed, a State rational or irrational, but in any case terrorist.' The counter-revolutions of fascism only serve to reinforce the general argument.

Camus shows the real quality of his thought in his final pages. It would have been easy, on the facts accumulated, to have retreated into despair or reaction. Camus substitutes the idea of 'limits'. 'Now, at the end of our long enquiry into revolt and nihilism, we realise that revolution without any limits other than historical efficacity signifies servitude without any limits. To escape this fate the revolutionary spirit, if it is to remain alive, should recruit its forces at the source of revolt and become inspired with the only idea which is true to these origins, the idea of limits.' To illustrate his meaning, Camus refers to syndicalism, that movement in politics which is based on the organic unity of the cell, and which is the negation of abstract and bureaucratic centralism. He quotes Tolain: '*Les êtres humains ne s'émancipent qu'au sein des groupes naturels*' – human beings only emancipate themselves on the basis of natural groups. 'The commune against the State, concrete society against absolutist society, considered liberty against rational tyranny, altruistic individualism against the colonisation of the masses – these are the antinomies which reflect once more the endless confrontation in the history of the Western world, of restraint and unrestraint.' The tradition of 'measure' belongs to the Mediterranean world, and has been destroyed by the excesses of German ideology and Christian otherworldliness.

Restraint is not the contrary of revolt. It is revolt that carries with it the very idea of restraint.

> 'Restraint, born from revolt, can only live by revolt. It is a continuous conflict, perpetually maintained and controlled by the intelligence.... Whatever we may do, lack of restraint will always find a place in the human breast, in the heart of solitude. We all carry within us our prisons, our crimes and our destructive instincts. But our task is not to let them loose on the world – to combat them in ourselves and in others. Revolt, the secular will not to go under of which Barrès speaks, is still today behind this struggle. The source of true life, it keeps us ever upright in the formless and furious stress of history.'

In his last pages, Camus rises to fine heights of eloquence which I will not attempt to translate. It is an inspiring book. It is particularly a book which should be read by all those who wish to see the movement of revolt inspired by a new spirit of idealism and action. Camus mentions, as an illustration of his final message, those condemned Catholics in the Spanish prisons who have recently refused to take communion because the priests of the régime have made it obligatory. 'They, too,' he says, 'refuse salvation if it must be paid for with injustice and oppression. Such mad generosity is of the spirit of revolt, which gives of its love without hesitation and rejects injustice without delay. Its honour is not to calculate, to give everything for the sake of the present life and the living brother. In that way it serves the life to come. True generosity towards the future consists in giving everything to the present.'

39
A Statement

THAT an anarchist should be offered a knighthood is a paradox that could only occur in England; that he should accept it is a decision which may give amusement to an indifferent public, dismay to his comrades, and pleasure only to those friends who have sufficient imagination to appreciate the dilemma in which he found himself.

The honour was given 'for services to literature'. It might have been given for services to art, for in that sphere I have been more publicly active, and have devoted much time and energy to the work of such bodies as the British Council and the Arts Council. But these services were not mentioned in the official announcement.

That neglect makes no difference to my attitude in the matter, nor to the reasons which led me to accept the honour. I accepted the honour (as I have accepted lesser honours in the past) because, though I am an anarchist, and was an anarchist before any of these unsought distinctions came my way, I have never renounced the society in which I have lived; and having lived in compromise with that society in big things and little, I cannot see why, logically, the empty question of a title should be made a matter of indignant protest.

I would ask my accusing comrades to examine their own consciences before condemning me. Daily and continually, almost every one of you accepts an order of living, which is integrally bourgeois and from which you cannot escape, unless you are prepared to go and live on a desert island. You accept the protection of the State's armed forces; you accept the benefits of the National Health Service; you use national roads and railways; you eat subsidised food. Moreover, unless you are too poor, you pay taxes which support all these State activities and benefits. Every glass of beer you drink, every cigarette you smoke, helps to sustain the bourgeois society which (in theory) you so rightly despise.

To contract out of that society is an idle gesture. It does not cost you anything to keep your seat at the picture-house when the National Anthem is played; it does not cost you anything to stand on a soapbox and shout insults at the Queen or her Government. So long as you keep within the law and pay your taxes, you are free to make an exhibition of your Ishmaelitish self, at the mere cost of embarrassment to your friends. But what positive good do you do? How much nearer do you bring an anarchist society?

Living is one activity, thought is another. Never do they correspond, except in the case of rare eremites, who flee society to live in the desert. Even Gandhi, the purest-minded man of our times – even Gandhi accepted the religious observances of his caste; even Gandhi accepted the title of Mahatma.

By thought one aims to transform the world. The ideas which we associate with names like Socrates, Buddha, Lao Tzu, Jesus, Francis of Assisi, Luther, Rousseau, Tolstoy – such ideas have transformed society. It did not follow from the fact that such men held such ideas, and even attempted to live lives in conformity with their principles, that they were not honoured by the people among whom they lived. When Tolstoy tried to get rid of his title and estate, he caused much suffering to his family and his dependents. He did not advance his ideas by such selfish intransigent conduct; on the contrary, the world has had to forgive him his actions before it could accept his ideas.

To renounce one's faith in order to find a position in society is the worst kind of treachery; but to take a position in society that will give force and authority to one's faith is an elementary duty.

Whatever the reaction of my comrades may be to the decision which I have taken, my own conduct will not be in doubt. My convictions have not changed and will not change. I regard war as the curse of humanity and governments as the instruments of war. I shall as always work unceasingly to abolish those social and economic institutions which exclude love and foster hatred.

AGAINST POWER AND DEATH
The Anarchist Articles and Pamphlets
of
Alex Comfort

edited with an introduction by
David Goodway

Alex Comfort, who was born in 1920, is best known nowadays as the author of the phenomenally successful *Joy of Sex*. But he is also a poet, novelist, critic, doctor, medical biologist, the pioneer of gerontology in Britain, a pacifist – and an anarchist.

From the early 1940s he was for a decade a prolific, combative and innovative writer on pacifism and anarchism.

This volume collects all the articles Comfort published in *War Commentary* and *Freedom*, most of his other social and political essays, as well as the most important of his Peace News pamphlets. The latter include *Peace and Disobedience*, the finest single statement of his highly individual and original anarchism.

David Goodway's wide-ranging introduction situates Comfort's politics in the context of his overall career.

168 pages   ISBN 0 900384 71 9   £5.00

Send for a list of publications and details of our journals
Freedom (fortnightly) and *The Raven* (quarterly)

FREEDOM PRESS
84b Whitechapel High Street, London E1 7QX